# Some Thoughts Concerning Education

and

# Of the Conduct of the Understanding

# John Locke

## Some Thoughts Concerning Education
and
## Of the Conduct of the Understanding

Edited, with Introduction, by
### Ruth W. Grant and Nathan Tarcov

Hackett Publishing Company, Inc.
Indianapolis/Cambridge

John Locke: 1632–1704

*Some Thoughts Concerning Education* was first published in 1693.

*Of the Conduct of the Understanding* was first published (posthumously) in 1706.

Introduction, Bibliography, and Notes copyright © 1996 by Hackett Publishing Company, Inc.

Printed in the United States of America

02 01 00 99 98 97 96    1 2 3 4 5 6 7

For further information, please address

Hackett Publishing Company, Inc.
P.O. Box 44937
Indianapolis, Indiana 46244–0937

Cover design by Listenberger Design & Associates
Text design by Dan Kirklin

**Library of Congress Cataloging-in-Publication Data**

Locke, John, 1632–1704.
    [Some thoughts concerning education]
    Some thoughts concerning education; and, Of the conduct of the understanding/John Locke; edited, with introduction and notes, by Ruth W. Grant and Nathan Tarcov.
        p.   cm.
    Includes bibliographical references (p.    ).
    ISBN 0-87220-335-2 (cloth)  ISBN 0-87220-334-4 (pbk.)
    1. Education—Philosophy.   2. Knowledge, Theory of.   3. Intellect.   4. Reasoning.   I. Grant, Ruth Weissbourd, 1951– .   II. Tarcov, Nathan.   III. Locke, John, 1632–1704. Of the conduct of the understanding.   IV. Title.   V. Title: Of the conduct of the understanding.
LB475.L6L63 1996
370'.1—dc20                            96–23832
                                                    CIP

# Contents

# Introduction

This volume brings together John Locke's two most important writings on education: *Some Thoughts Concerning Education* and *Of the Conduct of the Understanding*. They complement each other well: the *Thoughts* focuses on the education of children by their parents, whereas the *Conduct* addresses the self-education of adults. The *Thoughts* is an early articulation of some of the most important presuppositions of modern education, whereas the *Conduct* indicates the ideal which is the aim of such an education: a person who is capable of judging independently his own and public affairs. The *Conduct* completes the picture of the sort of person Locke is aiming to produce with the educational method of the *Thoughts*. And while the *Conduct* lays out in universal terms the standards of intellectual integrity and independence, the *Thoughts* describes the particular methods for realizing those standards in the education of the sons of English gentlemen of the seventeenth century. Together these writings illuminate the wide range of educational, philosophical, moral, religious, and political issues that concerned their remarkable author. Moreover, they highlight both the foundation for and the problems of education in a liberal political society.

Among Americans, John Locke is known as the philosopher most closely associated with their fundamental political principles. Natural equality, individual rights, the legitimacy of government grounded in consent, the popular right of resistance to unjust government, separation of church and state, and the rule of law—these are the principles of America's founding documents, and they are each developed and defended in the seventeenth-century British philosopher's political writings. Together these principles constitute the doctrine of self-government central to modern liberalism, that political tradition which includes both what is called "liberalism" and what is called "conservatism" in contemporary political debate.

It has often been said that modern liberal governments are impressively stable and enduring precisely because the political institutions of self-government can function well without particularly virtuous citizens and politicians. According to this view, we do not need any particular upbringing or special education as the foundation for healthy politics. Indeed, it would be dangerous to rely on the personal virtues produced by education to guarantee decent politics and to protect against injustice. Individuals will tend to seek their own advantage and join with others who share their interests into parties and groups to press their advantage. It is best therefore to rely on well-structured political institutions to shape group conflicts and check excessive demands so as to produce fair accommodations of competing claims. Moral matters can remain outside of the public sphere, more or less, and individuals can make their own judgments concerning upbringing and education. In short, it seems to some to be an advantage of liberal politics that it does not require too much thought about morality, education, or character development.

Yet in the works published here, morality, education, and character development are exactly the subjects that receive Locke's concerted attention. The education described in the *Thoughts* aims at virtue, duty, and self-restraint. It even includes a criticism, on moral and psychological grounds, of the impulse to acquire property beyond what is necessary (§110). The *Conduct* repeatedly stresses the importance of nonpartisanship, open-mindedness, and fair-mindedness, not only for inquiring after truth, but also for the proper conduct of politics. It outlines the requirements for the mental discipline necessary to combat the spirit of partisanship and to think independently. Neither of these works lends much support to the view that a society of self-interested individuals pressing partisan demands is sufficient to sustain Lockean liberal politics. On the contrary, they suggest that Locke sought methods of educating individuals to be able to submit their desires to rational control, to be concerned for others as well as for their own advantage, and to be intellectually independent of public authorities. These works demonstrate Locke's concern with individual self-government both for its political consequences and for its own sake.

Locke understood personal freedom, as he understood political freedom, to be a matter of self-government. But what does it mean to be self-governing, to be free in this sense? What sort of education produces adults who are capable of it? What are the psychological prerequisites of this possibility? Is reason capable of guiding our conduct, or does desire alone determine our goals? These are questions central to the texts published here, and they are questions that remain critically important for us. The reader will find Locke's reflections on them sometimes useful, sometimes provocative, and often problematic.

Many of the problems these texts raise are inherent in the effort to provide an education appropriate for a liberal society. There are certain paradoxes that liberal educators must confront that do not arise for their illiberal counterparts. For example, in an illiberal regime, it would be taken for granted that the state has a crucial role in shaping the character, preferences, and opinions of the next generation of citizens. But liberal societies limit the extent to which public authority may interfere in the private sphere, particularly with respect to religious and political opinions. Consequently, Americans, for example, are perennially engaged in conflicts over issues like teaching Darwinism, school prayer, and the education of Amish children. Locke does note in the dedicatory letter to the *Thoughts* that "the welfare and prosperity of the nation" depend on the proper education of children. Nonetheless, he concludes that education is "the duty and concern" of parents. He recommends against school in favor of private education by parents and tutors in the home (§70). Apparently, the state has no role as educator at all. Yet, Locke seems to acknowledge that liberal societies do require certain kinds of "liberal" people. And if this is so, the question remains: what sort of public effort might be made to produce them?

There is another paradox for liberal education, more profound though less often remarked. All education begins with children who are entirely dependent on adults and subject to their authority. A liberal education aims to produce adults who are independent and self-governing as far as is possible. How do you govern children when they are in need of government and at the same time avoid establishing either habits of subservience or a taste for dominance unsuitable for a society of independent adults? Again, in illiberal societies, particularly traditional patriarchal ones, the difficulty may not exist. Where adults remain subject to their father's authority until his death and where adults are understood to be subject to political authorities in the same way that children are subject to parents, the necessary experience of childhood dependence may be a perfectly appropriate preparation for adult life. The point can perhaps be made most clearly by considering the education of women in a society where women remain dependent throughout life. In such a situation, there is a continuity between a young girl's dependence on her parents and her later dependence on her husband that simplifies the task of education considerably. But education is a more complicated matter where the goal is to allow a fully independent adult to emerge after years of childhood dependence. This is the difficulty that lies behind Locke's condemnation of corporal punishment in the *Thoughts*, for example. Discipline of this sort will produce habits of character unfit for an independent adult. There must be ways to exercise authority without authoritarianism in the family as well as in the polity. To deal with this problem in the upbringing of children, Locke allows as much liberty and encourages as much reasoning as possible, appealing to our natural love of liberty and the pride we take in our rationality. But he also relies on our concern for esteem and disgrace and the cultivation of good habits. And the gentleman who is the adult product of a Lockean education remains concerned with his reputation, with custom and civility, and is still a creature of habit in some respects.

One might well wonder whether this is a model entirely consistent with independence in the fullest sense. Dependence on reputation is still a form of dependence, after all. The problem arises in considering the relation between the *Thoughts* and the *Conduct*. The ideal independent-minded man of the *Conduct* takes nothing for granted in forming the opinions that guide his actions, while the gentleman of the *Thoughts* takes a great deal for granted indeed. The latter has been educated to take his place in society, while the former subjects the common opinions of his day to the strictest scrutiny. Their differences reflect the tension between an education for good citizenship in a particular society and an education for intellectual freedom. Again, this is a problem that is particularly paradoxical for a liberal society, where freedom of thought is valued and even considered politically necessary and where the society appeals to universalistic principles of right, and not to tradition, for its legitimacy. In a liberal society, it should be possible in principle for an education for citizenship and an education for intellectual freedom to converge. But in practice, liberal education sometimes offers less a true resolution than a masking of the parochialism that is present even in liberal societies. Even liberal societies tend to require that their principles be embraced as unquestioned matters of habit, rather than be subjected to open scrutiny. To read the *Thoughts* and the *Conduct* together and consider their relation is to confront this issue.

Moreover, the *Thoughts*, unlike the *Conduct*, is specifically addressed to the education of the sons of the English gentry of the late seventeenth century, and thus its content is limited by gender, class, and era in certain respects. Clearly, many particulars of the *Thoughts* pertain to the situation of the gentry. For example, the *Thoughts* recommends private tutoring in the home, which is no longer a practical possibility on any large scale. Yet, as much as the current class structure differs from that of seventeenth-century England, in reading the *Thoughts* it is worth considering the extent to which middle-class mores are a democratized form of the traditional responsibilities of the gentry class. It should be noted also that the work is not directed exclusively to any particular class. Its moral virtues are for "a man or a gentleman" (§135), and its intellectual virtues are for "a gentleman or a lover of truth" (§189). Similarly, Locke did not think that gender made a crucial difference to education, though different subjects would be useful to boys and to girls, as they were expected to play different roles in adult life. Locke wrote to Mrs. Clarke in a letter of January 7, 1684, that since he acknowledged "no difference of sex in your mind relating to truth, virtue and obedience," he thought nothing in his previous letter, about the education of her son, need be altered for her daughters, including the same meat, drink, lodging, clothing, and exercise (though he was willing to make concessions to beauty "as much as health will permit" and have them exercise in the shade, indoors, or before sunrise). In cautioning against excessive reliance on public dancing schools, Locke remarks that "too much shamefacedness better becomes a girl than too much confidence," but his recommendation in the *Thoughts* (§70) that boys should be educated at home explicitly states that they too would be better off with the bashfulness of homebred girls than with the roughness and overconfidence of schoolboys. He modestly admitted to Mrs. Clarke that he had "more admired than considered your sex" and that he might therefore be mistaken in matters pertaining to the education of girls, and he suggested that the upbringing of daughters properly belongs more to the mother than to the father. The reader of the *Thoughts* will need to judge the extent to which time and place circumscribe its teachings.

Undoubtedly, these texts will strike the contemporary reader as quaint and outmoded in certain respects. Yet Locke's positions and many of the arguments with which he defends them are also almost eerily modern. The *Conduct* contains passages that could be found in the welcoming address to freshmen at a liberal arts college today, for example, on the importance of diversity of studies to open the mind, on the need to combat bias and prejudice, and on the creation of perpetual learners as the goal of education. The *Thoughts* includes familiar precepts such as that children learn best through play and that they must learn not only to do the right thing but to do it for the right reason.

At the same time, there are certainly some striking differences between a Lockean liberal education and a modern one. Preeminent among them is Locke's denigration of education in the arts and total silence on the development of creativity and imagination. In striking contrast to that other great

modern work on education, Rousseau's *Émile*, Locke's are entirely unconcerned with the education of eros or with the development of an aesthetic
sense. His educational recommendations are always to be judged by their
utility. His is an education for individual independence and self-mastery,
but certainly not for individuality and self-expression. The difference high-
lights the centrality of reason and the rational faculties in Locke's writings.

This is a crucial emphasis in all of Locke's writings, epistemological,
political, and educational. But the *Conduct* particularly reveals the structure of relations between reason, freedom, and morality that Locke pre-
supposes. We have already said that, in Locke's view, to be free is to be
self-governing. But to be self-governing is to be guided by reason. To be
guided by reason, in turn, is to judge fairly and hence to act fairly; it is to
overcome the effects of interest, passion, and prejudice that are the obsta-
cles to morality. Locke conceives of rationality as fairness. Each of us thus
has a *moral* responsibility to cultivate our rational faculties and to overcome those moral failings that stand in the way of reasonableness. The
*Conduct* is a manual of instruction in that task as well as a delightful attack
on the smugness of narrow-minded specialists and parochial partisans.
Throughout the work, Locke draws the connections between rational
deliberation, on the one hand, and impartiality, toleration, distrust of
authority, and personal liberation from authoritative opinion, on the other.
The capacity for independent judgment and reasonable conduct is the crucial capacity for both freedom and morality.

To emphasize reason in this way could produce a great deal of optimism about what education can accomplish. To the extent that our moral
and political failings are failings of the understanding, they might be overcome by improvements in education and the cultivation of rational public
discourse. This is a liberal hope which often finds expression today. But
the experience of political evil and fanaticism in the twentieth century
indicates the seriousness and the difficulty of the issue. Is the optimism
warranted? If we were to eliminate error and ignorance, would we have
eliminated evil too? The *Conduct* and the *Thoughts* offer ambiguous testimony on this question. There is much in Locke's writing to support the
optimistic view, but there is also an acknowledgment of the presence of
dangerous passions even in children that must be controlled by something
more than reasoning. In reading these works, we are likely to find ourselves asking whether Locke gives an adequate account of the sources of
evil and whether he overestimates the power of reason in human affairs.

Readers interested in John Locke, in liberalism, in education, or in the
philosophic consideration of rationalism and morality should find much

food for thought in the *Thoughts* and in the *Conduct*. In studying these works, questions will inevitably arise about their relation to Locke's political theory and his philosophy more generally. For example, does the successful implementation of Locke's political theory require members of civil society and their representatives to have the qualities inculcated by the *Thoughts* and the *Conduct*: justice as respect for the rights of others, civility, liberality, humanity, self-denial, industry, thrift, courage, truthfulness, and a willingness to question prejudice, authority, and the biases of one's own interest? What are the philosophical bases of the notions of liberty and rationality employed in Locke's educational as well as his political works? How is the use of habituation and reputation in the practice of moral education in the *Thoughts* related to the critical analyses of the association of ideas and of the domination of common opinion in the *Essay* and the *Conduct*? Questions such as these enrich the study of Locke's educational writings, and so we provide a brief summary of his major political and philosophic works in the next section, followed by a biographical sketch that should help the reader to see Locke's writings in the context of his activities as a political actor, scientist, and educator.

## Politics, Philosophy, and Education

In order to assess the relation of the educational advice Locke offers to the political liberty he advocated, we must turn to his most important work of political theory, the *Two Treatises of Government*. It was published to vindicate the English Revolution of 1688, though most of it had been written earlier to justify revolutionary action. In the *First Treatise*, he refuted Sir Robert Filmer's (1588–1653) theory of divine-right patriarchal monarchy, a theory which was invoked by the Tory advocates of royal power against the Whig proponents of parliamentary control. Locke rejected Filmer's derivation of political principles from obscure scriptural passages, his assumption that a particular form of government and even particular rulers were divinely ordained, and his acceptance of the patriarchal family as the model for politics. Locke thus cleared the ground for his presentation of his own political theory in the *Second Treatise*, which derived political principles from natural human reason, relegated forms of government and rulers to human choice, and sharply distinguished between family and politics. (Readers of the *Thoughts* should bear in mind Locke's antipatriarchal politics in considering his depiction of relationships within the family.)

The fundamental hypothesis of the *Second Treatise* was what Locke called the state of nature, his claim that the condition all human beings are naturally in is one of freedom and equality, constrained only by their own reason (the dictates of which Locke called the law of nature). Locke argued that in such a state of nature, in the absence of government, individuals could acquire property through their own labor for the sake of their own preservation and comfort, without any specific donation by God or a human sovereign. He justified such natural economic rights on the grounds that human labor produced almost all value and that such private appropriation did not lessen, but increased the amount left for others. These economic views are reflected in the passages in the *Thoughts* about industry and thrift, though they may also be modified by those about liberality and humanity. Locke's claims concerning property led to his being considered one of the originators of the spirit of capitalism and (also because of his arguments in his *Several Papers Relating to Money, Interest, and Trade* of 1696) one of the founders of modern political economy.

According to the *Second Treatise*, families would be formed in a state of nature through voluntary conjugal contracts between men and women and the duty of parents to preserve, nourish, and educate their children until they reach the age of reason. Locke's account of these natural relations gives the economy and the family a priority to and independence of government. It also helps to clarify the distinctive features of political power. Unlike economic and familial power, political power includes power over life and death; but political power does not belong to its holders as a kind of property to be used or sold for their own benefit, nor does it involve paternalistic education by the more rational. Once again we note the problematic relation between education of dependent children and the political liberty properly enjoyed by adults.

Since adult human beings are by nature free and equal, without any subordination of one to another, for Locke all rightful political power exists only by consent. As individuals consent to become members of civil society only to secure the rights to life, liberty, and property that they possess in a state of nature, so the end of government is the protection of the lives, liberties, and properties of all the members of society, as far as possible. (Locke sometimes called the end of government the preservation of "property," referring to all three of these rights collectively, since each of them is conceived of as property, i.e., something belonging to individuals that they cannot be rightfully deprived of without their own consent.) This limited end of government is the heart of modern liberalism and contrasts sharply with classical and medieval conceptions of the end of government as the improvement or salvation of our souls, the punishment of vice or sin, the propagation of the truth, or the glorification of God.

This limitation and contrast are especially clear and important in Locke's *Letter Concerning Toleration*, where he argued explicitly that the civil power is confined solely to the care and advancement of civil goods (such as life, liberty, bodily health and freedom from pain, and possession of external things such as land, money, and furniture) and that it neither can nor ought to be extended to the salvation of souls. From this he concluded that government should tolerate all religious opinions and practices except for those that interfere with the civil rights of others or with the preservation of civil society and except for those that reject the duty of such toleration. While few denominations might have met that test in Locke's time, through *The Reasonableness of Christianity* he contributed immensely to the modern liberalization of religion that allows it to meet those conditions for toleration. That liberalization is clearly applied to religious education in the *Thoughts*.

In the *Second Treatise*, Locke limited not only the end but the power of legitimate government. It cannot possess absolute arbitrary power over the lives and property of the people, rule by decree without promulgated laws and authorized judges, or take any part of anyone's property without the consent of the majority or their representatives. Locke's political theory allowed the people by majority decision to establish the form of government they think best through an original constitution which no inferior power can alter. But Locke ruled out absolute monarchy as inconsistent with civil society and required every legitimate form of government to include one elected representative branch (such as the English House of Commons) for purposes of taxation and perhaps for all legislation. Reading Locke's educational writings, one might consider whether the products of the education he describes would be effective representatives of the people in such a government.

[Whatever the form of government, the same persons should not have in their hands the legislative and executive powers, allowing them to exempt themselves from the laws they make. The rule of law must be guaranteed. The people give the legislative power as a trust to be employed only for their good, and they retain the power to remove or alter it when it is used contrary to that trust; this is the right of revolution.] Readers of the works printed here may therefore also consider whether Locke's educational program would enhance the capacity of the people to question, judge, and finally resist abuses of power by the authorities.

In his major work of philosophy, Locke used his pen to combat authoritarianism on another level. In his *Essay Concerning Human Understanding*, Locke encouraged his readers to question the opinions others would

impose on them by authority and to refrain from imposing their own opinions on others by authority. He refuted the doctrine of innate ideas, which
he regarded as a justification for subservience to prejudice, superstition,
and intellectual tyranny, and argued instead that we acquire all our knowledge from experience and reflection on the operations of our own minds.
Our ideas of good and evil in particular are derived from our experience of
pleasure and pain, and so are very different for different people (*Essay* II
xx 2, xxi 42, 54–55). Pain or uneasiness rather than a conception of good is
the chief spur to human industry and action (II xx 6, xxi 29, 31–39). Moral
good and evil are the pleasure and pain resulting from the conformity or
disagreement of our actions with some law, whether the natural or divine
law, the civil law, or the law of opinion or reputation, as Locke calls the
approval or disapproval of one's society (II xxviii 5–14). He considers the
last to be not only a law but the most powerful law governing human conduct, since most people fear the dislike of their fellows more than the
penalities of the natural, divine, or civil laws. It is no wonder that praise
and blame play a major role in the educational method of the *Thoughts*.
The idea of liberty, so crucial to all Locke's writings on politics and education, is traced in the *Essay* to reflection on the power of the mind over
one's own actions, especially the power to suspend action in pursuit of the
satisfaction of one's desires until after a full consideration of their objects
(II xxi 7, 47, 51–52). The *Essay* thus shows how the independence of mind
pursued in the *Conduct* is possible.

The *Essay* also offers a critique of the errors into which we are led by
the association of ideas that have no natural connection (II xxxiii) and by
the imperfection and abuse of words (III ix–x). It recommends that we
attach words to distinct ideas to prevent the latter errors (III xi). All of
these themes recur in the *Conduct*. Finally, the *Essay* distinguishes demonstrative, intuitive, and self-evident knowledge, and it also distinguishes all
knowledge from assent to probability in general and from religious faith in
particular. The *Essay*'s investigation of what we can know and how we can
know it lies at the basis of Locke's educational reflections.

Readers will find in the *Thoughts* and the *Conduct* more concrete applications and a more richly detailed picture of human life than the abstract
and formal analysis of the *Essay*. They will gain a better understanding of
the conceptions of reason and freedom so central to Locke's work. They
will see the moral and intellectual qualities, as well as the relations
between individuals presupposed by the political doctrines of the *Two
Treatises*. As a result, perhaps they will see the *Two Treatises* in a fresh
light as well. The works published here, read together with Locke's better-

known political and philosophic writings, will allow the reader to develop a deeper appreciation of the various interconnected concerns at the core of Lockean liberalism.

## Locke's Life

The author of these works was by no means a merely academic philosopher—he was a practicing physician, an experimenting scientist, an adviser to statesmen, and a tutor of young children, engagements that resonate throughout these texts. Locke was born on August 29, 1632, at Wrington, a little village in Somerset, in the West country near Bristol. His family background was Puritan and commercial. His father was a local lawyer and small landowner; his grandfathers, a clothier and a tanner. The English Civil War broke out when Locke was ten; his father fought briefly on the Parliamentary side. Locke attended the prestigious Westminster School in London from 1647 to 1652, where he was a schoolmate of the dominant literary figure of his age, John Dryden. There Locke studied Latin, Greek, some Hebrew, classical literature, history, philosophy, geography, and scripture. He attended Christ Church College at Oxford from 1652 to 1658, continuing his Greek and Hebrew and studying scholastic philosophy. He then commenced an academic career which included a senior studentship in 1658 and a lectureship in Greek in 1660, which required supervising the education of his teenaged pupils in Latin, Greek, philosophy, ethics, and religion. But Locke focused his own interests on medicine and the new natural science of his unofficial mentor, the pioneering chemist Robert Boyle. In 1660–61 he wrote two tracts, one in English and one in Latin, supporting the authority of the civil magistrate to regulate religious worship, published in 1967 as *Two Tracts on Government*. In 1664 he served as Censor of Moral Philosophy, in which capacity he wrote the Latin disputation recently published as *Questions Concerning the Law of Nature*.

Locke's academic career was interrupted by service in 1665–66 on a diplomatic mission to the court of Brandenburg at Cleves. Shortly after his return to Oxford, his medical practice brought him a distinguished collaborator, the greatest English physician of his time, Thomas Sydenham, and, more important, a distinguished patient, Anthony Ashley Cooper, a leading politician and later the Whig leader and first earl of Shaftesbury. Locke left Oxford to join the latter as secretary, intellectual collaborator, and tutor to his teenaged son and later to his grandchildren, including Anthony Ashley Cooper, the third earl of Shaftesbury and future deist philosopher. He also continued his medical and scientific activities, being elected to the recently formed Royal Society in 1668. As Shaftesbury rose politically, Locke held a series of posts that further involved him in the high politics of the day, as secretary to the proprietors of Carolina, secretary to the Board of trade, and secretary for ecclesiastical patronage to Shaftesbury as Lord Chancellor. He became, like Shaftesbury, an advocate of religious toleration, writing a powerful argument in its favor in 1667, which was published only centuries later as "An Essay Concerning Toleration" (not to be confused with the later Letter). It was in Shaftesbury's household, while engaged in partisan struggle for political liberty, that Locke seems to have begun the early drafts of his great liberating works on politics, philosophy, and economics.

After Shaftesbury went into opposition, Locke received his medical degree in 1675 and a post as a teacher of medicine at Christ Church, but he spent his time traveling in France, part of the time as tutor to Caleb Banks, the son of a wealthy merchant. Locke thereby missed Shaftesbury's arrest in 1677 and his confinement in the Tower, but he returned in time for Shaftesbury's return to power in 1679. He seems to have begun work on the *Two Treatises of Government* during the Exclusion Crisis of 1679–81, the unsuccessful struggle by Shaftesbury's Whigs to exclude Charles II's younger brother, the Roman Catholic Duke of York and future James II, from the succession to the throne. In July 1681, Shaftesbury was again arrested and confined to the Tower on a charge of high treason. After his release, he began to plot to put the king's illegitimate but Protestant son, the Duke of Monmouth, on the throne, a plot that Locke may have been involved in. Upon the failure of this effort, Shaftesbury fled to Holland in 1682, where he died shortly thereafter. After the failure of a further Whig plot to kidnap both Charles and James in 1683, more prominent Whigs were arrested, among them Algernon Sydney, who was executed on a charge of treason, partly for having written a manuscript that, like Locke's *Two Treatises*, refuted Filmer's divine-right theory. Locke fled to Holland in 1683 and was expelled from Oxford for political reasons in 1684.

While in exile in Holland, Locke wrote in Latin his first *Letter Concerning Toleration* and the final draft of the *Essay Concerning Human Understanding*. He also wrote a series of letters of advice to his friend Edward Clarke on the education of his children. It was these letters that Locke revised and expanded into *Some Thoughts Concerning Education*, published in 1693 and considerably expanded further in the edition of 1695.

After the successful Revolution of 1688 that expelled James II and installed William and Mary on the throne, Locke returned to England in

February 1689. The *Letter Concerning Toleration*, the *Two Treatises*, and the *Essay* were all published in 1689, the first two anonymously. The *Essay* was published over Locke's name and made him famous. He became a friend of the great scientist and mathematician Isaac Newton, an adviser to the Whig leader Lord John Somers, and from 1696 to 1700 a member of the Board of Trade. His lifelong asthma having worsened, Locke left London to live at Oates, in Essex, in the household of Sir Francis Masham. In the early 1680s, Locke had become a close friend of Masham's wife, Damaris, daughter of the Platonist philosopher Ralph Cudworth. At the Masham home, Locke wrote his pamphlets on interest, money, and trade; the *Reasonableness of Christianity* (1695) and the *Vindications* in its defense; his *Letters to the Bishop of Worcester* (1697), defending the *Essay*; the *Second*, *Third*, and *Fourth Letters Concerning Toleration*, defending the earlier *Letter*; and *A Paraphrase and Notes on the Epistles of St. Paul* (1705–7). He wrote *Of the Conduct of the Understanding* in 1697, originally intending it as the largest chapter of the *Essay*, but it was published separately and posthumously in 1706. He died on October 28, 1704, the most famous and influential philosopher of his age.

# Selected Bibliography

## Locke's Major Works

*The Correspondence of John Locke*, 8 vols., ed. by E. S. De Beer, (Oxford: Clarendon Press, 1976–85).

*An Early Draft of Locke's Essay*, ed. by R. I. Aaron and Jocelyn Gibb (Oxford: Clarendon Press, 1936).

*An Essay Concerning Human Understanding*, ed. with introduction by Peter H. Nidditch (Oxford: Clarendon Press, 1975).

*An Essay Concerning Toleration*, in David Wootton, ed. *The Political Writings of John Locke* (New York: Mentor, 1993).

*A Letter Concerning Toleration*, ed. by James Tully, translated by William Popple for the 1689 edition (Indianapolis and Cambridge, Mass.: Hackett Publishing, 1983).

*Locke on Money*, 2 vols., ed. by Patrick H. Kelly (Oxford: Clarendon Edition of the Works of John Locke, 1991).

*A Paraphrase and Notes on the Epistles of St. Paul*, 2 vols., ed. by Arthur W. Wainright (Oxford: Clarendon Edition of the Works of John Locke Ser., 1988).

*Questions Concerning the Law of Nature*, ed. and translated by Robert Horwitz, Jenny Strauss Clay, and Diskin Clay (Ithaca: Cornell University Press, 1990).

*Reasonableness of Christianity and A Discourse of Miracles*, ed. by I. T. Ramsey (Stanford: Stanford University Press, 1958).

*Two Tracts on Government*, ed. with introduction, notes, and translation by Philip Abrams (Cambridge: Cambridge University Press, 1967).

*Two Treatises of Government*, ed. with introduction by Peter Laslett (Cambridge: Cambridge University Press, 1960; student edition 1988).

*The Works of John Locke in Ten Volumes*, 12th ed. (London: Thomas Davison, 1823).

# Works on Locke

Ashcraft, Richard. *Revolutionary Politics and Locke's "Two Treatises of Government"* (Princeton: Princeton University Press, 1986).

——————, ed. *John Locke: Critical Assessments*, 4 vols. (London: Routledge Press, 1991).

Axtell, James L., ed. Introduction, *The Educational Writings of John Locke* (Cambridge: Cambridge University Press, 1968).

Cranston, Maurice. *John Locke: A Biography* (New York: Macmillan Press, 1957).

Dunn, John. *The Political Thought of John Locke: An Historical Account of the Argument of the "Two Treatises of Government"* (Cambridge: Cambridge University Press, 1969).

Gibson, James. *Locke's Theory of Knowledge and Its Historical Relations* (Cambridge: Cambridge University Press, 1917, 1968).

Grant, Ruth W. *John Locke's Liberalism* (Chicago: University of Chicago Press, 1987).

Laslett, Peter, ed. Introduction, John Locke's *Two Treatises of Government* (Cambridge: Cambridge University Press, 1963, 1988).

Macpherson, C. Brough. *The Political Theory of Possessive Individualism: Hobbes to Locke*, chap. V (Oxford: Clarendon Press, 1962).

Mehta, Uday Singh. *The Anxiety of Freedom: Imagination and Individuality in Locke's Political Thought* (Ithaca: Cornell University Press, 1992).

Pangle, Thomas. *The Spirit of Modern Republicanism: The Moral Vision of the American Founders and the Philosophy of Locke* (Chicago: University of Chicago Press, 1988).

Schouls, Peter A. *Reasoned Freedom: John Locke and Enlightenment* (Ithaca: Cornell University Press, 1992).

Seliger, Martin. *The Liberal Politics of John Locke* (London: Allen & Unwin, 1968).

Strauss, Leo. *Natural Right and History*, chap. V (Chicago: University of Chicago Press, 1953).

Tarcov, Nathan. *Locke's Education for Liberty* (Chicago: University of Chicago Press, 1984).

Tully, James H. *A Discourse on Property: John Locke and His Adversaries* (Cambridge: Cambridge University Press, 1980).

Wood, Neal. *The Politics of Locke's Philosophy: a Social Study of "An Essay Concerning Human Understanding"* (Berkeley: University of California Press, 1983)

Yolton, John W. *John Locke and the Way of Ideas* (Oxford: Clarendon Press, 1956).

——————. *John Locke and Education* (New York: Random House, 1971).

# Bibliographies

Christopherson, H. O. *A Bibliographical Introduction to the Study of John Locke* (Oslo: I Kommisjon Hos Jacob Dybwad, 1930).

Hall, Roland, and Roger Woolhouse. *Eighty Years of Locke Scholarship* (Edinburgh: Edinburgh University Press, 1983). Updated listings are published periodically in the *Locke Newsletter*, edited by Roland Hall, University of York, York, England.

Yolton, Jean, and John Yolton. *John Locke: A Reference Guide* (Boston, Mass.: G. K. Hall, 1985).

# Note on the Texts

*Some Thoughts Concerning Education* was first published in 1693, based on a series of letters of advice Locke had written between 1684 and 1691 to his friend Edward Clarke on the education of his children, and expanded further by Locke for the editions of 1695, 1699, and 1705. In preparing this edition, the editors used an electronic text prepared by Mark Rooks of InteLex Corporation, comparing the version in *The Clarendon Edition of the Works of John Locke*, edited by John W. and Jean S. Yolton (Oxford: Oxford University Press, 1989), with the 1695 edition and the version in the twelfth edition of Locke's *Collected Works* of 1824. *Of the Conduct of the Understanding* was first published in 1706, in the *Posthumous Works of John Locke*, edited by Peter King. InteLex provided the editors with an electronic text of the version edited by Thomas Fowler (Oxford: 1901), which was compared with the facsimile edition of the original 1706 version, currently published by Thoemmes Press.

The editors' intention was to provide texts for the contemporary reader that would be as readable as possible while remaining true to the originals. We resisted the temptation to break up or rewrite Locke's often lengthy and complicated sentences, with their flexible and informal syntax. We merely modernized capitalization, spelling, verbal forms, and punctuation, and established grammatical agreement where required for readability. We provided explanatory notes for words not easily found in common dictionaries, and where required for ease of comprehension, we occasionally added words between brackets that can readily be identified as our insertions.

The editors have supplied a table of contents for each work, based on the original headings in each text.

# Some Thoughts Concerning Education

Doctrina vires promovet insitas,
rectique cultus pectora roborant:
utcunque defecere mores,
dedecorant bene nata culpae.[1]

Horace Bk. IV Ode 4

John Locke

---

1. "Teaching improves implanted strength, and right cultivation strengthens the heart; whenever morals fail, the faults dishonor the wellborn."

# Contents of
## *Some Thoughts Concerning Education*

# To
# Edward Clarke
# of *Chipley*, Esquire

Sir,

These *Thoughts Concerning Education,* which now come abroad into the world, do of right belong to you, being written several years since for your sake, and are no other than what you have already by you in my letters. I have so little varied anything, but only the order of what was sent you at different times and on several occasions, that the reader will easily find, in the familiarity and fashion of the style, that they were rather the private conversation of two friends than a discourse designed for public view.

The importunity of friends is the common apology for publications men are afraid to own themselves forward to. But you know I can truly say that if some who, having heard of these papers of mine, had not pressed to see them and afterwards to have them printed, they had lain dormant still in that privacy they were designed for. But those whose judgment I defer much to, telling me that they were persuaded that this rough draft of mine might be of some use if made more public, touched upon what will always be very prevalent with me. For I think it every man's indispensable duty to do all the service he can to his country; and I see not what difference he puts between himself and his cattle, who lives without that thought. This subject is of so great concernment, and a right way of education is of so general advantage, that did I find my abilities answered my wishes, I should not have needed exhortations or importunities from others. However, the meanness of these papers and my just distrust of them shall not keep me, by the shame of doing so little, from contributing my mite when there is no more required of me than my throwing it into the public receptacle. And if there be any more of their size[2] and notions who liked them

2.  Mental or moral qualities, or possibly social rank or position.

7

so well that they thought them worth printing, I may flatter myself they will not be lost labor to everybody.

I myself have been consulted of late by so many who profess themselves at a loss how to breed their children, and the early corruption of youth is now become so general a complaint, that he cannot be thought wholly impertinent who brings the consideration of this matter on the stage and offers something, if it be but to excite others or afford matter of correction. For errors in education should be less indulged than any: these, like faults in the first concoction that are never mended in the second or third, carry their afterwards incorrigible taint with them through all the parts and stations of life.

I am so far from being conceited of anything I have here offered, that I should not be sorry, even for your sake, if someone abler and fitter for such a task would in a just treatise of education, suited to our English gentry, rectify the mistakes I have made in this; it being much more desirable to me that young gentlemen should be put into (that which everyone ought to be solicitous about) the best way of being formed and instructed than that my opinion should be received concerning it. You will, however, in the meantime bear me witness, that the method here proposed has had no ordinary effects upon a gentleman's son it was not designed for. I will not say the good temper of the child did not very much contribute to it, but this I think you and the parents are satisfied of, that a contrary usage according to the ordinary disciplining of children would not have mended that temper, nor have brought him to be in love with his book, to take a pleasure in learning, and to desire as he does to be taught more than those about him think fit always to teach him.

But my business is not to recommend this treatise to you, whose opinion of it I know already, nor it to the world, either by your opinion or patronage. The well educating of their children is so much the duty and concern of parents, and the welfare and prosperity of the nation so much depends on it, that I would have everyone lay it seriously to heart and, after having well examined and distinguished what fancy, custom, or reason advises in the case, set his helping hand to promote everywhere that way of training up youth with regard to their several conditions[3] which is the easiest, shortest, and likeliest to produce virtuous, useful, and able men in their distinct callings: though that most to be taken care of is the gentleman's calling. For if those of that rank are by their education once set right, they will quickly bring all the rest into order.

3. Social classes.

I know not whether I have done more than shown my good wishes towards it in this short discourse; such as it is, the world now has it, and if there be anything in it worth their acceptance, they owe their thanks to you for it. My affection to you gave the first rise to it, and I am pleased that I can leave to posterity this mark of the friendship [that] has been between us. For I know no greater pleasure in this life, nor a better remembrance to be left behind one, than a long continued friendship with an honest, useful, and worthy man and lover of his Country. I am,

Sir,

Your most humble and most faithful Servant,

7 March 1690.

JOHN LOCKE.

§1. A sound mind in a sound body[4] is a short but full description of a happy state in this world: he that has these two has little more to wish for, and he that wants either of them will be but little the better for anything else. Men's happiness or misery is most part of their own making. He whose mind directs not wisely will never take the right way; and he whose body is crazy[5] and feeble will never be able to advance in it. I confess there are some men's constitutions of body and mind so vigorous and well framed by nature that they need not much assistance from others, but by the strength of their natural genius they are from their cradles carried towards what is excellent, and by the privilege of their happy constitutions are able to do wonders; but examples of this kind are but few, and I think I may say that of all the men we meet with, nine parts of ten are what they are, good or evil, useful or not, by their education. 'Tis that which makes the great difference in mankind. The little and almost insensible impressions on our tender infancies have very important and lasting consequences: and there it is as in the fountains of some rivers, where a gentle application of the hand turns the flexible waters into channels that make them take quite contrary courses, and by this little direction given them at first in the source, they receive different tendencies and arrive at last at very remote and distant places.

§2. I imagine the minds of children as easily turned this or that way as water itself; and though this be the principal part, and our main care should be about the inside, yet the clay cottage is not to be neglected. I shall therefore begin with the case, and consider first the *health* of the body as that which perhaps you may rather expect from that study I have been thought more peculiarly to have applied myself to, and that also which will be soonest dispatched, as lying, if I guess not amiss, in a very little compass.

*Health.*

§3. How necessary *health* is to our business and happiness, and how requisite a strong constitution, able to endure hardships and fatigue, is to one that will make any figure in the world, is too obvious to need any proof.

§4. The consideration I shall here have of *health* shall be not what a physician ought to do with a sick or crazy child, but what the parents without the help of physic should do for the *preservation and improvement of a healthy*, or at least *not sickly constitution* in their children: and this perhaps might be all dispatched in this one short rule, viz. that gentlemen should use their children as the honest farmers and substantial yeomen do theirs. But because the mothers possibly may think this a little too hard, and the

4. Juvenal *Satires* x 356.
5. Unsound.

10

fathers too short, I shall explain myself more particularly; only laying down this as a general and certain observation for the women to consider, viz. that most children's constitutions are either spoiled, or at least harmed, by *cockering* and *tenderness*.

*Tenderness.*

§5. The first thing to be taken care of is that children be not too *warmly* *clad or covered,* winter or summer. The face, when we are born, is no less tender than any other part of the body: 'tis use alone hardens it and makes it more able to endure the cold. And therefore the Scythian philosopher gave a very significant answer to the Athenian who wondered how he could go naked in frost and snow: How, said the Scythian, can you endure your face exposed to the sharp winter air? My face is used to it, said the Athenian. Think me all face, replied the Scythian. Our bodies will endure anything that from the beginning they are accustomed to.

*Warmth.*

An eminent instance of this, though in the contrary excess of heat, being to our present purpose, to show what use can do, I shall set down in the author's words, as I meet with it in a late ingenious voyage.[6] 'The heats,' says he, 'are more violent in Malta than in any part of Europe; they exceed those of Rome itself, and are perfectly stifling; and so much the more because there are seldom any cooling breezes here. This makes the common people as black as Gypsies: but yet the peasants defy the sun; they work on in the hottest part of the day, without intermission or sheltering themselves from his scorching rays. This has convinced me that nature can bring itself to many things which seem impossible, provided we accustom ourselves from our infancy. The Maltese do so, who harden the bodies of their children and reconcile them to the heat, by making them go stark naked without shirt, drawers, or anything on their heads from their cradles till they are ten years old.'

Give me leave therefore to advise you not to fence too carefully against the cold of this our climate. There are those in England who wear the same clothes winter and summer, and that without any inconvenience or more sense of cold than others find. But if the mother will needs have an allowance for frost and snow for fear of harm, and the father for fear of censure, be sure let not his winter clothing be too warm; and amongst other things remember, that when nature has so well covered his head with hair and strengthened it with a year or two's age that he can run about by day without a cap, it is best that by night a child should also lie without one; there being nothing that more exposes to headache, colds, catarrhs, coughs, and several other diseases than keeping the *head warm.*

6. *Nouveau Voyage du Levant* (1694), p. 150 [Locke's note].

§6. I have said *he* here because the principal aim of my discourse is how a young gentleman should be brought up from his infancy, which, in all things, will not so perfectly suit the education of *daughters;* though where the difference of sex requires different treatment, it will be no hard matter to distinguish.

*Feet.*  §7. I would also advise his *feet to be washed* every day in cold water, and to have his *shoes* so thin that they might leak and *let in water* whenever he comes near it. Here, I fear, I shall have the mistress and maids too against me. One will think it too filthy; and the other, perhaps, too much pains to make clean his stockings. But yet truth will have it that his health is much more worth than all such considerations, and ten times as much more. And he that considers how mischievous and mortal a thing taking *wet in the feet* is to those who have been bred nicely, will wish he had with the poor people's children gone *barefoot*, who by that means come to be so reconciled by custom to wet in their feet that they take no more cold or harm by it than if they were wet in their hands. And what is it, I pray, that makes this great difference between the hands and the feet in others, but only custom? I doubt not but if a man from his cradle had been always used to go barefoot, whilst his hands were constantly wrapped up in warm mittens and covered with *hand-shoes*, as the Dutch call gloves, I doubt not, I say, but such a custom would make taking wet in his hands as dangerous to him as now taking wet in their feet is to a great many others. The way to prevent this is to have his shoes made so as to leak water and his feet washed constantly every day in cold water. It is recommendable for its cleanliness, but that which I aim at in it is health. And therefore I limit it not precisely to any time of the day. I have known it used every night with very good success, and that all the winter, without the omitting it so much as one night in extreme cold weather when thick ice covered the water, the child bathed his legs and feet in it though he was of an age not big enough to rub and wipe them himself, and when he began this custom was puling and very tender. But the great end being to harden those parts by a frequent and familiar use of cold water, and thereby to prevent the mischiefs that usually attend accidental taking wet in the feet in those who are bred otherwise, I think it may be left to the prudence and convenience of the parents to choose either night or morning. The time I deem indifferent so the thing be effectually done. The health and hardiness procured by it would be a good purchase at a much dearer rate. To which, if I add the preventing of corns, that to some men would be a very valuable consideration. But begin first in the spring, with lukewarm, and so colder and colder every night, till in a few days you come to perfectly cold water, and then continue it so winter and summer. For it is to be observed in this, as in all other *alterations* from our ordinary way of living, the changes must be made by gentle and insensible degrees; and so we may bring our bodies to anything without pain and without danger.                                   *Alterations.*

How fond mothers are likely to receive this doctrine is not hard to foresee. What can it be less than to murder their tender babes to use them thus? What! Put their feet in cold water in frost and snow, when all one can do is little enough to keep them warm? A little to remove their fears by examples, without which the plainest reason is seldom hearkened to: Seneca tells us of himself, *Epistles* 53 and 83, that he used to bathe himself in cold spring water in the midst of winter. This, if he had not thought it not only tolerable but healthy too, he would scarce have done in an exuberant fortune that could well have borne the expense of a warm bath, and in an age (for he was then old) that would have excused greater indulgence. If we think his Stoical principles led him to this severity, let it be so that his sect reconciled cold water to his sufferance; what made it agreeable to his health? For that was not impaired by this hard usage. But what shall we say to Horace, who warmed not himself with the reputation of any sect and least of all affected Stoical austerities? Yet he assures us he was wont in the winter season to bathe himself in cold water.[7] But perhaps Italy will be thought much warmer than England, and the chillness of their waters not to come near ours in winter. If the rivers of Italy are warmer, those of Germany and Poland are much colder than any in this our country; and yet in these, the Jews, both men and women, bathe all over at all seasons of the year without any prejudice to their health. And everyone is not apt to believe it is a miracle or any peculiar virtue of St. Winifred's Well that makes the cold waters of that famous spring do no harm to the tender bodies that bathe in it. Everyone is now full of the miracles done by cold baths on decayed and weak constitutions for the recovery of health and strength, and therefore they cannot be impracticable or intolerable for the improving and hardening the bodies of those who are in better circumstances.

If these examples of grown men be not thought yet to reach the case of children, but that they may be judged still to be too tender and unable to bear such usage, let them examine what the Germans of old and the Irish now do to them; and they will find, that infants too, as tender as they are thought, may without any danger endure bathing not only of their feet, but of their whole bodies, in cold water; and there are at this day ladies in the Highlands of Scotland who use this discipline to their children in the

---

7. *Epistles* I 15.4–5.

midst of winter and find that cold water does them no harm even when there is ice in it.

*Swimming.*    §8. I shall not need here to mention *swimming* when he is of an age able to learn and has anyone to teach him. 'Tis that saves many a man's life: and the Romans thought it so necessary that they ranked it with letters; and it was the common phrase to mark one ill educated and good for nothing that he had neither learned to read nor to swim. *Nec literas didicit nec natare.* But besides the gaining a skill which may serve him at need, the advantages to health, by often *bathing in cold water* during the heat of summer, are so many that I think nothing need to be said to encourage it, provided this one caution be used that he never go into the water when exercise has at all warmed him or left any emotion in his blood or pulse.

*Air.*    §9. Another thing that is of great advantage to everyone's health, but especially children's, is to be much in the *open air* and very little as may be by the fire even in winter. By this he will accustom himself also to heat and cold, shine and rain; all which, if a man's body will not endure, it will serve him to very little purpose in this world; and when he is grown up, it is too late to begin to use[8] him to it; it must be got early, and by degrees. Thus the body may be brought to bear almost anything. If I should advise him to play in the *wind and sun without a hat*, I doubt whether it could be borne. There would a thousand objections be made against it, which at last would amount to no more, in truth, than being sunburnt. And if my young master be to be kept always in the shade and never exposed to the sun and wind for fear of his complexion, it may be a good way to make him a *beau*, but not a man of business. And although greater regard be to be had to beauty in the daughters, yet I will take the liberty to say that the more they are in the *air*, without prejudice to their faces, the stronger and healthier they will be; and the nearer they come to the hardships of their brothers in their education, the greater advantage will they receive from it all the remaining part of their lives.

§10. Playing in the *open air* has but this one danger in it that I know; and that is that when he is hot with running up and down he should sit or lie down on the cold or moist earth. This, I grant, and drinking cold drink when they are hot with labor or exercise, brings more people to the grave, or to the brink of it, by fevers and other diseases than anything I know. These mischiefs are easily enough prevented whilst he is little, being then seldom out of sight. And if, during his childhood, he be constantly and rigorously kept from sitting on the ground or drinking any cold liquor whilst

8. Accustom.

he is hot, the custom of forbearing, grown into a habit, will help much to preserve him when he is no longer under his maid's or tutor's eye. This is *Habits.* all I think can be done in the case; for, as years increase, liberty must come with them, and in a great many things he must be trusted to his own conduct, since there cannot always be a guard upon him, except what you have put into his own mind by good principles and established habits, which is the best and surest, and therefore most to be taken care of. For from repeated cautions and rules, ever so often inculcated, you are not to expect anything either in this or any other case farther than practice has established them into habits.

§11. One thing the mention of the girls brings into my mind, which *Clothes.* must not be forgot, and that is that your son's *clothes* be *never* made *strait,* especially about the breast. Let nature have scope to fashion the body as she thinks best. She works of herself a great deal better and exacter than we can direct her. And if women were themselves to frame the bodies of their children in their wombs, as they often endeavor to mend their shapes when they are out, we should as certainly have no perfect children born, as we have few well-shaped that are *strait-laced* or much tampered with. This consideration should, me thinks, keep busy people (I will not say ignorant nurses and bodice-makers) from meddling in a matter they understand not; and they should be afraid to put nature out of her way in fashioning the parts when they know not how the least and meanest is made. And yet I have seen so many instances of children receiving great harm from *strait-lacing* that I cannot but conclude there are other creatures, as well as monkeys, who, little wiser than they, destroy their young ones by senseless fondness and too much embracing.

§12. Narrow breasts, short and stinking breath, ill lungs, and crookedness, are the natural and almost constant effects of *hard bodices* and *clothes that pinch.* That way of making slender waists and fine shapes serves but the more effectually to spoil them. Nor can there indeed but be disproportion in the parts when the nourishment prepared in the several offices of the body cannot be distributed as nature designs; and therefore what wonder is it, if it being laid, where it can, on some part not so *braced*, it often makes a shoulder or a hip higher or bigger than its just proportion. It is generally known that the women of China (imagining I know not what kind of beauty in it), by bracing and binding them hard from their infancy, have very little feet. I saw lately a pair of China shoes, which I was told were for a grown woman; they were so exceedingly disproportioned to the feet of one of the same age amongst us, that they would scarce have been big enough for one of our little girls. Besides this, it is observed that their women are also very little and short-lived whereas the men are of the ordinary stature of other men and live to a proportionable age. These defects in the female sex in that country are by some imputed to the unreasonable binding of their feet, whereby the free circulation of the blood is hindered, and the growth and health of the whole body suffers. And how often do we see that some small part of the foot being injured by a wrench or a blow, the whole leg and thigh thereby lose their strength and nourishment and dwindle away? How much greater inconveniences may we expect when the *thorax*, wherein is placed the heart and seat of life, is unnaturally *compressed* and hindered from its due expansion?

*Diet.*      §13. As for his *diet*, it ought to be very *plain* and simple; and, if I might advise, flesh should be forborne as long as he is in [petti]coats, or at least till he is two or three years old. But whatever advantage this may be to his present and future health and strength, I fear it will hardly be consented to by parents, misled by the custom of eating too much flesh themselves, who will be apt to think their children, as they do themselves, in danger to be starved if they have not flesh at least twice a day. This I am sure, children would breed their teeth with much less danger, be freer from diseases whilst they were little, and lay the foundations of a healthy and strong constitution much surer, if they were not crammed so much as they are by fond mothers and foolish servants and were kept wholly from flesh the first three or four years of their lives.

But if my young master must needs have flesh, let it be but once a day, and of one sort at a meal. Plain beef, mutton, veal, etc., without other sauce than hunger, is best; and great care should be used that he eat *bread* plentifully both alone and with everything else. And whatever he eats that is solid, make him *chew* it well. We English are often negligent herein; from whence follow indigestion and other great inconveniences.

§14. For *breakfast* and *supper, milk, milk-pottage, water-gruel, flummery,* and twenty other things that we are wont to make in England are very fit for children; only, in all these, let care be taken that they be plain and without much mixture, and very sparingly seasoned with *sugar,* or rather none at all; especially all *spice* and other things that may heat the blood are carefully to be avoided. Be sparing also of *salt* in the seasoning of all his victuals, and use him not to high-seasoned meats. Our palates grow into a relish and liking of the seasoning and cookery which by custom they are set to, and an overmuch use of salt, besides that it occasions thirst and overmuch drinking, has other ill effects upon the body. I should think that a good piece of well-made, and well-baked *brown bread*, sometimes with and sometimes without *butter* or *cheese*, would be often the best breakfast for my young master. I am sure it is as wholesome and will make him as strong a man as greater delicacies; and if he be used to it, it will be as pleasant to him. If he at any time calls for victuals between meals, use him to nothing but dry *bread*. If he be hungry more than wanton, *bread* alone will down; and if he be not hungry, it is not fit he should eat. By this you will obtain two good effects: 1. that by custom he will come to be in love with *bread*, for, as I said, our palates and stomachs too are pleased with the things we are used to. [2.] Another good you will gain hereby is that you will not teach him to eat more nor oftener than nature requires. I do not think that all people's appetites are alike: some have naturally stronger, and some weaker stomachs. But this I think, that many are made *gourmands* and *gluttons* by custom that were not so by nature: and I see in some countries men as lusty and strong that eat but two meals a day as others that have set their stomachs by a constant usage, like alarms, to call on them for four or five. The Romans usually fasted till supper, the only set meal even of those who ate more than once a day; and those who used breakfasts (as some did at eight, some at ten, others at twelve of the clock, and some later) neither ate flesh nor had anything made ready for them. Augustus, when the greatest monarch on the Earth, tells us, he took a bit of dry bread in his chariot.[9] And Seneca, in his 83rd Epistle, giving an account how he managed himself even when he was old and his age permitted indulgence, says that he used to eat a piece of dry bread for his dinner without the formality of sitting to it, though his estate would have as well paid for a better meal (had health required it) as any subject's in England were it doubled. The masters of the world were bred up with this spare diet: and the young gentlemen of Rome felt no want of strength or spirit because they ate but once a day. Or if it happened by chance that anyone could not fast so long as till supper, their only set meal, he took nothing but a bit of dry bread or at most a few raisins or some such slight thing with it to stay his stomach. This part of temperance was found so necessary both for health and business, that the custom of only one meal a day held out against that prevailing luxury which their Eastern conquests and spoils had brought in amongst them; and those who had given up their old frugal eating and made feasts yet began them not till the evening. And more than one set meal a day was thought so monstrous that it was a reproach as low down as Caesar's time to make an entertainment or sit down to a full table till towards sunset. And therefore if it would not be thought too severe, I should judge it most convenient that my young master should have noth-

9. Suetonius, *Augustus* 76.

ing but *bread* too for *breakfast*. You cannot imagine of what force custom is: and I impute a great part of our diseases in England to our eating too much *flesh* and too little *bread*.

*Meals.*     §15. As to his *meals*, I should think it best that, as much as it can be conveniently avoided, they should not be kept constantly to an hour. For when custom has fixed his eating to certain stated periods, his stomach will expect victuals at the usual hour and grow peevish if he passes it, either fretting itself into a troublesome excess or flagging into a downright want of appetite. Therefore I would have no time kept constantly to for his breakfast, dinner, and supper, but rather varied almost every day. And if between these, which I call *meals*, he will eat, let him have, as often as he calls for it, good dry bread. If anyone think this too hard and sparing a diet for a child, let them know that a child will never starve nor dwindle for want of nourishment who, besides flesh at dinner and spoonmeat[10] or some such other thing at supper, may have good bread and beer as often as he has a stomach: for thus, upon second thoughts, I should judge it best for children to be ordered. The morning is generally designed for study, to which a full stomach is but an ill preparation. Dry bread, though the best nourishment, has the least temptation: and nobody would have a child crammed at breakfast who has any regard to his mind or body and would not have him dull and unhealthy. Nor let anyone think this unsuitable to one of estate and condition.[11] A gentleman, in any age, ought to be so bred as to be fitted to bear arms and be a soldier. But he that, in this, breeds his son so as if he designed him to sleep over his life in the plenty and ease of a full fortune he intends to leave him, little considers the examples he has seen or the age he lives in.

*Drink.*     §16. His *drink* should be only small beer; and that too he should never be suffered to have between meals, but after he had eaten a piece of bread. The reasons why I say this, are these:

§17. 1. More fevers and surfeits are got by people's drinking when they are hot than by any one thing I know. Therefore, if by play he be hot and dry, bread will ill go down; and so if he cannot have *drink* but upon that condition, he will be forced to forbear. For if he be very hot, he should by no means *drink*. At least, a good piece of bread first to be eaten, will gain time to warm the beer *blood-hot,* which then he may drink safely. If he be very dry, it will go down so warmed and quench his thirst better: and if he will not drink it so warmed, abstaining will not hurt him. Besides, this will

10.  Soft food to be eaten with a spoon by infants or invalids.
11.  High social class.

teach him to forbear, which is a habit of greatest use for health of body and mind too.

§18. 2. Not being permitted to *drink* without eating will prevent the custom of having the cup often at his nose, a dangerous beginning and preparation to *good-fellowship*. Men often bring habitual hunger and thirst on themselves by custom. And if you please to try, you may, though he be weaned from it, bring him by use to such a necessity again of *drinking* in the night that he will not be able to sleep without it. It being the lullaby used by nurses to still crying children, I believe mothers generally find some difficulty to wean their children from *drinking* in the night when they first take them home. Believe it, custom prevails as much by day as by night; and you may, if you please, bring anyone to be thirsty every hour.

I once lived in a house where, to appease a froward child, they gave him *drink* as often as he cried, so that he was constantly bibbing; and though he could not speak, yet he drank more in twenty-four hours than I did. Try it when you please, you may with small as well as with strong beer drink yourself into a drought. The great thing to be minded in education is what *habits* you settle: and therefore in this, as all other things, do not begin to make anything *customary* the practice whereof you would not have continue and increase. It is convenient for health and sobriety to *drink* no more than natural thirst requires: and he that eats not salt meats nor drinks strong drink will seldom thirst between meals, unless he has been accustomed to such unseasonable *drinking*. *Habits.*

§19. Above all, take great care that he seldom, if ever, taste any *wine* or *strong drink*. There is nothing so ordinarily given children in England, *Strong Drink.* and nothing so destructive to them. They ought *never* to drink any *strong liquor* but when they need it as a cordial and the doctor prescribes it. And in this case it is that servants are most narrowly to be watched, and most severely to be reprehended when they transgress. Those mean sort of people, placing a great part of their happiness in *strong drink*, are always forward to make court to my young master by offering him that which they love best themselves; and finding themselves made merry by it, they foolishly think it will do the child no harm. This you are carefully to have your eye upon and restrain with all the skill and industry you can; there being nothing that lays a surer foundation of mischief, both to body and mind, than children's being used to *strong drink*, especially to drink in private *with the servants*.

§20. Fruit makes one of the most difficult chapters in the government *Fruit.* of health, especially that of children. Our first parents ventured Paradise for it: and it is no wonder our children cannot stand the temptation, though it cost them their health. The regulation of this cannot come under any one general rule. For I am by no means of their mind who would keep children almost wholly from *fruit* as a thing totally unwholesome for them, by which strict way they make them but the more ravenous after it and to eat good and bad, ripe or unripe, all that they can get, whenever they come at it. *Melons, peaches,* most sorts of *plums,* and all sorts of *grapes* in England, I think children should be *wholly kept from* as having a very tempting taste in a very unwholesome juice; so that, if it were possible, they should never so much as see them or know there were any such thing. But *strawberries, cherries, gooseberries,* or *currants,* when thoroughly ripe, I think may be very safely allowed them, and that with a pretty liberal hand, if they be eaten with these cautions: 1. not after meals, as we usually do, when the stomach is already full of other food, but I think they should be eaten rather before or between meals, and children should have them for their breakfasts; 2. bread eaten with them; 3. perfectly ripe. If they are thus eaten, I imagine them rather conducing than hurtful to our health. *Summer fruits,* being suited to the hot season of the year they come in, refresh our stomachs, languishing and fainting under it: and therefore I should not be altogether so strict in this point as some are to their children, who, being kept so very short, instead of a moderate quantity of well-chosen *fruit,* which being allowed them would content them, whenever they can get loose or bribe a servant to supply them, satisfy their longing with any trash they can get and eat to a surfeit.

*Apples* and *pears* too, which are thoroughly ripe and have been gathered some time, I think may be safely eaten at any time and in pretty large quantities, especially *apples,* which never did anybody hurt that I have heard after October.

*Fruits* also *dried* without sugar I think very wholesome. But *sweetmeats* of all kinds are to be avoided, which whether they do more harm to the maker or eater is not easy to tell. This I am sure, it is one of the most inconvenient ways of expense that vanity has yet found out; and so I leave them to the ladies.

*Sleep.*  §21. Of all that looks soft and effeminate, nothing is more to be indulged children than *sleep.* In this alone they are to be permitted to have their full satisfaction; nothing contributing more to the growth and health of children than *sleep.* All that is to be regulated in it is in what part of the twenty-four hours they should take it: which will easily be resolved by only saying that it is of great use to accustom them to rise early in the morning. It is best so to do for health: and he that from his childhood has, by a settled custom, made *rising betimes* easy and familiar to him will not when he is a man waste the best and most useful part of his life in drowsiness and lying abed. If children therefore are to be called up early in the morning, it will follow of course that they must go to bed betimes; whereby they will be accustomed to avoid the unhealthy and unsafe hours of debauchery, which are those of the evenings; and they who keep good hours seldom are guilty of any great disorders. I do not say this as if your son, when grown up, should never be in company past eight nor ever chat over a glass of wine till midnight. You are now, by the accustoming of his tender years, to indispose him to those inconveniences as much as you can; and it will be no small advantage that, contrary practice having made sitting up uneasy to him, it will make him often avoid and very seldom propose midnight revels. But if it should not reach so far, but fashion and company should prevail and make him live as others do about twenty, it is worth the while to accustom him to *early rising* and early going to bed between this and that [age] for the present improvement of his health and other advantages.

Though I have said a large allowance of *sleep*, even as much as they will take, should be made to children when they are little, yet I do not mean that it should always be continued to them in so large a proportion, and they suffered to indulge a drowsy laziness in their beds as they grow up bigger. But whether they should begin to be restrained at seven, or ten years old, or any other time, is impossible to be precisely determined. Their tempers, strength, and constitutions must be considered. But sometime between seven and fourteen, if they are too great lovers of their beds, I think it may be seasonable to begin to reduce them by degrees to about eight hours, which is generally rest enough for healthy grown people. If you have accustomed him, as you should do, to rise constantly very early in the morning, this fault of being too long in bed will easily be reformed; and most children will be forward enough to shorten that time themselves by coveting to sit up with the company at night; though if they be not looked after, they will be apt to take it out in the morning, which should by no means be permitted. They should constantly be called up and made to rise at their early hour: but great care should be taken in waking them that it be not done hastily, nor with a loud or shrill voice or any other sudden violent noise. This often affrights children and does them great harm. And sound *sleep* thus broken off, with sudden alarms, is apt enough to discompose anyone. When children are to be wakened out of their *sleep*, be sure to begin with a low call and some gentle motion, and so draw them out of it by degrees, and give them none but kind words and usage till they are come perfectly to themselves, and being quite dressed, you are sure they are thoroughly awake. The being forced from their *sleep*, how gently soever you do it, is pain enough to them: and care should be taken not to add any other uneasiness to it, especially such that may terrify them.

*Bed.*     §22. Let his *bed* be *hard*, and rather quilts than feathers. Hard lodging strengthens the [bodily] parts; whereas being buried every night in feathers melts and dissolves the body, [and] is often the cause of weakness and the forerunner of an early grave. And besides the [kidney] stone, which has often its rise from this warm wrapping of the reins, several other indispositions, and that which is the root of them all, a tender weakly constitution, is very much owing to *down beds*. Besides, he that is used to hard lodging at home will not miss his sleep (where he has most need of it) in his travels abroad for want of his soft bed and his pillows laid in order. And therefore I think it would not be amiss to *make* his *bed* after different fashions, sometimes lay his head higher, sometimes lower, that he may not feel every little change he must be sure to meet with who is not designed to lie always in my young master's bed at home and to have his maid lay all things in print[12] and tuck him in warm. The great cordial of nature is sleep. He that misses that will suffer by it: and he is very unfortunate who can take his cordial only in his mother's fine gilt cup, and not in a wooden dish. He that can sleep soundly takes the cordial: and it matters not whether it be on a soft *bed* or the hard boards. It is sleep only that is the thing necessary.

*Costiveness.*     §23. One thing more there is, which has a great influence upon the health, and that is *going to stool* regularly. People that are very *loose* have seldom strong thoughts or strong bodies. But the cure of this, both by diet and medicine, being much more easy than the contrary evil, there needs not much to be said about it: for if it come to threaten either by its violence or duration, it will soon enough, and sometimes too soon, make a physician be sent for; and if it be moderate or short, it is commonly best to leave it to nature. On the other side, *costiveness* has too its ill effects and is much harder to be dealt with by physic; purging medicines, which seem to give relief, rather increasing than removing the evil.

§24. It being an indisposition I had a particular reason to inquire into and not finding the cure of it in books, I set my thoughts on work, believing that greater changes than that might be made in our bodies, if we took the right course and proceeded by rational steps.

1. Then I considered that *going to stool* was the effect of certain motions of the body, especially of the peristaltic motion of the guts.

2. I considered that several motions that were not perfectly voluntary might yet by use and constant application be brought to be habitual if by

12. In exact order.

an unintermitted custom they were at certain seasons endeavored to be constantly produced.

3. I had observed some men who, by taking after supper a pipe of tobacco, never failed of a *stool*, and began to doubt with myself whether it were not more custom than the tobacco that gave them the benefit of nature; or at least if the tobacco did it, it was rather by exciting a vigorous motion in the guts than by any purging quality, for then it would have had other effects.

Having thus once got the opinion that it was possible to make it habitual, the next thing was to consider what way and means was the likeliest to obtain it.

4. Then I guessed that if a man after his first eating in the morning would presently solicit nature and try whether he could strain himself so as to obtain a *stool*, he might in time, by a constant application, bring it to be habitual.

§25. The reasons that made me choose this time were:

1. Because the stomach being then empty, if it received anything grateful[13] to it (for I would never, but in case of necessity, have anyone eat but what he likes and when he has an appetite), it was apt to embrace it close by a strong constriction of its fibers; which constriction, I supposed, might probably be continued on in the guts and so increase their peristaltic motion; as we see in the *ileus* that an inverted motion, being begun anywhere below, continues itself all the whole length and makes even the stomach obey that irregular motion.

2. Because when men eat they usually relax their thoughts, and the spirits, then free from other employments, are more vigorously distributed into the lower belly, which thereby contribute to the same effect.

3. Because whenever men have leisure to eat they have leisure enough also to make so much court to Madam Cloacina[14] as would be necessary to our present purpose; but else, in the variety of human affairs and accidents, it was impossible to affix it to any hour certain, whereby the custom would be interrupted. Whereas men in health seldom failing to eat once a day, though the hour changed, the custom might still be preserved.

§26. Upon these grounds, the experiment began to be tried; and I have known none who have been steady in the prosecution of it and taken care to go constantly to the necessary house after their first eating, whenever that happened, whether they found themselves called on or no, and there

13. Pleasing.

14. From the Latin for "sewer."

endeavored to put nature upon her duty, but in a few months they obtained the desired success, and brought themselves to so regular a habit that they seldom ever failed of a *stool* after their first eating, unless it were by their own neglect. For whether they have any motion or no, if they go to the place and do their part, they are sure to have nature very obedient.

§27. I would therefore advise that this course should be taken with a child every day presently after he has eaten his breakfast. Let him be set upon the stool as if disburdening were as much in his power as filling his belly; and let not him or his maid know anything to the contrary but that it is so: and if he be forced to endeavor, by being hindered from his play or eating again till he has been effectually at *stool* or at least done his utmost, I doubt not but in a little while it will become natural to him. For there is reason to suspect that children, being usually intent on their play and very heedless of anything else, often let pass those motions of nature when she calls them but gently; and so they, neglecting the seasonable offers, do by degrees bring themselves into a habitual costiveness. That by this method costiveness may be prevented, I do more than guess; having known, by the constant practice of it for some time, a child brought to have a *stool* regularly after his breakfast every morning.

§28. How far any grown people will think fit to make trial of it must be left to them, though I cannot but say that, considering the many evils that come from that defect of a requisite easing of nature, I scarce know anything more conducing to the preservation of health than this is. Once in four and twenty hours, I think, is enough; and nobody, I guess, will think it too much. And by this means it is to be obtained without physic, which commonly proves very ineffectual in the cure of a settled and habitual costiveness.

*Physic.*  §29. This is all I have to trouble you with concerning his management in the ordinary course of his health. Perhaps it will be expected from me that I should give some directions of *physic* to prevent diseases, for which I have only this one very sacredly to be observed: never to give children any *physic* for prevention. The observation of what I have already advised will, I suppose, do that better than the ladies' diet drinks or apothecary's medicines. Have a great care of tampering that way lest instead of preventing you draw on diseases. Nor even upon every little indisposition is *physic* to be given or the physician to be called to children, especially if he be a busy man that will presently fill their windows with gallipots and their stomachs with drugs. It is safer to leave them wholly to nature than to put them into the hands of one forward to tamper or that thinks children are to be cured in ordinary distempers by anything but diet or by a method very little distant from it. It seeming suitable both to my reason and experience that the tender constitutions of children should have as little done to them as is possible and as the absolute necessity of the case requires. A little cold distilled red *poppy-water*, which is the true surfeit-water, with ease and abstinence from flesh, often puts an end to several distempers in the beginning which, by too forward applications, might have been made lusty diseases. When such a gentle treatment will not stop the growing mischief nor hinder it from turning into a formed disease, it will be time to seek the advice of some sober and discreet physician. In this part, I hope I shall find an easy belief; and nobody can have a pretence to doubt the advice of one who has spent some time in the study of physic when he counsels you not to be too forward in making use of *physic* and *physicians*.

§30. And thus I have done with what concerns the body and health, which reduces itself to these few and easily observable rules: plenty of open *air, exercise,* and *sleep*; plain *diet*, no *wine* or *strong drink*, and very little or no *physic*; not too warm and straight *clothing*, especially the *head* and *feet* kept cold, and the *feet* often used to cold water and exposed to wet.

§31. Due care being had to keep the body in strength and vigor so that it may be able to obey and execute the orders of the *mind*, the next and principal business is to set the *mind* right, that on all occasions it may be disposed to consent to nothing but what may be suitable to the dignity and excellency of a rational creature. <sub></sub>*Mind.*

§32. If what I have said in the beginning of this discourse[15] be true, as I do not doubt but it is, viz. that the difference to be found in the manners and abilities of men is owing more to their *education* than to anything else, we have reason to conclude that great care is to be had of the forming children's *minds* and giving them that seasoning early which shall influence their lives always after. For when they do well or ill the praise or blame will be laid there: and when anything is done untowardly, the common saying will pass upon them, that it is suitable to their *breeding*.

§33. As the strength of the body lies chiefly in being able to endure hardships, so also does that of the mind. And the great principle and foundation of all virtue and worth is placed in this, that a man is able to *deny himself* his own desires, cross his own inclinations, and purely follow what reason directs as best though the appetite lean the other way.

§34. The great mistake I have observed in people's breeding their children has been that this has not been taken care enough of in its *due season*, that the mind has not been made obedient to discipline and pliant to reason *Early.*

15. §1.

when at first it was most tender, most easy to be bowed. Parents, being wisely ordained by nature to love their children, are very apt, if reason watch not that natural affection very warily, are apt, I say, to let it run into fondness. They love their little ones, and 'tis their duty; but they often, with them, cherish their faults too. They must not be crossed, forsooth; they must be permitted to have their wills in all things; and they being in their infancies not capable of great vices, their parents think they may safely enough indulge their little irregularities and make themselves sport with that pretty perverseness, which, they think, well enough becomes that innocent age. But to a fond parent, that would not have his child corrected for a perverse trick but excused it, saying it was a small matter, Solon very well replied, aye, but custom is a great one.[16]

§35. The fondling must be taught to strike and call names, must have what he cries for, and do what he pleases. Thus parents, by humoring and cockering them when *little*, corrupt the principles of nature in their children, and wonder afterwards to taste the bitter waters, when they themselves have poisoned the fountain. For when their children are grown up, and these ill habits with them; when they are now too big to be dandled, and their parents can no longer make use of them as playthings; then they complain that the brats are untoward and perverse; then they are offended to see them willful and are troubled with those ill humors which they themselves infused and fomented in them; and then, perhaps too late, would be glad to get out those weeds which their own hands have planted, and which now have taken too deep root to be easily extirpated. For he that has been used to have his will in everything as long as he was in [petti]coats, why should we think it strange that he should desire it and contend for it still when he is in breeches? Indeed, as he grows more towards a man, age shows his faults the more, so that there be few parents then so blind as not to see them, few so insensible as not to feel the ill effects of their own indulgence. He had the will of his maid before he could speak or go; he had the mastery of his parents ever since he could prattle; and why, now he is grown up, is stronger and wiser than he was then, why now of a sudden must he be restrained and curbed? Why must he at seven, fourteen, or twenty years old lose the privilege which the parent's indulgence, till then, so largely allowed him? Try it in a dog or a horse or any other creature, and see whether the ill and restive tricks they have learned when young are easily to be mended when they are knit: and yet none of

16. Diogenes Laertius III 38, told of the philosopher Plato not the Athenian legislator Solon.

those creatures are half so willful and proud or half so desirous to be masters of themselves and others as man.

§36. We are generally wise enough to begin with them when they are *very young* and discipline *betimes* those other creatures we would make useful and good for somewhat. They are only our own offspring that we neglect in this point; and having made them ill children, we foolishly expect they should be good men. For if the child must have grapes or sugarplumbs when he has a mind to them rather than make the poor baby cry or be out of humor; why, when he is grown up, must he not be satisfied too if his desires carry him to wine or women? They are objects as suitable to the longing of one of more years as what he cried for when little was to the inclinations of a child. The having desires accommodated to the apprehensions and relish of those several ages is not the fault, but the not having them subject to the rules and restraints of reason; the difference lies not in the having or not having appetites, but in the power to govern and deny ourselves in them. He that is not used to submit his will to the reason of others *when* he is *young*, will scarce hearken or submit to his own reason when he is of an age to make use of it. And what kind of a man such a one is likely to prove is easy to foresee.

§37. These are oversights usually committed by those who seem to take the greatest care of their children's education. But if we look into the common management of children, we shall have reason to wonder, in the great dissoluteness of manners which the world complains of, that there are any footsteps at all left of virtue. I desire to know what vice can be named, which parents and those about children do not season them with and drop into them the seeds of as soon as they are capable to receive them? I do not mean by the examples they give and the patterns they set before them, which is encouragement enough, but that which I would take notice of here is the downright teaching them vice and actual putting them out of the way of virtue. Before they can go, they principle them with violence, revenge, and cruelty. *Give me a blow that I may beat him,* is a lesson which most children every day hear: and it is thought nothing because their hands have not strength to do any mischief. But I ask, does not this corrupt their minds? Is not this the way of force and violence that they are set in? And if they have been taught when little to strike and hurt others by proxy, and encouraged to rejoice in the harm they have brought upon them and see them suffer, are they not prepared to do it when they are strong enough to be felt themselves and can strike to some purpose?

The coverings of our bodies, which are for modesty, warmth, and defense, are by the folly or vice of parents recommended to their children for other uses. They are made matter of vanity and emulation. A child is set a longing after a new suit for the finery of it; and when the little girl is tricked up in her new gown and commode, how can her mother do less than teach her to admire herself by calling her *her little queen* and *her princess?* Thus the little ones are taught to be *proud* of their clothes before they can put them on. And why should they not continue to value themselves for this outside fashionableness of the tailor or attire-woman's making, when their parents have so early instructed them to do so?

*Lying* and equivocations, and excuses little different from lying, are put into the mouths of young people and commended in apprentices and children whilst they are for their master's or parent's advantage. And can it be thought that he that finds the straining of truth dispensed with and encouraged whilst it is for his godly master's turn will not make use of that privilege for himself when it may be for his own profit?

Those of the meaner sort are hindered by the straightness of their fortunes from encouraging *intemperance* in their children by the temptation of their diet or invitations to eat or drink more than enough; but their own ill examples, whenever plenty comes in their way, show that it is not the dislike of drunkenness and gluttony that keeps them from excess, but want of materials. But if we look into the houses of those who are a little warmer in their fortunes, there eating and drinking are made so much the great business and happiness of life that children are thought neglected if they have not their share of it. Sauces and ragouts and food disguised by all the arts of cookery must tempt their palates when their bellies are full; and then, for fear the stomach should be over-charged, a pretence is found for another glass of wine to help digestion, though it only serves to increase the surfeit.

Is my young master a little out of order, the first question is *What will my dear eat? what shall I get for thee?* Eating and drinking are instantly pressed; and everybody's invention is set on work to find out something luscious and delicate enough to prevail over that want of appetite which nature has wisely ordered in the beginning of distempers as a defence against their increase, that being freed from the ordinary labor of digesting any new load in the stomach, she may be at leisure to correct and master the peccant humors.

And where children are so happy in the care of their parents as by their prudence to be kept from the excess of their tables to the sobriety of a plain and simple diet, yet there too they are scarce to be preserved from the contagion that poisons the mind. Though by a discreet management, whilst they are under tuition, their healths perhaps may be pretty well secured, yet their desires must needs yield to the lessons which everywhere will be read to them upon this part of epicurism. The commendation that *eating well* has everywhere cannot fail to be a successful incentive to natural appetite and bring them quickly to the liking and expense of a fashionable table. This shall have from everyone, even the reprovers of vice, the title of *living well*. And what shall sullen reason dare to say against the public testimony? Or can it hope to be heard if it should call that *luxury*, which is so much owned and universally practiced by those of the best quality?[17]

This is now so grown a vice and has so great supports that I know not whether it do not put in for the name of virtue, and whether it will not be thought folly or want of knowledge of the world to open one's mouth against it. And truly I should suspect that what I have here said of it might be censured as a little satire out of my way, did I not mention it with this view: that it might awaken the care and watchfulness of parents in the education of their children when they see how they are beset on every side not only with temptations, but instructors to vice, and that perhaps in those they thought places of security.

I shall not dwell any longer on this subject, much less run over all the particulars that would show what pains are used to corrupt children and instill principles of vice into them; but I desire parents soberly to consider what irregularity or vice there is which children are not visibly taught, and whether it be not their duty and wisdom to provide them other instructions.

§38. It seems plain to me that the principle of all virtue and excellency *Craving.* lies in a power of denying ourselves the satisfaction of our own desires where reason does not authorize them. This power is to be got and improved by custom, made easy and familiar by an *early* practice. If therefore I might be heard, I would advise that, contrary to the ordinary way, children should be used to submit their desires and go without their longings even *from their very cradles*. The first thing they should learn to know should be that they were not to have anything because it pleased them, but because it was thought fit for them. If things suitable to their wants were supplied to them, so that they were never suffered to have what they once cried for, they would learn to be content without it, would never with bawling and peevishness contend for mastery, nor be half so uneasy to themselves and others as they are because *from the first* beginning they are not thus handled. If they were never suffered to obtain their desire by the

17. High social class.

impatience they expressed for it, they would no more cry for other things than they do for the moon.

§39. I say not this as if children were not to be indulged in anything; or that I expected they should in hanging sleeves[18] have the reason and conduct of councillors. I consider them as children, who must be tenderly used, who must play, and have playthings. That which I mean is that, whenever they craved what was not fit for them to have or do, they should not be permitted it because they were *little* and desired it: nay, whatever they were importunate for, they should be sure, for that very reason, to be denied. I have seen children at a table who, whatever was there, never asked for anything, but contentedly took what was given them; and at another place I have seen others cry for everything they saw, must be served out of every dish, and that first too. What made this vast difference but this: that one was accustomed to have what they called or cried for, the other to go without it? The *younger* they are, the less, I think, are their unruly and disorderly appetites to be complied with; and the less reason they have of their own, the more are they to be under the absolute power and restraint of those in whose hands they are. From which, I confess, it will follow that none but discreet people should be about them. If the world commonly does otherwise, I cannot help that. I am saying what I think should be: which, if it were already in fashion, I should not need to trouble the world with a discourse on this subject. But yet I doubt not but when it is considered, there will be others of opinion with me, that the *sooner* this way is begun with children, the easier it will be for them and their governors too; and that this ought to be observed as an inviolable maxim, that whatever once is denied them, they are certainly not to obtain by crying or importunity, unless one has a mind to teach them to be impatient and troublesome by rewarding them for it when they are so.

*Early.*    §40. Those therefore that intend ever to govern their children should begin it whilst they are *very little*, and look that they perfectly comply with the will of their parents. Would you have your son obedient to you when past a child? Be sure then to establish the authority of a father *as soon* as he is capable of submission and can understand in whose power he is. If you would have him stand in awe of you, imprint it *in his infancy*, and as he approaches more to a man admit him nearer to your familiarity; so shall you have him your obedient subject (as is fit) whilst he is a child, and your affectionate friend when he is a man. For, methinks, they mightily misplace the treatment due to their children who are indulgent and familiar

18. Loose open sleeves worn by children.

when they are little, but severe to them and keep them at a distance when they are grown up. For liberty and indulgence can do no good to *children:* their want of judgment makes them stand in need of restraint and discipline. And, on the contrary, imperiousness and severity is but an ill way of treating men, who have reason of their own to guide them, unless you have a mind to make your children, when grown up, weary of you and secretly to say within themselves, *When will you die, Father?*

§41. I imagine everyone will judge it reasonable that their children *when little* should look upon their parents as their lords, their absolute governors, and, as such, stand in awe of them; and that when they come to riper years, they should look on them as their best, as their only sure friends, and, as such, love and reverence them. The way I have mentioned, if I mistake not, is the only one to obtain this. We must look upon our children, when grown up, to be like ourselves: with the same passions, the same desires. We would be thought rational creatures, and have our freedom; we love not to be uneasy under constant rebukes and browbeatings; nor can we bear severe humors and great distance in those we converse with. Whoever has such treatment when he is a man will look out other company, other friends, other conversation,[19] with whom he can be at ease. If therefore a strict hand be kept over children *from the beginning,* they will in that age be tractable and quietly submit to it, as never having known any other; and if, as they grow up to the use of reason, the rigor of government be, as they deserve it, gently relaxed, the father's brow more smoothed to them, and the distance by degrees abated, his former restraints will increase their love when they find it was only a kindness to them and a care to make them capable to deserve the favor of their parents and the esteem of everybody else.

§42. Thus much for the settling your authority over your children in general. Fear and awe ought to give you the first power over their minds, and love and friendship in riper years to hold it: for the time must come when they will be past the rod and correction, and then if the love of you make them not obedient and dutiful, if the love of virtue and reputation keep them not in laudable courses, I ask, what hold will you have upon them to turn them to it? Indeed, fear of having a scanty portion if they displease you may make them slaves to your estate, but they will be never the less ill and wicked in private; and that restraint will not last always. Every man must sometime or other be trusted to himself and his own conduct; and he that is a good, a virtuous and able man must be made so within.

19. Social intercourse.

And, therefore, what he is to receive from education, what is to sway and influence his life, must be something put into him betimes: habits woven into the very principles of his nature, and not a counterfeit carriage[20] and dissembled outside put on by fear only to avoid the present anger of a father who perhaps may disinherit him.

*Punishments.*    §43. This being laid down in general as the course [that] ought to be taken, 'tis fit we now come to consider the parts of the discipline to be used a little more particularly. I have spoken so much of carrying a *strict hand* over children, that perhaps I shall be suspected of not considering enough what is due to their tender ages and constitutions. But that opinion will vanish when you have heard me a little farther. For I am very apt to think that *great severity* of punishment does but very little good, nay, great harm in education; and I believe it will be found that, *ceteris paribus*, those children who have been most *chastised* seldom make the best men. All that I have hitherto contended for is that, whatsoever *rigor* is necessary, it is more to be used the younger children are; and having by a due application wrought its effect, it is to be relaxed and changed into a milder sort of government.

*Awe.*    §44. A compliance and suppleness of their wills, being by a steady hand introduced by parents before children have memories to retain the beginnings of it, will seem natural to them and work afterwards in them as if it were so, preventing all occasions of struggling or repining. The only care is that it be begun early and inflexibly kept to till *awe* and *respect* be grown familiar and there appears not the least reluctancy in the submission and ready obedience of their minds. When this *reverence* is once thus established (which it must be early or else it will cost pains and blows to recover it, and the more, the longer it is deferred), 'tis by it, mixed still with as much indulgence as they make not an ill use of, and not by *beating, chiding,* or other *servile punishments,* they are for the future to be governed as they grow up to more understanding.

§45. That this is so will be easily allowed when it is but considered what is to be aimed at in an ingenuous education and upon what it turns.

*Self-denial.*    1. He that has not a mastery over his inclinations, he that knows not how to *resist* the importunity of *present pleasure or pain* for the sake of what reason tells him is fit to be done, wants the true principle of virtue and industry and is in danger never to be good for anything. This temper, therefore, so contrary to unguided nature, is to be got betimes; and this habit, as the true foundation of future ability and happiness, is to be

20. Deportment.

wrought into the mind as early as may be, even from the first dawnings of any knowledge or apprehension in children, and so to be confirmed in them by all the care and ways imaginable by those who have the oversight of their education.

§46. 2. On the other side, if the *mind* be curbed and *humbled* too much   *Dejected* in children, if their *spirits* be abased and *broken* much by too strict a hand over them, they lose all their vigor and industry, and are in a worse state than the former. For extravagant young fellows that have liveliness and spirit come sometimes to be set right, and so make able and great men; but *dejected minds*, timorous and tame, and *low spirits* are hardly ever to be raised and very seldom attain to anything. To avoid the danger that is on either hand is the great art; and he that has found a way how to keep up a child's spirit easy, active, and free and yet at the same time to restrain him from many things he has a mind to and to draw him to things that are uneasy to him, he, I say, that knows how to reconcile these seeming contradictions has in my opinion got the true secret of education.

§47. The usual lazy and short way by chastisement and the rod, which   *Beating* is the only instrument of government that tutors generally know or ever think of, is the most unfit of any to be used in education because it tends to both those mischiefs; which, as we have shown, are the Scylla and Charybdis, which on the one hand or the other ruin all that miscarry.

§48. 1. This kind of punishment contributes not at all to the mastery of our natural propensity to indulge corporal and present pleasure and to avoid pain at any rate; but rather encourages it and thereby strengthens that in us which is the root from whence spring all vicious actions and the irregularities of life. For what other motive but of sensual pleasure and pain does a child act by who drudges at his book against his inclination or abstains from eating unwholesome fruit that he takes pleasure in only out of fear of *whipping*? He in this only prefers the greater *corporal pleasure* or avoids the greater *corporal pain*. And what is it to govern his actions and direct his conduct by such motives as these? What is it, I say, but to cherish that principle in him, which it is our business to root out and destroy? And therefore I cannot think any correction useful to a child where the shame of suffering for having done amiss does not work more upon him than the pain.

§49. 2. This sort of correction naturally breeds an aversion to that which it is the tutor's business to create a liking to. How obvious is it to observe that children come to hate things which were at first acceptable to them when they find themselves *whipped*, and *chid*, and *teased* about them? And it is not to be wondered at in them when grown men would not be able to be reconciled to anything by such ways. Who is there that would not be disgusted with any innocent recreation, in itself indifferent to him, if he should with *blows,* or ill language be *haled* to it when he had no mind? Or be constantly so treated for some circumstance in his application to it? This is natural to be so. Offensive circumstances ordinarily infect innocent things which they are joined with: and the very sight of a cup, wherein anyone uses to take nauseous physic, turns his stomach; so that nothing will relish well out of it, though the cup be ever so clean, and well shaped, and of the richest materials.

§50. 3. Such a sort of *slavish discipline* makes a *slavish temper.* The child submits and dissembles obedience whilst the fear of the rod hangs over him; but when that is removed, and by being out of sight he can promise himself impunity, he gives the greater scope to his natural inclination; which by this way is not at all altered, but on the contrary heightened and increased in him, and after such restraint breaks out usually with the more violence; or:

§51. 4. If *severity* carried to the highest pitch does prevail, and works a cure upon the present unruly distemper, it is often by bringing in the room of it a worse and more dangerous disease by breaking the mind, and then in the place of a disorderly young fellow, you have a *low spirited, moped* creature: who, however with his unnatural sobriety he may please silly people, who commend tame inactive children because they make no noise nor give them any trouble, yet at last will probably prove as uncomfortable a thing to his friends, as he will be all his life a useless thing to himself and others.

*Rewards.* §52. Beating, then, and all other sorts of slavish and corporal punishments are not the discipline fit to be used in the education of those we would have wise, good, and ingenuous men; and therefore [are] very rarely to be applied, and that only in great occasions and cases of extremity. On the other side, to flatter children by *rewards* of things that are pleasant to them is as carefully to be avoided. He that will give his son *apples,* or *sugarplumbs,* or what else of this kind he is most delighted with, to make him learn his book, does but authorize his love of pleasure and cocker up that dangerous propensity which he ought by all means to subdue and stifle in him. You can never hope to teach him to master it whilst you compound for the check you give his inclination in one place by the satisfaction you propose to it in another. To make a good, a wise, and a virtuous man, it is fit he should learn to cross his appetite and deny his inclination to *riches, finery,* or *pleasing his palate* etc. whenever his reason advises the contrary and his duty requires it. But when you draw him to do anything that is fit by the offer of *money* or reward the pains of learning his book by the pleasure of a luscious morsel; when you promise him a *lace-cravat* or a *fine new suit* upon the performance of some of his little tasks; what do you by proposing these as *rewards* but allow them to be the good things he should aim at, and thereby encourage his longing for them and accustom him to place his happiness in them? Thus people, to prevail with children to be industrious about their grammar, dancing, or some other such matter of no great moment to the happiness or usefulness of their lives, by misapplied *rewards* and *punishments* sacrifice their virtue, invert the order of their education, and teach them luxury, pride, or covetousness etc. For in this way, flattering those wrong inclinations which they should restrain and suppress, they lay the foundations of those future vices, which cannot be avoided but by curbing our desires and accustoming them early to submit to reason.

§53. I say not this that I would have children kept from the conveniences or pleasures of life that are not injurious to their health or virtue. On the contrary, I would have their lives made as pleasant and as agreeable to them as may be in a plentiful enjoyment of whatsoever might innocently delight them: provided it be with this caution, that they have those enjoyments only as the consequences of the state of esteem and acceptation they are in with their parents and governors; but they should *never* be offered or bestowed on them as the *rewards of this or that particular performance* that they show an aversion to or to which they would not have applied themselves without that temptation.

§54. But if you take away the rod, on one hand, and these little encouragements, which they are taken with, on the other, how then (will you say) shall children be governed? Remove hope and fear, and there is an end of all discipline. I grant that good and evil, *reward* and *punishment*, are the only motives to a rational creature; these are the spur and reins whereby all mankind are set on work and guided, and therefore they are to be made use of to children too. For I advise their parents and governors always to carry this in their minds, that children are to be treated as rational creatures.

§55. *Rewards*, I grant, and *punishments* must be proposed to children, if we intend to work upon them. The mistake, I imagine, is that those that are generally made use of are *ill chosen*. The pains and pleasures of the body are, I think, of ill consequence when made the rewards and punishments whereby men would prevail on their children: for, as I said before,[21] they serve but to increase and strengthen those inclinations which it is our

21. §§47, 52.

business to subdue and master. What principle of virtue do you lay in a child if you will redeem his desires of one pleasure by the proposal of another? This is but to enlarge his appetite and instruct it to wander. If a child cries for an unwholesome and dangerous fruit, you purchase his quiet by giving him a less hurtful sweetmeat. This perhaps may preserve his health, but spoils his mind and sets that farther out of order. For here you only change the object, but flatter still his *appetite* and allow that must be satisfied wherein, as I have showed, lies the root of the mischief; and till you bring him to be able to bear a denial of that satisfaction, the child may at present be quiet and orderly, but the disease is not cured. By this way of proceeding you foment and cherish in him that which is the spring from whence all the evil flows, which will be sure on the next occasion to break out again with more violence, give him stronger longings, and you more trouble.

*Reputation.*      §56. The *rewards* and *punishments* then, whereby we should keep children in order, *are* quite of another kind and of that force, that when we can get them once to work, the business, I think, is done and the difficulty is over. *Esteem* and *disgrace* are, of all others, the most powerful incentives to the mind, when once it is brought to relish them. If you can once get into children a love of credit and an apprehension of shame and disgrace, you have put into them the true principle, which will constantly work and incline them to the right. But it will be asked, how shall this be done?

I confess it does not at first appearance want some difficulty; but yet I think it worth our while to seek the ways (and practice them when found) to attain this, which I look on as the great secret of education.

§57. *First,* children (earlier perhaps than we think) are very sensible of *praise* and commendation. They find a pleasure in being esteemed and valued, especially by their parents and those whom they depend on. If therefore the father *caress and commend them when they do well, show a cold and neglectful countenance to them upon doing ill,* and this accompanied by a like carriage of the mother and all others that are about them, it will in a little time make them sensible of the difference; and this, if constantly observed, I doubt not but will of itself work more than threats or blows, which lose their force when once grown common and are of no use when shame does not attend them and therefore are to be forborne and never to be used but in the case hereafter mentioned,[22] when it is brought to extremity.

§58. But *secondly,* to make the sense of *esteem* or *disgrace* sink the deeper and be of the more weight, other *agreeable or disagreeable things should con-*

22. §78.

*stantly accompany these different states,* not as particular rewards and punishments of this or that particular action, but as necessarily belonging to and constantly attending one who by his carriage has brought himself into a state of disgrace or commendation. By which way of treating them, children may, as much as possible, be brought to conceive that those that are commended and in esteem for doing well will necessarily be beloved and cherished by everybody and have all other good things as a consequence of it; and, on the other side, when anyone by miscarriage falls into disesteem, and cares not to preserve his credit, he will unavoidably fall under neglect and contempt, and in that state the want of what ever might satisfy or delight him will follow. In this way the objects of their desires are made assisting to virtue, when a settled experience from the beginning teaches children that the things they delight in belong to and are to be enjoyed by those only who are in a state of reputation. If by these means you can come once to shame them out of their faults (for besides that, I would willingly have no punishment) and make them in love with the pleasure of being well thought on, you may turn them as you please, and they will be in love with all the ways of virtue.

§59. The great difficulty here is, I imagine, from the folly and perverseness of servants, who are hardly to be hindered from crossing herein the design of the father and mother. Children, discountenanced by their parents for any fault, find usually a refuge and relief in the caresses of those foolish flatterers, who thereby undo whatever the parents endeavor to establish. When the father or mother looks sour on the child, everybody else should put on the same coldness to him and nobody give him countenance, till forgiveness asked and a reformation of his fault has set him right again and restored him to his former credit. If this were constantly observed, I guess there would be little need of blows or chiding: their own ease and satisfaction would quickly teach children to court commendation and avoid doing that which they found everybody condemned and they were sure to suffer for, without being chid or beaten. This would teach them modesty and shame; and they would quickly come to have a natural abhorrence for that which they found made them slighted and neglected by everybody. But how this inconvenience from servants is to be remedied, I must leave to parents' care and consideration. Only I think it of great importance and that they are very happy who can get discreet people about their children.

§60. Frequent *beating* or *chiding* is therefore carefully *to be avoided.*   *Shame.* Because this sort of correction never produces any good farther than it serves to raise *shame* and abhorrence of the miscarriage that brought it on them. And if the greatest part of the trouble be not the sense that they have done amiss and the apprehension that they have drawn on themselves the just displeasure of their best friends, the pain of whipping will work but an imperfect cure. It only patches up for the present and skins it over, but reaches not to the bottom of the sore. Ingenuous *shame* and the apprehension of displeasure are the only true restraint: these alone ought to hold the reins and keep the child in order. But corporal punishments must necessarily lose that effect and wear out the sense of *shame* where they frequently return. Shame in children has the same place that modesty has in women, which cannot be kept and often transgressed against. And as to the apprehension of *displeasure in the parents*, that will come to be very insignificant if the marks of that displeasure quickly cease and a few blows fully expiate. Parents should well consider what faults in their children are weighty enough to deserve the declaration of their anger: but when their displeasure is once declared to a degree that carries any punishment with it, they ought not presently to lay by the severity of their brows, but to restore their children to their former grace with some difficulty and delay a full reconciliation till their conformity and more than ordinary merit make good their amendment. If this be not so ordered, *punishment* will by familiarity become a mere thing of course and lose all its influence: offending, being chastised, and then forgiven, will be thought as natural and necessary as noon, night, and morning following one another.

*Reputation.*     §61. Concerning reputation, I shall only remark this one thing more of it: that though it be not the true principle and measure of virtue (for that is the knowledge of a man's duty and the satisfaction it is to obey his Maker in following the dictates of that light God has given him with the hopes of acceptation and reward), yet it is that which comes nearest to it; and being the testimony and applause that other people's reason, as it were by common consent, gives to virtuous and well-ordered actions, it is the proper guide and encouragement of children, till they grow able to judge for themselves and to find what is right by their own reason.

§62. This consideration may direct parents, how to manage themselves in reproving and commending their children. The rebukes and chiding, which their faults will sometimes make hardly to be avoided, should not only be in sober, grave, and dispassionate words, but also alone and in private; but the commendations children deserve, they should receive before others. This doubles the reward by spreading their praise; but the backwardness parents show in divulging their faults will make them set a greater value on their credit themselves and teach them to be the more careful to preserve the good opinion of others whilst they think they have it; but when being exposed to shame by publishing their miscarriages, they give it up for lost, that check upon them is taken off; and they will be the less careful to preserve others' good thoughts of them, the more they suspect that their reputation with them is already blemished.

§63. But if a right course be taken with children, there will not be so *Childishness.* much need of the application of the common rewards and punishments as we imagine and as the general practice has established. For all their innocent folly, playing, and *childish actions are to be* left perfectly free and *unrestrained* as far as they can consist with the respect due to those that are present, and that with the greatest allowance. If these faults of their age rather than of the children themselves were, as they should be, left only to time and imitation and riper years to cure, children would escape a great deal of misapplied and useless correction, which either fails to overpower the natural disposition of their childhood and so by an ineffectual familiarity makes correction in other necessary cases of less use; or else, if it be of force to restrain the natural gaiety of that age, it serves only to spoil the temper both of body and mind. If the noise and bustle of their play prove at any time inconvenient or unsuitable to the place or company they are in (which can only be where their parents are), a look or a word from the father or mother, if they have established the authority they should, will be enough either to remove or quiet them for that time. But this gamesome humor, which is wisely adapted by nature to their age and temper, should rather be encouraged to keep up their spirits and improve their strength and health than curbed or restrained: and the chief art is to make all that they have to do sport and play too.

§64. And here give me leave to take notice of one thing I think a fault in *Rules.* the ordinary method of education; and that is the charging of children's memories, upon all occasions, with *rules* and precepts, which they often do not understand and constantly as soon forget as given. If it be some action you would have done, or done otherwise, whenever they forget or do it awkwardly, make them do it over and over again till they are perfect, whereby you will get these two advantages: *first*, to see whether it be an action they can do or is fit to be expected of them. For sometimes children are bid to do things which upon trial they are found not able to do and had need be taught and exercised in before they are required to do them. But it is much easier for a tutor to command than to teach. *Secondly*, another thing got by it will be this: that by repeating the same action, till it be grown habitual in them, the performance will not depend on memory or reflection, the concomitant of prudence and age and not of childhood, but will be natural in them. Thus bowing to a gentleman when he salutes him and looking in his face when he speaks to him is by constant use as natural to a well-bred man as breathing; it requires no thought, no reflection. Having this way cured in your child any fault, it is cured forever: and thus one by one you may weed them out all and plant what habits you please.

§65. I have seen parents so heap *rules* on their children that it was impossible for the poor little ones to remember a tenth part of them, much less to observe them. However, they were either by words or blows corrected for the breach of those multiplied and often very impertinent precepts. Whence it naturally followed that the children minded not what was said to them when it was evident to them that no attention they were capable of was sufficient to preserve them from transgression and the rebukes which followed it.

Let therefore your *rules* to your son be as few as is possible, and rather fewer than more than seem absolutely necessary. For if you burden him with many *rules*, one of these two things must necessarily follow: that either he must be very often punished, which will be of ill consequence by making punishment too frequent and familiar, or else you must let the transgressions of some of your rules go unpunished, whereby they will of course grow contemptible and your authority become cheap to him. Make but few *laws*, but see they be well observed when once made. Few years require but few laws, and as his age increases, when one rule is by practice well established you may add another.

Habits.     §66. But pray remember, children are *not* to be *taught by rules*, which will be always slipping out of their memories. What you think necessary for them to do, settle in them by an indispensable practice as often as the occasion returns; and if it be possible, make occasions. This will beget habits in them, which, being once established, operate of themselves easily and naturally without the assistance of the memory. But here let me give two cautions: 1. The one is that you keep them to the practice of what you would have grow into a habit in them by kind words and gentle admonitions, rather as minding them of what they forget than by harsh rebukes and chiding as if they were willfully guilty. Secondly, another thing you are to take care of is not to endeavor to settle too many habits at once, lest by variety you confound them, and so perfect none. When constant custom has made any one thing easy and natural to them, and they practice it without reflection, you may then go on to another.

Practice.     This method of teaching children by a repeated practice, and the same action done over and over again under the eye and direction of the tutor till they have got the habit of doing it well, and not by relying on *rules* trusted to their memories, has so many advantages whichever way we consider it that I cannot but wonder (if ill customs could be wondered at in anything) how it could possibly be so much neglected. I shall name one more that comes now in my way. By this method we shall see whether what is required of him be adapted to his capacity and anyway suited to the child's natural genius and constitution; for that too must be considered in a right education. We must not hope wholly to change their original tempers nor make the gay pensive and grave, nor the melancholy sportive, without spoiling them. God has stamped certain characters upon men's minds, which, like their shapes, may perhaps be a little mended but can hardly be totally altered and transformed into the contrary.

He, therefore, that is about children should well study their natures and aptitudes and see, by often trials, what turn they easily take and what becomes them, observe what their native stock is, how it may be improved, and what it is fit for; he should consider what they want, whether they be capable of having it wrought into them by industry and incorporated there by practice, and whether it be worthwhile to endeavor it. For in many cases, all that we can do or should aim at is to make the best of what nature has given, to prevent the vices and faults to which such a constitution is most inclined, and give it all the advantages it is capable of. Everyone's natural genius should be carried as far as it could, but to attempt the putting another upon him will be but labor in vain: and what is so plastered on will at best sit but untowardly and have always hanging to it the ungracefulness of constraint and affectation.

*Affectation* is not, I confess, an early fault of childhood or the product    *Affectation.* of untaught nature; it is of that sort of weeds which grow not in the wild uncultivated waste, but in garden plots under the negligent hand or unskillful care of a gardener. Management, and instruction, and some sense of the necessity of breeding are requisite to make anyone capable of *affectation*, which endeavors to correct natural defects and has always the laudable aim of pleasing, though it always misses it; and the more it labors to put on gracefulness, the farther it is from it. For this reason it is the more carefully to be watched, because it is the proper fault of education, a perverted education indeed but such as young people often fall into either by their own mistake or the ill conduct of those about them.

He that will examine wherein that gracefulness lies which always pleases will find it arises from that natural coherence which appears between the thing done and such a temper of mind as cannot but be approved of as suitable to the occasion. We cannot but be pleased with a humane, friendly, civil temper wherever we meet with it. A mind free and master of itself and all its actions, not low and narrow, not haughty and insolent, not blemished with any great defect, is what everyone is taken with. The actions which naturally flow from such a well-formed mind please us also as the genuine marks of it and, being as it were natural emanations from the spirit and disposition within, cannot but be easy and unconstrained. This seems to me to be that beauty which shines through some men's actions, sets off all that they do, and takes all they come near when, by a constant practice, they have fashioned their carriage and made all those little expressions of civility and respect, which nature or custom has established in conversation, so easy to themselves that they seem not artificial or studied, but naturally to flow from a sweetness of mind and a well-turned disposition.

On the other side, *affectation* is an awkward and forced imitation of what should be genuine and easy, wanting the beauty that accompanies what is natural, because there is always a disagreement between the outward action and the mind within one of these two ways: 1. Either when a man would outwardly put on a disposition of mind which then he really has not, but endeavors by a forced carriage to make show of, yet so that the constraint he is under discovers itself; and thus men affect sometimes to appear sad, merry, or kind when in truth they are not so.

2. The other is when they do not endeavor to make show of dispositions of mind which they have not, but to express those they have by a carriage not suited to them: and such in conversation are all constrained motions, actions, words, or looks, which though designed to show either their respect or civility to the company or their satisfaction and easiness in it, are not yet natural nor genuine marks of the one or the other, but rather of some defect or mistake within. Imitation of others, without discerning what is graceful in them or what is peculiar to their characters, often makes a great part of this. But *affectation* of all kinds, whencesoever it proceeds, is always offensive because we naturally hate whatever is counterfeit and contemn those who have nothing better to recommend themselves by.

Plain and rough nature, left to itself, is much better than an artificial ungracefulness and such studied ways of being ill fashioned. The want of an accomplishment or some defect in our behavior coming short of the utmost gracefulness often escapes observation and censure. But *affectation* in any part of our carriage is lighting up a candle to our defects and never fails to make us be taken notice of, either as wanting sense or wanting sincerity. This governors ought the more diligently to look after because, as I above observed, it is an acquired ugliness, owing to mistaken education, few being guilty of it but those who pretend to breeding and would not be thought ignorant of what is fashionable and becoming in conversation;

and, if I mistake not, it has often its rise from the lazy admonitions of those who give rules and propose examples without joining practice with their instructions and making their pupils repeat the action in their sight that they may correct what is indecent or constrained in it till it be perfected into a habitual and becoming easiness.

§67. *Manners,* as they call it, about which children are so often per- *Manners.* plexed and have so many goodly exhortations made them by their wise maids and governesses, I think, are rather to be learned by example than rules; and then children, if kept out of ill company, will take a pride to behave themselves prettily, after the fashion of others, perceiving themselves esteemed and commended for it. But if by a little negligence in this part, the boy should not put off his hat nor make legs[23] very gracefully, a dancing master will cure that defect and wipe off all that plainness of nature, which the a-la-mode people call clownishness. And since nothing appears to me to give children so much becoming confidence and behavior and so to raise them to the conversation of those above their age as *dancing,* *Dancing.* I think they should be taught to dance as soon as they are capable of learning it. For though this consist only in outward gracefulness of motion, yet, I know not how, it gives children manly thoughts and carriage more than anything. But otherwise I would not have little children much tormented about punctilios or niceties of breeding.

Never trouble yourself about those faults in them which you know age *Manners.* will cure. And therefore want of well-fashioned civility in the carriage, whilst *civility* is not wanting in the mind (for there you must take care to plant it early), should be the parent's least care whilst they are young. If his tender mind be filled with a veneration for his parents and teachers, which consists in love and esteem and a fear to offend them, and with *respect and good will* to all people, that respect will of itself teach those ways of expressing it which he observes most acceptable. Be sure to keep up in him the principles of good nature and kindness; make them as habitual as you can, by credit and commendation and the good things accompanying that state; and when they have taken root in his mind and are settled there by a continued practice, fear not, the ornaments of conversation and the outside of fashionable manners will come in their due time if, when they are removed out of their maid's care, they are put into the hands of a well-bred man to be their governor. Whilst they are very young, any *carelessness* is to be borne with in children that carries not with it the marks of pride or ill nature: but those, whenever they appear

23. Bow.

in any action, are to be corrected immediately by the ways mentioned above.[24]

What I have said concerning manners, I would not have so understood, as if I meant that those who have the judgment to do it should not gently fashion the motions and carriage of children when they are very young. It would be of great advantage if they had people about them from their being first able to go that had the skill and would take the right way to do it. That which I complain of is the wrong course is usually taken in this matter. Children who were never taught any such thing as behavior are often (especially when strangers are present) chid for having some way or other failed in good manners, and have thereupon reproofs and precepts heaped upon them concerning putting off their hats, or making of legs, etc. Though in this those concerned pretend to correct the child, yet in truth, for the most part, it is but to cover their own shame: and they lay the blame on the poor little ones, sometimes passionately enough, to divert it from themselves for fear the bystanders should impute to their want of care or skill the child's ill behavior. For, as for the children themselves, they are never one jot bettered by such occasional lectures. They at other times should be shown what to do and by reiterated actions be fashioned beforehand into the practice of what is fit and becoming, and not told and talked to upon the spot of what they have never been accustomed nor know how to do as they should. To hare[25] and rate them thus at every turn is not to teach them, but to vex and torment them to no purpose. They should be let alone, rather than chid for a fault which is none of theirs nor is in their power to mend for speaking to. And it were much better their natural childish negligence or plainness should be left to the care of riper years than that they should frequently have rebukes misplaced upon them which neither do nor can give them graceful motions. If their minds are well disposed and principled with inward civility, a great part of the roughness which sticks to the outside for want of better teaching, time and observation will rub off as they grow up if they are bred in good company; but if in ill, all the rules in the world, all the correction imaginable, will not be able to polish them. For you must take this for a certain truth, that let them have what instructions you will, and ever so learned lectures of breeding daily inculcated into them, that which will most influence their carriage will be the company they converse with and the fashion of those about them. Children (nay, and men too) do most by example. We are all a sort of chameleons that still take a tincture

24. §§56–58.
25. Harry or harass.

from things near us; nor is it to be wondered at in children, who better understand what they see than what they hear.

§68. I mentioned above one great mischief that came by servants to children when by their flatteries they take off the edge and force of the parents' rebukes and so lessen their authority.[26] And here is another great inconvenience which children receive from the ill examples which they meet with amongst the meaner servants. They are wholly, if possible, to be kept from such conversation for the contagion of these ill precedents, both in civility and virtue, horribly infects children as often as they come within reach of it. They frequently learn from unbred or debauched servants such language, untowardly tricks, and vices as otherwise they possibly would be ignorant of all their lives.

§69. 'Tis a hard matter wholly to prevent this mischief. You will have very good luck if you never have a clownish or vicious servant, and if from them your children never get any infection. But yet as much must be done towards it as can be; and the children kept as much as may be[27] in *the company of their parents* and those to whose care they are committed. To this purpose, their being in their presence should be made easy to them: they should be allowed the liberties and freedom suitable to their ages, and not be held under unnecessary restraints when in their parent's or governor's sight. If it be a prison to them, it is no wonder they should not like it. They must not be hindered from being children or from playing or doing as children, but from doing ill: all other liberty is to be allowed them. Next, to make them in love with the *company of their parents* they should receive all their good things there and from their hands. The servants should be hindered from making court to them by giving them strong drink, wine, fruit, playthings, and other such matters, which may make them in love with their conversation.

§70. Having named *company*, I am almost ready to throw away my pen and trouble you no farther on this subject. For since that does more than all precepts, rules, and instructions, methinks it is almost wholly in vain to make a long discourse of other things and to talk of that almost to no purpose. For you will be ready to say, What shall I do with my son? If I keep him always at home, he will be in danger to be my young master; and if I

*Company.*

26. §59.

27. How much the Romans thought the education of their children a business that properly belonged to the parents themselves, see in Suetonius *Augustus* §64, Plutarch *in vitā Catonis Censoris [Life of Cato the Censor]*, Diodorus Siculus, *bk. 2. chap. 3* [Locke's note].

send him abroad, how is it possible to keep him from the contagion of
rudeness and vice, which is so everywhere in fashion? In my house he will
perhaps be more innocent, but more ignorant too of the world: wanting
there change of company and being used constantly to the same faces, he
will, when he comes abroad, be a sheepish or conceited creature.

I confess both sides have their inconveniences. Being abroad, it is true,
will make him bolder and better able to bustle and shift amongst boys of
his own age; and the emulation of schoolfellows often puts life and industry into young lads. But till you can find a school wherein it is possible for
the master to look after the manners of his scholars and can show as great
effects of his care of forming their minds to virtue and their carriage to
good breeding as of forming their tongues to the learned languages, you
must confess that you have a strange value for words, when preferring the
languages of the ancient Greeks and Romans to that which made them
such brave men, you think it worthwhile to hazard your son's innocence
and virtue for a little Greek and Latin. For, as for that boldness and spirit
which lads get amongst their playfellows at school, it has ordinarily such a
mixture of rudeness and an ill-turned confidence that those misbecoming
and disingenuous ways of shifting in the world must be unlearned and all
the tincture washed out again to make way for better principles and such
manners as make a truly worthy man. He that considers how diametrically
opposite the skill of living well and managing as a man should do his affairs
in the world is to that malapertness, tricking, or violence learned amongst
schoolboys will think the faults of a privater education infinitely to be preferred to such improvements and will take care to preserve his child's
innocence and modesty at home, as being nearer of kin and more in the
way of those qualities which make a useful and able man. Nor does anyone
find or so much as suspect that that retirement and bashfulness which
their daughters are brought up in make them less knowing or less able
women. Conversation, when they come into the world, soon gives them a
becoming assurance; and whatsoever, beyond that, there is of rough and
boisterous may in men be very well spared too; for courage and steadiness,
as I take it, lie not in roughness and ill breeding.

*Virtue.*          Virtue is harder to be got than a knowledge of the world, and if lost in
a young man is seldom recovered. Sheepishness and ignorance of the
world, the faults imputed to a private education, are neither the necessary
consequences of being bred at home nor, if they were, are they incurable
evils. Vice is the more stubborn as well as the more dangerous evil of the
two and therefore in the first place to be fenced against. If that sheepish
softness, which often enervates those who are bred like fondlings at home,

be carefully to be avoided, it is principally so for virtue's sake: for fear lest such a yielding temper should be too susceptible of vicious impressions and expose the novice too easily to be corrupted. A young man, before he leaves the shelter of his father's house and the guard of a tutor, should be fortified with resolution and made acquainted with men to secure his virtue, lest he should be led into some ruinous course or fatal precipice before he is sufficiently acquainted with the dangers of conversation and has steadiness enough not to yield to every temptation. Were it not for this, a young man's bashfulness and ignorance of the world would not so much need an early care. Conversation would cure it in great measure; or if that will not do it early enough, it is only a stronger reason for a good tutor at home. For if pains be to be taken to give him a manly air and assurance betimes, it is chiefly as a fence to his virtue when he goes into the world under his own conduct.

It is preposterous therefore to sacrifice his innocency to the attaining of confidence and some little skill of bustling for himself amongst others by his conversation with ill-bred and vicious boys when the chief use of that sturdiness and standing upon his own legs is only for the preservation of his virtue. For if confidence or cunning come once to mix with vice and support his miscarriages, he is only the surer lost: and you must undo again and strip him of all that he has got from his companions or give him up to ruin. Boys will unavoidably be taught assurance by conversation with men when they are brought into it; and that is time enough. Modesty and submission, till then, better fits them for instruction; and therefore there needs not any great care to stock them with confidence beforehand. That which requires most time, pains, and assiduity is to work into them the principles and practice of virtue and good breeding. This is the seasoning they should be prepared with so as not easily to be got out again. This they had need to be well provided with. For conversation, when they come into the world, will add to their knowledge and assurance but be too apt to take from their virtue; which therefore they ought to be plentifully stored with, and have that tincture sunk deep into them.

How they should be fitted for conversation and entered into the world when they are ripe for it, we shall consider in another place. But how anyone's being put into a mixed herd of unruly boys and there learning to wrangle at trap or rook at span-farthing[28] fits him for civil conversation or

28. Trap or trap-ball was a game in which a ball was hit with a bat after being propelled off a wooden pivot or trap; span-farthing, a game in which one tried to toss a coin within a hand's span of the other player's.

business, I do not see. And what qualities are ordinarily to be got from such a troop of playfellows as schools usually assemble together from parents of all kinds that a father should so much covet, is hard to divine. I am sure he who is able to be at the charge of a tutor at home may there give his son a more genteel carriage, more manly thoughts, and a sense of what is worthy and becoming, with a greater proficiency in learning into the bargain, and ripen him up sooner into a man, than any at school can do. Not that I blame the schoolmaster in this or think it to be laid to his charge. The difference is great between two or three pupils in the same house and three- or fourscore boys lodged up and down. For let the master's industry and skill be ever so great, it is impossible he should have fifty or a hundred scholars under his eye any longer than they are in the school together; nor can it be expected that he should instruct them successfully in anything but their books, the forming of their minds and manners requiring a constant attention and particular application to every single boy which is impossible in a numerous flock and would be wholly in vain (could he have time to study and correct everyone's particular defects and wrong inclinations) when the lad was to be left to himself or the prevailing infection of his fellows the greatest part of the four and twenty hours.

But fathers, observing that fortune is often most successfully courted by bold and bustling men, are glad to see their sons pert and forward betimes, take it for a happy omen that they will be thriving men, and look on the tricks they play their schoolfellows or learn from them as a proficiency in the art of living and making their way through the world. But I must take the liberty to say that he that lays the foundation of his son's fortune in virtue and good breeding takes the only sure and warrantable way. And 'tis not the waggeries or cheats practiced amongst schoolboys, 'tis not their roughness one to another, nor the well-laid plots of robbing an orchard together that make an able man, but the principles of justice, generosity and sobriety, joined with observation and industry, qualities which I judge schoolboys do not learn much of one another. And if a young gentleman, bred at home, be not taught more of them than he could learn at school, his father has made a very ill choice of a tutor. Take a boy from the top of a grammar school and one of the same age bred, as he should be, in his father's family, and bring them into good company together, and then see which of the two will have the more manly carriage and address himself with the more becoming assurance to strangers. Here I imagine the schoolboy's confidence will either fail or discredit him: and if it be such as fits him only for the conversation of boys, he were better be without it.

Vice, if we may believe the general complaint, ripens so fast nowadays and runs up to seed so early in young people that it is impossible to keep a lad from the spreading contagion if you will venture him abroad in the herd and trust to chance or his own inclination for the choice of his company at school. By what fate vice has so thriven amongst us these years past, and by what hands it has been nursed up into so uncontrolled a dominion, I shall leave to others to inquire. I wish that those who complain of the great decay of Christian piety and virtue everywhere and of learning and acquired improvements in the gentry of this generation would consider how to retrieve them in the next. This I am sure, that if the foundation of it be not laid in the education and principling of the youth, all other endeavors will be in vain. And if the innocence, sobriety, and industry of those who are coming up be not taken care of and preserved, it will be ridiculous to expect that those who are to succeed next on the stage should abound in that virtue, ability, and learning which has hitherto made England considerable in the world. I was going to add courage too, though it has been looked on as the natural inheritance of Englishmen. What has been talked of some late actions at sea, of a kind unknown to our ancestors, gives me occasion to say that debauchery sinks the courage of men, and when dissoluteness has eaten out the sense of true honor, bravery seldom stays long after it. And I think it impossible to find an instance of any nation, however renowned for their valor, who ever kept their credit in arms or made themselves redoubtable amongst their neighbors after corruption had once broke through and dissolved the restraint of discipline and vice was grown to such a head that it dared show itself barefaced without being out of countenance.

'Tis virtue then, direct virtue, which is the hard and valuable part to be aimed at in education, and not a forward pertness or any little arts of shifting. All other considerations and accomplishments should give way and be postponed to this. This is the solid and substantial good which tutors should not only read lectures and talk of, but the labor and art of education should furnish the mind with and fasten there, and never cease till the young man had a true relish of it and placed his strength, his glory, and his pleasure in it.

The more this advances, the easier way will be made for all other accomplishments in their turns. For he that is brought to submit to virtue will not be refractory or restive in anything that becomes him. And therefore I cannot but prefer breeding of a young gentleman at home, in his father's sight under a good governor, as much the best and safest way to this great and main end of education, when it can be had and is ordered as it should be. Gentlemen's houses are seldom without variety of company: they should use their sons to all the strange faces that come there and engage them in conversation with men of parts[29] and breeding as soon as they are capable of it. And why those who live in the country should not take them with them when they make visits of civility to their neighbors, I know not. This I am sure, a father that breeds his son at home has the opportunity to have him more in his own company and there give him what encouragement he thinks fit, and can keep him better from the taint of servants and the meaner sort of people than is possible to be done abroad. But what shall be resolved in the case must in great measure be left to the parents to be determined by their circumstances and conveniences. Only I think it the worst sort of good husbandry for a father not to strain himself a little for his son's breeding, which, let his condition be what it will, is the best portion he can leave him. But if, after all, it shall be thought by some that the breeding at home has too little company and that at ordinary schools not such as it should be for a young gentleman, I think there might be ways found out to avoid the inconveniences on the one side and the other.

*Example.*    §71. Having under consideration how great the influence of *company* is and how prone we are all, especially children, to imitation, I must here take the liberty to mind parents of this one thing, viz. that he that will have his son have a respect for him and his orders must himself have a great reverence for his son. *Maxima debetur pueris reverentia.*[30] You must do nothing before him which you would not have him imitate. If anything escape you which you would have pass for a fault in him, he will be sure to shelter himself under your example, and shelter himself so as that it will not be easy to come at him to correct it in him the right way. If you punish him for what he sees you practice yourself, he will not think that severity to proceed from kindness in you, careful to amend a fault in him, but will be apt to interpret it [as] the peevishness and arbitrary imperiousness of a father who, without any ground for it, would deny his son the liberty and pleasures he takes himself. Or if you assume to yourself the liberty you have taken as a privilege belonging to riper years to which a child must not aspire, you do but add new force to your example and recommend the action the more powerfully to him. For you must always remember that children affect to be men earlier than is thought: and they love breeches

29. Talents, or abilities.

30. "The greatest reverence is owed to children," Juvenal *Satires* xiv 47, dealing with the influence of parental example on children.

not for their cut or ease, but because the having them is a mark of a step towards manhood. What I say of the father's carriage before his children must extend itself to all those who have any authority over them or for whom he would have them have any respect.

§72. But to return to the businesses of rewards and punishments. All *Punishment.* the actions of childishness, and unfashionable carriage, and whatever time and age will of itself be sure to reform, being (as I have said[31]) exempt from the discipline of the rod, there will not be so much need of beating children as is generally made use of. To which if we add learning to read, write, dance, foreign languages, etc. as under the same privilege, there will be but very rarely any occasion for blows or force in an ingenuous education. The right way to teach them those things is to give them a liking and inclination to what you propose to them to be learned; and that will engage their industry and application. This I think no hard matter to do if children be handled as they should be, and the rewards and punishments mentioned above[32] be carefully applied and with them these few rules observed in the method of instructing them.

§73. 1. None of the things they are to learn should ever be made a bur- *Task.* den to them or imposed on them as a *task*. Whatever is so proposed presently becomes irksome: the mind takes an aversion to it, though before it were a thing of delight or indifference. Let a child be but ordered to whip his top at a certain time every day, whether he has or has not a mind to it; let this be but required of him as a duty wherein he must spend so many hours morning and afternoon, and see whether he will not soon be weary of any play at this rate? Is it not so with grown men? What they do cheerfully of themselves, do they not presently grow sick of and can no more endure as soon as they find it is expected of them as a duty? Children have as much a mind to show that they are free, that their own good actions come from themselves, that they are absolute and independent, as any of the proudest of you grown men, think of them as you please.

§74. 2. As a consequence of this, they should seldom be put about *Disposition.* doing even those things you have got an inclination in them to but when they have a mind and *disposition* to it. He that loves reading, writing, music, etc. finds yet in himself certain seasons wherein those things have no relish to him; and if at that time he forces himself to it, he only pothers and wearies himself to no purpose. So it is with children. This change of temper should be carefully observed in them, and the favorable *seasons of*

31. §§63, 67.
32. §§56–58.

*aptitude and inclination* be heedfully laid hold of: and if they are not often
enough forward of themselves, a good disposition should be talked into
them before they be set upon anything. This I think no hard matter for a
discreet tutor to do, who has studied his pupil's temper and will be at [a]
little pains to fill his head with suitable ideas, such as may make him in love
with the present business. By this means a great deal of time and tiring
would be saved. For a child will learn three times as much when he is *in
tune* as he will with double the time and pains when he goes awkwardly or
is dragged unwillingly to it. If this were minded as it should, children
might be permitted to weary themselves with play and yet have time
enough to learn what is suited to the capacity of each age. But no such
thing is considered in the ordinary way of education, nor can it well be.
That rough discipline of the rod is built upon other principles, has no
attraction in it, regards not what humor children are in, nor looks after
favorable seasons of inclination. And indeed it would be ridiculous, when
compulsion and blows have raised an aversion in the child to his task, to
expect he should freely of his own accord leave his play and with pleasure
court the occasions of learning. Whereas were matters ordered right,
learning anything they should be taught might be made as much a recreation to their play as their play is to their learning. The pains are equal on
both sides: nor is it that which troubles them, for they love to be busy, and
the change and variety is that which naturally delights them. The only
odds is, in that which we call play they act at liberty and employ their pains
(whereof you may observe them never sparing) freely, but what they are to
learn is forced upon them: they are called, compelled, and driven to it.
This is that that at first entrance balks and cools them; they want their liberty; get them but to ask their tutor to teach them, as they do often their
playfellows, instead of his calling upon them to learn, and they being satisfied that they act as freely in this as they do in other things, they will go
on with as much pleasure in it and it will not differ from their other sports
and play. By these ways, carefully pursued, a child may be brought to
desire to be taught anything you have a mind he should learn. The hardest
part, I confess, is with the first or eldest; but when once he is set right it is
easy by him to lead the rest whither one will.

§75. Though it be past doubt that the fittest time for children to learn
anything is when their *minds* are *in tune and well-disposed* to it, when neither flagging of spirit nor intentness of thought upon something else
makes them awkward and averse; yet two things are to be taken care of: 1.
That, these seasons either not being warily observed and laid hold on as
often as they return or else not returning as often as they should, the

improvement of the child be not thereby neglected, and so he be let grow into a habitual idleness and confirmed in this indisposition. 2. That though other things are ill learned when the mind is either indisposed or otherwise taken up, yet it is of great moment and worth our endeavors to teach the mind to get the mastery over itself, and to be able upon choice to take itself off from the hot pursuit of one thing and set itself upon another with facility and delight, or at any time to shake off its sluggishness and vigorously employ itself about what reason or the advice of another shall direct. This is to be done in children by trying them sometimes, when they are by laziness unbent or by avocation bent another way, and endeavoring to make them buckle to the thing proposed. If by this means the mind can get a habitual dominion over itself, lay by *ideas* or business as occasion requires, and betake itself to new and less acceptable employments without reluctancy or discomposure, it will be an advantage of more consequence than Latin or logic or most of those things children are usually required to learn.

§76. Children being more active and busy in that age than in any *Compulsion.* other part of their life, and being indifferent to anything they can do, so they may be but doing, *dancing* and *Scotch-hoppers* would be the same thing to them were the encouragements and discouragements equal. But to things we would have them learn, the great and only discouragement I can observe is that they are called to it; it is *made their business;* they are *teased* and *chid* about it, and do it with trembling and apprehension; or when they come willingly to it, are kept too long at it till they are quite tired; all which entrenches too much on that natural freedom they extremely affect. And 'tis that liberty alone which gives the true relish and delight to their ordinary play-games. Turn the tables, and you will find they will soon change their application especially if they see the examples of others whom they esteem and think above themselves. And if the things which they observed others to do be ordered so that they insinuate themselves into them as the privilege of an age or condition above theirs, then ambition and the desire still to get forward and higher and to be like those above them will set them on work and make them go on with vigor and pleasure, pleasure in what they have begun by their own desire. In which way the enjoyment of their dearly beloved freedom will be no small encouragement to them. To all which, if there be added the satisfaction of credit and reputation, I am apt to think there will need no other spur to excite their application and assiduity as much as is necessary. I confess there needs patience and skill, gentleness and attention, and a prudent conduct to attain this at first. But why have you a tutor if there needed no pains? But when this is once established, all the rest will follow more easily than in any more severe and imperious discipline. And I think it no hard matter to gain this point; I am sure it will not be where children have no ill examples set before them. The great danger therefore I apprehend is only from servants, and other ill-ordered children, or such other vicious or foolish people who spoil children both by the ill pattern they set before them in their own ill manners and by giving them together the two things they should never have at once: I mean, vicious pleasures and commendation.

*Chiding.*     §77. As children should very seldom be corrected by blows, so I think frequent and especially passionate *chiding* of almost as ill consequence. It lessens the authority of the parents and the respect of the child; for I bid you still remember, they distinguish early between passion and reason; and as they cannot but have a reverence for what comes from the latter, so they quickly grow into a contempt of the former or if it causes a present terror, yet it soon wears off and natural inclination will easily learn to slight such scarecrows, which make a noise but are not animated by reason. Children being to be restrained by the parents only in vicious (which, in their tender years, are only a few) things, a look or nod only ought to correct them when they do amiss; or if words are sometimes to be used, they ought to be grave, kind, and sober, representing the ill or unbecomingness of the fault, rather than a *hasty rating* of the child for it, which makes him not sufficiently distinguish whether your dislike be not more directed to him than his fault. Passionate chiding usually carries rough and ill language with it, which has this further ill effect that it teaches and justifies it in children; and the names that their parents or preceptors give them they will not be ashamed or backward to bestow on others, having so good authority for the use of them.

*Obstinacy.*     §78. I foresee here it will be objected to me: What then, will you have children never beaten nor chid for any fault? This will be to let loose the reins to all kinds of disorder. Not so much as is imagined if a right course has been taken in the first seasoning of their minds and implanting that awe of their parents mentioned above.[33] For beating, by constant observation, is found to do little good where the smart of it is all the punishment is feared or felt in it; for the influence of that quickly wears out with the memory of it. But yet there is one, and but one fault, for which I think children should be beaten; and that is *obstinacy* or *rebellion*. And in this too I would have it ordered so, if it can be, that the shame of the whipping, and not the pain, should be the greatest part of the punishment. Shame of

33. §§40–44.

doing amiss and deserving chastisement is the only true restraint belonging to virtue. The smart of the rod, if shame accompanies it not, soon ceases and is forgotten, and will quickly by use lose its terror. I have known the children of a person of quality kept in awe by the fear of having their shoes pulled off as much as others by apprehensions of a rod hanging over them. Some such punishment I think better than beating; for it is shame of the fault and the disgrace that attends it that they should stand in fear of rather than pain, if you would have them have a temper truly ingenuous. But *stubbornness* and an *obstinate disobedience* must be mastered with force and blows: for this there is no other remedy. Whatever particular action you bid him do or forbear, you must be sure to see yourself obeyed; no quarter in this case, no resistance. For when once it comes to be a trial of skill, a contest for mastery between you, as it is if you command and he refuses, you must be sure to carry it, whatever blows it costs, if a nod or words will not prevail; unless forever after you intend to live in obedience to your son. A prudent and kind mother of my acquaintance was, on such an occasion, forced to whip her little daughter at her first coming home from nurse eight times successively the same morning before she could master her *stubbornness* and obtain a compliance in a very easy and indifferent matter. If she had left off sooner and stopped at the seventh whipping, she had spoiled the child forever and by her unprevailing blows only confirmed her *refractoriness*, very hardly afterwards to be cured; but wisely persisting till she had bent her mind and suppled her will, the only end of correction and chastisement, she established her authority thoroughly in the very first occasion and had ever after a very ready compliance and obedience in all things from her daughter. For as this was the first time, so, I think, it was the last too she ever struck her.

The pain of the rod *the first* occasion that requires it, continued and increased without leaving off till it has thoroughly prevailed, should first bend the mind and settle the parents' authority; and then gravity mixed with kindness should forever after keep it.

This, if well reflected on, would make people more wary in the use of the rod and the cudgel and keep them from being so apt to think beating the safe and universal remedy to be applied at random on all occasions. This is certain, however, if it does no good, it does great harm; if it reaches not the mind and makes not the will supple, it hardens the offender; and whatever pain he has suffered for it, it does but endear to him his beloved *stubbornness*, which has got him this time the victory, and prepares him to contest and hope for it for the future. Thus I doubt not but by ill-ordered correction many have been taught to be *obstinate* and *refractory* who otherwise would have been very pliant and tractable. For if you punish a child so, as if it were only to revenge the past fault which has raised your choler, what operation can this have upon his mind, which is the part to be amended? If there were no *sturdy humor* or *willfulness* mixed with his fault, there was nothing in it that required the severity of blows. A kind or grave admonition is enough to remedy the slips of frailty, forgetfulness, or inadvertency, and is as much as they will stand in need of. But if there were a *perverseness* in the will, if it were a designed, resolved disobedience, the punishment is not to be measured by the greatness or smallness of the matter wherein it appeared, but by the opposition it carries and stands in to that respect and submission [that] is due to the father's orders; which must always be rigorously exacted, and the blows by pauses laid on till they reach the mind and you perceive the signs of a true sorrow, shame, and purpose of obedience.

This, I confess, requires something more than setting children a task and whipping them without any more ado if it be not done, and done to our fancy. This requires care, attention, observation, and a nice study of children's tempers, and weighing their faults well, before we come to this sort of punishment. But is not that better than always to have the rod in hand as the only instrument of government? And by frequent use of it on all occasions misapply and render inefficacious this last and useful remedy where there is need of it? For what else can be expected when it is promiscuously used upon every little slip? When a mistake in *concordance*[34] or a wrong *position* in verse shall have the severity of the lash in a well-tempered and industrious lad as surely as a willful crime in an obstinate and perverse offender, how can such a way of correction be expected to do good on the mind, and set that right? Which is the only thing to be looked after, and when set right brings all the rest that you can desire along with it.

§79. Where a *wrong bent of the will* wants not amendment there can be no need of blows. All other faults, where the mind is rightly disposed and refuses not the government and authority of the father or tutor, are but mistakes and may often be overlooked; or when they are taken notice of need no other but the gentler remedies of advice, direction and reproof till the repeated and willful neglect of those shows the fault to be in the mind and that a manifest *perverseness* of the will lies at the root of their disobedience. But whenever *obstinacy*, which is an open defiance, appears, that cannot be winked at or neglected but must in the first instance be subdued

34. Grammatical agreement.

and mastered: only care must be had that we mistake not, and we must be sure it is obstinacy and nothing else.

§80. But since the occasions of punishment, especially beating, are as much to be avoided as may be, I think it should not be often brought to this point. If the awe I spoke of[35] be once got, a look will be sufficient in most cases. Nor indeed should the same carriage, seriousness, or application be expected from young children as from those of riper growth. They must be permitted, as I said,[36] the foolish and childish actions suitable to their years without taking notice of them. Inadvertency, carelessness, and gaiety is the character of that age. I think the severity I spoke of is not to extend itself to such unseasonable restraints. Nor is that hastily to be interpreted [as] obstinacy or willfulness which is the natural product of their age or temper. In such miscarriages they are to be assisted and helped towards an amendment as weak people under a natural infirmity, which though they are warned of, yet every relapse must not be counted a perfect neglect and they presently treated as obstinate. Faults of frailty, as they should never be neglected or let pass without minding, so, unless the will mix with them, they should never be exaggerated or very sharply reproved, but with a gentle hand set right as time and age permit. By this means children will come to see what it is in any miscarriage that is chiefly offensive and so learn to avoid it. This will encourage them to keep their wills right, which is the great business, when they find that it preserves them from any great displeasure and that in all their other failings they meet with the kind concern and help rather than the anger and passionate reproaches of their tutor and parents. Keep them from vice and vicious dispositions, and such a kind of behavior in general will come, with every degree of their age, as is suitable to that age and the company they ordinarily converse with; and as they grow in years they will grow in attention and application. But that your words may always carry weight and authority with them, if it shall happen, upon any occasion, that you bid him leave off the doing of any even childish thing, you must be sure to carry the point and not let him have the mastery. But yet, I say, I would have the father seldom interpose his authority and command in these cases or in any other but such as have a tendency to vicious habits. I think there are better ways of prevailing with them: and a gentle persuasion in reasoning (when the first point of submission to your will is got) will most times do much better.

35. §§40–44.
36. §63.

*Reasoning.*    §81. It will perhaps be wondered that I mention *reasoning* with children: and yet I cannot but think that the true way of dealing with them. They understand it as early as they do language; and, if I misobserve not, they love to be treated as rational creatures sooner than is imagined. 'Tis a pride should be cherished in them and, as much as can be, made the great instrument to turn them by.

But when I talk of *reasoning* I do not intend any other but such as is suited to the child's capacity and apprehension. Nobody can think a boy of three or seven years old should be argued with as a grown man. Long discourses and philosophical reasonings at best amaze and confound, but do not instruct children. When I say therefore that they must be *treated as rational creatures* I mean that you should make them sensible by the mildness of your carriage and the composure even in your correction of them that what you do is reasonable in you and useful and necessary for them and that it is not out of *caprichio*,[37] passion, or fancy that you command or forbid them anything. This they are capable of understanding; and there is no virtue they should be excited to nor fault they should be kept from which I do not think they may be convinced of, but it must be by such *reasons* as their age and understanding are capable of and those proposed always in very *few and plain words*. The foundations on which several duties are built and the fountains of right and wrong from which they spring are not perhaps easily to be let into the minds of grown men not used to abstract their thoughts from common received opinions. Much less are children capable of *reasonings* from remote principles. They cannot conceive the force of long deductions: the *reasons* that move them must be *obvious* and level to their thoughts, and such as may (if I may so say) be felt and touched. But yet, if their age, temper, and inclinations be considered, there will never want such motives as may be sufficient to convince them. If there be no other more particular, yet these will always be intelligible and of force to deter them from any fault fit to be taken notice of in them, viz. that it will be a discredit and disgrace to them, and displease you.

*Examples.*    §82. But of all the ways whereby children are to be instructed and their manners formed, the plainest, easiest, and most efficacious is to set before their eyes the *examples* of those things you would have them do or avoid. Which, when they are pointed out to them in the practice of persons within their knowledge with some reflection on their beauty or unbecomingness, are of more force to draw or deter their imitation than any discourses which can be made to them. Virtues and vices can by no words be

37. Caprice.

so plainly set before their understandings as the actions of other men will show them, when you direct their observation and bid them view this or that good or bad quality in their practice. And the beauty or uncomeliness of many things in good and ill breeding will be better learned and make deeper impressions on them in the *examples* of others than from any rules or instructions can be given about them.

This is a method to be used not only whilst they are young, but to be continued even as long as they shall be under another's tuition or conduct. Nay, I know not whether it be not the best way to be used by a father as long as he shall think fit, on any occasion, to reform anything he wishes mended in his son: nothing sinking so gently and so deep into men's minds as *example*. And what ill they either overlook or indulge in them themselves, they cannot but dislike and be ashamed of when it is set before them in another.

§83. It may be doubted concerning *whipping*, when as the last remedy it comes to be necessary, at what time and by whom it should be done: whether presently upon the committing the fault, whilst it is yet fresh and hot; and whether parents themselves should beat their children. As to the first, I think it should *not* be done *presently* lest passion mingle with it and so, though it exceed the just proportion, yet it lose of its due weight: for even children discern when we do things in passion. But, as I said before,[38] that has most weight with them that appears sedately to come from their parents' reason, and they are not without this distinction. Next, if you have any discreet servant capable of it and [who] has the place of governing your child (for if you have a tutor, there is no doubt), I think it is best the *smart* should come more immediately *from another's hand*, though by the parent's order who should see it done; whereby the parent's authority will be preserved and the child's aversion for the pain it suffers rather be turned on the person that immediately inflicts it. For I would have a *father seldom strike his child* but upon very urgent necessity and as the last remedy: and then perhaps it will be fit to do it so that the child should not quickly forget it.

§84. But, as I said before,[39] *beating* is the worst and therefore the last means to be used in the correction of children and that only in cases of extremity after all gentler ways have been tried and proved unsuccessful; which, if well observed, there will be very seldom any need of blows. For, it not being to be imagined that a child will often, if ever, dispute his

*Whipping.*

38. §81.
39. §§47–52, 60.

father's present command in any particular instance, and the father not interposing his absolute authority in peremptory rules concerning either childish or indifferent actions, wherein his son is to have his liberty, or concerning his learning or improvement, wherein there is no compulsion to be used, there remains only the prohibition of some vicious actions, wherein a child is capable of *obstinacy* and consequently can deserve beating: and so there will be but very few occasions of that discipline to be used by anyone who considers well and orders his child's education as it should be. For the first seven years, what vices can a child be guilty of but lying or some ill-natured tricks, the repeated commission whereof, after his father's direct command against it, shall bring him into the condemnation of *obstinacy* and the chastisement of the rod? If any vicious inclination in him be in the first appearance and instances of it treated as it should be first with your wonder and then, if returning again a second time, discountenanced with the severe brow of the father, tutor, and all about him and a treatment suitable to the state of discredit before mentioned,[40] and this continued till he be made sensible and ashamed of his fault, I imagine there will be no need of any other correction nor ever any occasion to come to blows. The necessity of such chastisement is usually the consequence only of former indulgences or neglects. If vicious inclinations were watched from the beginning and the first irregularities which they caused corrected by those gentler ways, we should seldom have to do with more than one disorder at once, which would be easily set right without any stir or noise and not require so harsh a discipline as beating. Thus one by one, as they appeared, they might all be weeded out without any signs or memory that ever they had been there. But we letting their faults (by indulging and humoring our little ones) grow up till they are sturdy and numerous and the deformity of them makes us ashamed and uneasy, we are fain[41] to come to the plough and the harrow, the spade and the pickax must go deep to come at the roots, and all the force, skill, and diligence we can use is scarce enough to cleanse the vitiated seed plot overgrown with weeds and restore us the hopes of fruits to reward our pains in its season.

§85. This course, if observed, will spare both father and child the trouble of repeated injunctions and multiplied rules of doing and forbearing. For I am of opinion that of those actions which tend to vicious habits (which are those alone that a father should interpose his authority and commands in) none should be forbidden children till they are found guilty

40. §§57–58.
41. Compelled.

of them. For such untimely prohibitions, if they do nothing worse, do at least so much towards teaching and allowing them that they suppose that children may be guilty of them who would possibly be safer in the ignorance of any such faults. And the best remedy to stop them is, as I have said,[42] to show *wonder and amazement* at any such action as has a vicious tendency when it is first taken notice of in a child. For example, when he is first found in a lie or any ill-natured trick, the first remedy should be to talk to him of it as a *strange monstrous matter* that it could not be imagined he would have done and so shame him out of it.

§86. It will be ('tis likely) objected that whatever I fancy of the tractableness of children and the prevalency of those softer ways of shame and commendation, yet there are many who will never apply themselves to their books and to what they ought to learn unless they are scourged to it. This I fear is nothing but the language of ordinary schools and fashion, which have never suffered the other to be tried as it should be in places where it could be taken notice of. *Why* else *does the learning of Latin and Greek need the rod, when French and Italian need it not?* Children learn to dance and fence without whipping; nay, arithmetic, drawing, etc. they apply themselves well enough to without beating, which would make one suspect that there is something strange, unnatural, and disagreeable to that age in the things required in grammar schools or in the methods used there that children cannot be brought to without the severity of the lash, and hardly with that too, or else that it is a mistake that those tongues could not be taught them without beating.

§87. But let us suppose some so negligent or idle that they will not be brought to learn by the gentler ways proposed, for we must grant that there will be children found of all tempers, yet it does not thence follow that the rough discipline of the cudgel is to be used to all. Nor can anyone be concluded unmanageable by the *milder methods* of government till they have been *thoroughly tried* upon him; and if they will not prevail with him to use his endeavors and do what is in his power to do, we make no excuses for the obstinate, blows are the proper remedies for those, but blows laid on in a way different from the ordinary. He that willfully neglects his book and stubbornly refuses anything he can do required of him by his father, expressing himself in a positive serious command, should not be corrected with two or three angry lashes for not performing his task, and the same punishment repeated again and again upon every the like default. But when it is brought to that pass that willfulness evidently shows itself and

42. §84.

makes blows necessary, I think the chastisement should be a little more
sedate and a little more severe, and the whipping (mingled with admonitions between) so continued till the impressions of it on the mind were
found legible in the face, voice, and submission of the child, not so sensible
of the smart as of the fault he has been guilty of and melting in true sorrow
under it. If such a correction as this, tried some few times at fit distances
and carried to the utmost severity, with the visible displeasure of the father
all the while, will not work the effect, turn the mind, and produce a future
compliance, what can be hoped from *blows*, and to what purpose should
they be any more used? *Beating*, when you can expect no good from it, will
look more like the fury of an enraged enemy than the good will of a compassionate friend; and such chastisement carries with it only provocation
without any prospect of amendment. If it be any father's misfortune to
have a son thus perverse and intractable, I know not what more he can do
but pray for him. But, I imagine, if a right course be taken with children
from the beginning, very few will be found to be such; and when there are
any such instances, they are not to be the rule for the education of those
who are better natured and may be managed with better usage.

Tutor.     §88. If a *tutor* can be got that, thinking himself in the father's place,
charged with his care, and relishing these things, will at the beginning
apply himself to put them in practice, he will afterwards find his work very
easy; and you will, I guess, have your son in a little time a greater proficient
in both learning and breeding than perhaps you imagine. But let him by no
means beat him at any time without your consent and direction, at least till
you have experience of his discretion and temper. But yet to keep up his
authority with his pupil, besides concealing that he has not the power of
the rod, you must be sure to use him with great respect yourself and cause
all your family to do so too. For you cannot expect your son should have
any regard for one whom he sees you or his mother or others slight. If you
think him worthy of contempt, you have chosen amiss; and if you show
any contempt of him, he will hardly escape it from your son; and whenever
that happens, whatever worth he may have in himself and abilities for this
employment, they are all lost to your child and can afterwards never be
made useful to him.

§89. As the father's example must teach the child respect for his tutor,
so the tutor's example must lead the child into those actions he would have
him do. His practice must by no means cross his precepts, unless he intend
to set him wrong. It will be to no purpose for the tutor to talk of the
restraint of the passions whilst any of his own are let loose; and he will in
vain endeavor to reform any vice or indecency in his pupil which he allows

in himself. Ill patterns are sure to be followed more than good rules; and therefore he must also carefully preserve him from the influence of ill precedents, especially the most dangerous of all, the examples of the servants, from whose company he is to be kept not by prohibitions, for that will but give him an itch after it, but by other ways I have mentioned.[43]

§90. In all the whole business of education, there is nothing likely to be less hearkened to or harder to be well observed than what I am now going to say: and that is, that I would from their first beginning to talk have some *discreet, sober,* nay, *wise* person about children, whose care it should be to fashion them aright and keep them from all ill, especially the infection of bad company. I think this province requires great *sobriety, temperance, tenderness, diligence,* and *discretion,* qualities hardly to be found united in persons that are to be had for ordinary salaries nor easily to be found anywhere. As to the charge of it, I think it will be the money best laid out that can be about our children, and therefore though it may be expensive more than is ordinary yet it cannot be thought dear. He that at any rate procures his child a good mind, well principled, tempered to virtue and usefulness, and adorned with civility and good breeding, makes a better purchase for him than if he laid out the money for an addition of more earth to his former acres. Spare it in toys and play-games, in silk and ribbons, laces and other useless expenses, as much as you please, but be not sparing in so necessary a part as this. It is not good husbandry to make his fortune rich and his mind poor. I have often with great admiration seen people lavish it profusely in tricking up their children in fine clothes, lodging and feeding them sumptuously, allowing them more than enough of useless servants, and yet at the same time starve their minds and not take sufficient care to cover that which is the most shameful nakedness, viz. their natural wrong inclinations and ignorance. This I can look on as no other than a sacrificing to their own vanity; it showing more their pride than true care of the good of their children. Whatsoever you employ to the advantage of your son's mind will show your true kindness, though it be to the lessening of his estate. A wise and good man can hardly want either the opinion or reality of being great and happy. But he that is foolish or vicious can be neither great nor happy, what estate soever you leave him; and I ask you, whether there be not men in the world whom you had rather have your son be with 500 £. per annum than some other you know with 5000 £.

§91. The consideration of charge ought not therefore to deter those who are able: the great difficulty will be where to find a *proper person.* For those

*Governor.*

43. §69.

of small age, parts, and virtue are unfit for this employment; and those that have greater will hardly be got to undertake such a charge. You must therefore look out early and inquire everywhere: for the world has people of all sorts. And I remember, Montaigne says in one of his Essays[44] that the learned Castalio was fain[45] to make trenches at Basle to keep himself from starving, when his father would have given any money for such a tutor for his son and Castalio have willingly embraced such an employment upon very reasonable terms: but this was for want of intelligence.[46]

*Tutor.*    §92. If you find it difficult to meet with such a tutor as we desire, you are not to wonder. I only can say, spare no care nor cost to get such a one. All things are to be had that way; and I dare assure you that if you get a good one, you will never repent the charge but will always have the satisfaction to think it the money of all other the best laid out. But be sure take nobody upon friends' or charitable, no, nor bare great recommendations. Nay, if you will do as you ought, the reputation of a sober man with a good stock of learning (which is all [that is] usually required in a tutor) will not be enough to serve your turn. In this choice be as curious as you would be in that of a wife for him, for you must not think of trial or changing afterwards; that will cause great inconvenience to you, and greater to your son. When I consider the scruples and cautions I here lay in your way, methinks it looks as if I advised you to something which I would have offered at but, in effect, not done. But he that shall consider how much the business of a tutor, rightly employed, lies out of the road, and how remote it is from the thoughts of many, even of those who propose to themselves this employment, will perhaps be of my mind that one fit to educate and form the mind of a young gentleman is not everywhere to be found, and that more than ordinary care is to be taken in the choice of him or else you may fail of your end.

§93. The character of a sober man and a scholar is, as I have above observed,[47] what everyone expects in a tutor. This generally is thought enough and is all that parents commonly look for. But when such a one has emptied out into his pupil all the Latin and logic he has brought from the university, will that furniture make him a fine gentleman? Or can it be expected that he should be better bred, better skilled in the world, better

44. I 35.
45. Compelled.
46. Information.
47. §90.

principled in the grounds and foundations of true virtue and generosity, than his young *tutor* is?

To form a young gentleman as he should be, 'tis fit his *governor* should himself be well-bred, understand the ways of carriage and measures of civility in all the variety of persons, times, and places, and keep his pupil, as much as his age requires, constantly to the observation of them. This is an art not to be learned nor taught by books. Nothing can give it but good company and observation joined together. The tailor may make his clothes modish, and the dancing master give fashion to his motions; yet neither of these, though they set off well, make a well-bred gentleman; no, though he have learning to boot, which if not well-managed makes him but the more impertinent and intolerable in conversation. Breeding is that which sets a gloss upon all his other good qualities and renders them useful to him in procuring him the esteem and good will of all that he comes near. Without good breeding his other accomplishments make him pass but for proud, conceited, vain, or foolish.

Courage in an ill-bred man has the air and escapes not the opinion of brutality; learning becomes pedantry; wit, buffoonery; plainness, rusticity; good nature, fawning. And there can be not a good quality in him which want of breeding will not warp and disfigure to his disadvantage. Nay, virtue and parts, though they are allowed their due commendation, yet are not enough to procure a man a good reception and make him welcome wherever he comes. Nobody contents himself with rough diamonds and wears them so, who would appear with advantage. When they are polished and set, then they give a lustre. Good qualities are the substantial riches of the mind, but it is good breeding [that] sets them off, and he that will be acceptable must give beauty as well as strength to his actions. Solidity or even usefulness is not enough: a graceful way and fashion in everything is that which gives the ornament and liking. And in most cases the manner of doing is of more consequence than the thing done; and upon that depends the satisfaction or disgust wherewith it is received. This therefore, which lies not in the putting off the hat nor making of compliments but in a due and free composure of language, looks, motion, posture, place, etc. suited to persons and occasions and can be learned only by habit and use, though it be above the capacity of children and little ones should not be perplexed about it, yet it ought to be begun and in a good measure learned by a young gentleman whilst he is under a tutor, before he comes into the world upon his own legs: for then usually it is too late to hope to reform several habitual indecencies which lie in little things. For the carriage is not as it should be till it is become natural in every part, falling, as skillful musicians' fingers do, into harmonious order without care and without thought. If in conversation a man's mind be taken up with a solicitous watchfulness about any part of his Behavior, instead of being mended by it, it will be constrained, uneasy, and ungraceful.

Besides, this part is most necessary to be formed by the hands and care of a *governor*: because, though the errors committed in breeding are the first that are taken notice of by others, yet they are the last that anyone is told of. Not but that the malice of the world is forward enough to tattle of them, but it is always out of his hearing who should make profit of their judgment and reform himself by their censure. And indeed, this is so nice a point to be meddled with that even those who are friends and wish it were mended scarce ever dare mention it and tell those they love that they are guilty in such or such cases of ill breeding. Errors in other things may often with civility be shown another, and it is no breach of good manners or friendship to set him right in other mistakes, but good breeding itself allows not a man to touch upon this or to insinuate to another that he is guilty of want of breeding. Such information can come only from those who have authority over them; and from them too it comes very hardly and harshly to a grown man and, however softened, goes but ill down with anyone who has lived ever so little in the world. Wherefore it is necessary that this part should be the *governor's* principal care: that a habitual gracefulness and politeness in all his carriage may be settled in his charge, as much as may be, before he goes out of his hands; and that he may not need advice in this point when he has neither time nor disposition to receive it, nor has anybody left to give it him. The *tutor* therefore ought in the first place to be well-bred: and a young gentleman who gets this one qualification from his *governor* sets out with great advantage and will find that this one accomplishment will more open his way to him, get him more friends, and carry him farther in the world than all the hard words or real knowledge he has got from the liberal arts or his *tutor's* learned *Encyclopedia*. Not that those should be neglected, but by no means preferred or suffered to thrust out the other.

§94. Besides being well-bred, the *tutor* should know the world well: the ways, the humors, the follies, the cheats, the faults of the age he is fallen into and particularly of the country he lives in. These he should be able to show to his pupil as he finds him capable, teach him skill in men and their manners, pull off the mask which their several callings and pretenses cover them with, and make his pupil discern what lies at the bottom under such appearances that he may not, as inexperienced young men are apt to do if they are unwarned, take one thing for another, judge by the outside, and give himself up to show and the insinuation of a fair carriage or an obliging application; a governor should teach his scholar to guess at and beware of the designs of men he has to do with neither with too much suspicion nor too much confidence, but as the young man is by nature most inclined to either side rectify him and bend him the other way. He should accustom him to make as much as is possible a true judgment of men by those marks which serve best to show what they are and give a prospect into their inside, which often shows itself in little things, especially when they are not on parade and upon their guard. He should acquaint him with the true state of the world and dispose him to think no man better or worse, wiser or foolisher, than really he is. Thus by safe and insensible degrees he will pass from a boy to a man, which is the most hazardous step in all the whole course of life. This therefore should be carefully watched, and a young man with great diligence handed over it and not, as now usually is done, be taken from a *governor's* conduct and all at once thrown into the world under his own not without manifest danger of immediate spoiling; there being nothing more frequent, than instances of the great looseness, extravagancy, and debauchery which young men have run into as soon as they have been let loose from a severe and strict education, which I think may be chiefly imputed to their wrong way of breeding, especially in this part; for having been bred up in a great ignorance of what the world truly is and finding it a quite other thing when they come into it than what they were taught it should be and so imagined it was, [they] are easily persuaded by other kind of tutors, which they are sure to meet with, that the discipline they were kept under and the lectures [that] were read to them were but the formalities of education and the restraints of childhood, that the freedom belonging to men is to take their swing in a full enjoyment of what was before forbidden them. They show the young novice the world full of fashionable and glittering examples of this everywhere, and he is presently dazzled with them. My young master, failing not to be willing to show himself a man as much as any of the sparks of his years, lets himself loose to all the irregularities he finds in the most debauched and thus courts credit and manliness in the casting off the modesty and sobriety he has till then been kept in and thinks it brave at his first setting out to signalize himself in running counter to all the rules of virtue which have been preached to him by his tutor.

The showing him the world as really it is, before he comes wholly into it, is one of the best means, I think, to prevent this mischief. He should by degrees be informed of the vices in fashion and warned of the applications and designs of those who will make it their business to corrupt him. He should be told the arts they use and the trains[48] they lay and now and then have set before him the tragical or ridiculous examples of those who are ruining or ruined this way. The age is not likely to want instances of this kind, which should be made landmarks to him that by the disgraces, diseases, beggary, and shame of hopeful young men thus brought to ruin, he may be precautioned and be made [to] see how those join in the contempt and neglect of them that are undone who by pretenses of friendship and respect lead them into it and help to prey upon them whilst they were undoing, that he may see before he buys it by a too dear experience that those who persuade him not to follow the sober advice he has received from his *governors* and the counsel of his own reason, which they call being governed by others, do it only that they may have the government of him themselves and make him believe he goes like a man of himself, by his own conduct and for his own pleasure, when, in truth, he is wholly as a child led by them into those vices which best serve their purposes. This is a knowledge which, upon all occasions, a *tutor* should endeavor to instill and by all methods try to make him comprehend and thoroughly relish.

I know it is often said that to discover to a young man the vices of the age is to teach them [to] him. That I confess is a good deal so, according as it is done, and therefore requires a discreet man of parts who knows the world and can judge of the temper, inclination, and weak side of his pupil. This farther is to be remembered, that it is not possible now (as perhaps formerly it was) to keep a young gentleman from vice by a total ignorance of it unless you will all his life mew him up in a closet and never let him go into company. The longer he is kept thus hoodwinked, the less he will see when he comes abroad into open daylight and be the more exposed to be a prey to himself and others. And an old boy at his first appearance, with all the gravity of his ivy-bush about him, is sure to draw on him the eyes and chirping of the whole town volary;[49] amongst which there will not be wanting some birds of prey that will presently be on the wing for him.

The only fence against the world is a thorough knowledge of it, into which a young gentleman should be entered by degrees as he can bear it, and the earlier the better, so he be in safe and skillful hands to guide him. The scene should be gently opened, and his entrance made step by step, and the dangers pointed out that attend him from the several degrees, tempers, designs, and clubs of men. He should be prepared to be shocked by some and caressed by others, warned who are likely to oppose, who to mis-

48. Traps or schemes.
49. A birdcage or the birds kept in it.

lead, who to undermine him, and who to serve him. He should be instructed how to know and distinguish them, where he should let them see, and when dissemble the knowledge of them and their aims and workings. And if he be too forward to venture upon his own strength and skill, the perplexity and trouble of a misadventure now and then that reaches not his innocence, his health, or his reputation may not be an ill way to teach him more caution.

This, I confess, containing one great part of wisdom, is not the product of some superficial thoughts or much reading, but the effect of experience and observation in a man who has lived in the world with his eyes open and conversed with men of all sorts. And therefore I think it of most value to be instilled into a young man, upon all occasions which offer themselves, that when he comes to launch into the deep himself he may not be like one at sea without a line, compass, or sea-chart, but may have some notice beforehand of the rocks and shoals, the currents and quicksands, and know a little how to steer, that he sink not before he get experience. He that thinks not this of more moment to his son and for which he more needs a governor than the languages and learned sciences, forgets of how much more use it is to judge right of men and manage his affairs wisely with them than to speak Greek and Latin, or argue in mood and figure, or to have his head filled with the abstruse speculations of natural philosophy and metaphysics, nay, than to be well-versed in the Greek and Roman writers, though that be much better for a gentleman than to be a good Peripatetic or Cartesian because those ancient authors observed and painted mankind well and give the best light into that kind of knowledge. He that goes into the eastern parts of Asia will find able and acceptable men without any of these; but without virtue, knowledge of the world, and civility, an accomplished, and valuable man can be found nowhere.

A great part of the learning now in fashion in the schools of Europe, and that goes ordinarily into the round of education, a gentleman may in a good measure be unfurnished with, without any great disparagement to himself or prejudice to his affairs. But prudence and good breeding are in all the stations and occurrences of life necessary, and most young men suffer in the want of them and come rawer and more awkward into the world than they should for this very reason: because these qualities, which are of all other the most necessary to be taught and stand most in need of the assistance and help of a teacher, are generally neglected and thought but a slight or no part of a *tutor's* business. Latin and learning make all the noise, and the main stress is laid upon his proficiency in things a great part whereof belong not to a gentleman's calling, which is to have the knowl-

edge of a man of business, a carriage suitable to his rank, and to be eminent
and useful in his country according to his station. Whenever either spare
hours from that, or an inclination to perfect himself in some parts of
knowledge which his *tutor* did but just enter him in, sets him upon any
study, the first rudiments of it, which he learned before, will open the way
enough for his own industry to carry him as far as his fancy will prompt or
his parts enable him to go. Or if he thinks it may save his time and pains to
be helped over some difficulties by the hand of a master, he may then take
a man that is perfectly well skilled in it or choose such a one as he thinks
fittest for his purpose. But to initiate his pupil in any part of learning as far
as is necessary for a young man in the ordinary course of his studies, an
ordinary skill in the *governor* is enough. Nor is it requisite that he should
be a thorough scholar or possess in perfection all those sciences which it is
convenient a young gentleman should have a taste of in some general view
or short system. A gentleman that would penetrate deeper must do it by
his own genius and industry afterwards: for nobody ever went far in
knowledge or became eminent in any of the sciences by the discipline and
constraint of a master.

The great work of a *governor* is to fashion the carriage and form the
mind, to settle in his pupil good habits and the principles of virtue and wisdom, to give him by little and little a view of mankind, and work him into
a love and imitation of what is excellent and praiseworthy, and in the prosecution of it to give him vigor, activity, and industry. The studies which
he sets him upon are but as it were the exercises of his faculties and
employment of his time to keep him from sauntering and idleness, to teach
him application, and accustom him to take pains, and to give him some little taste of what his own industry must perfect. For who expects that
under a *tutor* a young gentleman should be an accomplished critic, orator,
or logician? Go to the bottom of metaphysics, natural philosophy, or mathematics? Or be a master in history or chronology? Though something of
each of these is to be taught him, but it is only to open the door that he may
look in and as it were begin an acquaintance, but not to dwell there; and a
*governor* would be much blamed that should keep his pupil too long and
lead him too far in most of them. But of good breeding, knowledge of the
world, virtue, industry, and a love of reputation, he cannot have too much;
and if he have these, he will not long want what he needs or desires of the
other.

And since it cannot be hoped he should have time and strength to learn
all things, most pains should be taken about that which is most necessary,

and that principally looked after which will be of most and frequentest use to him in the world.

Seneca complains of the contrary practice in his time and yet the Burgersdiciuses and the Scheiblers[50] did not swarm in those days as they do now in these. What would he have thought if he had lived now, when the *tutors* think it their great business to fill the studies and heads of their pupils with such authors as these? He would have had more reason to say, as he does, *Non vitae sed scholae discimus,*[51] we learn not to live but to dispute; and our education fits us rather for the university than the world. But it is no wonder if those who make the fashion suit it to what they have and not to what their pupils want. The fashion being once established, who can think it strange that in this, as well as in all other things, it should prevail, and that the greatest part of those who find their account in an easy submission to it should be ready to cry out *heresy* when anyone departs from it? It is nevertheless matter of astonishment that men of quality and parts should suffer themselves to be so far misled by custom and implicit faith. Reason, if consulted with, would advise that their children's time should be spent in acquiring what might be useful to them when they come to be men rather than to have their heads stuffed with a deal of trash, a great part whereof they usually never do ('tis certain they never need to) think on again as long as they live; and so much of it as does stick by them, they are only the worse for. This is so well known that I appeal to parents themselves who have been at cost to have their young heirs taught it, whether it be not ridiculous for their sons to have any tincture of that sort of learning when they come abroad into the world, whether any appearance of it would not lessen and disgrace them in company. And that certainly must be an admirable acquisition and deserves well to make a part in education, which men are ashamed of where they are most concerned to show their parts and breeding.

There is yet another reason why politeness of manners and knowledge of the world should principally be looked after in a *tutor*: and that is because a man of parts and years may enter a lad far enough in any of those sciences which he has no deep insight into himself. Books in these will be able to furnish him and give him light and precedence enough to go before a young follower; but he will never be able to set another right in the knowledge of the world and above all in breeding who is a novice in them himself.

50. Seventeenth-century textbook writers.
51. Seneca, *Epistle* 106, "we learn not for life but for school."

This is a knowledge he must have about him, worn into him by use and conversation and a long forming himself by what he has observed to be practiced and allowed in the best company. This, if he has it not of his own, is nowhere to be borrowed for the use of his pupil; or if he could find pertinent treatises of it in books that would reach all the particulars of an English gentleman's behavior, his own ill-fashioned example, if he be not well-bred himself, would spoil all his lectures; it being impossible that anyone should come forth well-fashioned out of unpolished ill-bred company.

I say this, not that I think such a *tutor* is every day to be met with or to be had at the ordinary rates. But that those who are able may not be sparing of inquiry or cost in what is of so great moment; and that other parents, whose estates will not reach to greater salaries, may yet remember what they should principally have an eye to in the choice of one to whom they would commit the education of their children, and what part they should chiefly look after themselves whilst they are under their care and as often as they come within their observation, and not think that all lies in Latin and French or some dry systems of logic and philosophy.

*Familiarity.*    §95. But to return to our method again. Though I have mentioned the severity of the father's brow and the awe settled thereby in the mind of children when young as one main instrument whereby their education is to be managed,[52] yet I am far from being of an opinion that it should be continued all along to them whilst they are under the discipline and government of pupilage. I think it should be relaxed as fast as their age, discretion, and good behavior could allow it; even to that degree that a father will do well, as his son grows up and is capable of it, to *talk familiarly* with him, nay, *ask his advice and consult* with him about those things wherein he has any knowledge or understanding. By this the father will gain two things, both of great moment. The one is that it will put serious considerations into his son's thoughts better than any rules or advice he can give him. The sooner you *treat him as a man,* the sooner he will begin to be one: and if you admit him into serious discourses sometimes with you, you will insensibly raise his mind above the usual amusements of youth and those trifling occupations which it is commonly wasted in. For it is easy to observe that many young men continue longer in the thoughts and conversation of schoolboys than otherwise they would because their parents keep them at that distance and in that low rank by all their carriage to them.

§96. Another thing of greater consequence which you will obtain by such a way of treating him will be *his friendship.* Many fathers, though they

52. §§40–44.

proportion to their sons liberal allowances, according to their age and condition, yet they keep the knowledge of their estates and concerns from them with as much reservedness as if they were guarding a secret of state from a spy or an enemy. This, if it looks not like jealousy, yet it wants those marks of kindness and intimacy which a father should show to his son and, no doubt, often hinders or abates that cheerfulness and satisfaction wherewith a son should address himself to and rely upon his father. And I cannot but often wonder to see fathers who love their sons very well yet so order the matter by a constant stiffness and a mien of authority and distance to them all their lives as if they were never to enjoy or have any comfort from those they love best in the world till they have lost them by being removed into another. Nothing cements and establishes friendship and good will so much as *confident communication* of concernments and affairs. Other kindnesses without this leave still some doubts: but when your son sees you open your mind to him, when he finds that you interest him in your affairs as things you are willing should in their turn come into his hands, he will be concerned for them as for his own, wait his season with patience, and love you in the meantime who keep him not at the distance of a stranger. This will also make him see that the enjoyment you have is not without care; which the more he is sensible of, the less will he envy you the possession and the more think himself happy under the management of so favorable a friend and so careful a father. There is scarce any young man of so little thought or so void of sense that would not be glad of a *sure friend* that he might have recourse to and freely consult on occasion. The reservedness and distance that fathers keep often deprive their sons of that refuge which would be of more advantage to them than a hundred rebukes and chidings. Would your son engage in some frolic or take a vagary, were it not much better he should do it with than without your knowledge? For since allowances for such things must be made to young men, the more you know of his intrigues and designs, the better will you be able to prevent great mischiefs and, by letting him see what is likely to follow, take the right way of prevailing with him to avoid less inconveniences. Would you have him open his heart to you and ask your advice? You must begin to do so with him first and by your carriage beget that confidence.

§97. But whatever he consults you about, unless it lead to some fatal and irremediable mischief, be sure you advise only as a friend of more experience but with your advice mingle nothing of command or authority, no more than you would to your equal or a stranger. That would be to drive him forever from any farther demanding or receiving advantage from your counsel. You must consider that he is a young man and has pleasures and fancies which you are passed. You must not expect his inclinations should be just as yours, nor that at twenty he should have the same thoughts you have at fifty. All that you can wish is that since youth must have some liberty, some outleaps, they might be with the ingenuousness of a son and *under the eye of a father,* and then no very great harm can come of it. The way to obtain this, as I said before,[53] is (according as you find him capable) to talk with him about your affairs, propose matters to him *familiarly,* and ask his advice; and whenever he lights on the right, follow it as his; and if it succeeds well, let him have the commendation. This will not at all lessen your authority, but increase his love and esteem of you. Whilst you keep your estate, the staff will still be in your own hands; and your authority the surer, the more it is strengthened with *confidence* and *kindness.* For you have not that power you ought to have over him till he comes to be more afraid of offending so good a friend than of losing some part of his future expectation.

§98. Familiarity of discourse, if it can become a father to his son, may much more be condescended to by a tutor to his pupil. All their time together should not be spent in reading of lectures and magisterially dictating to him what he is to observe and follow; hearing him in his turn and using him to reason about what is proposed makes the rules go down the easier and sink the deeper and gives him a liking to study and instruction; and he will then begin to value knowledge when he sees that it enables him to discourse and he finds the pleasure and credit of bearing a part in the conversation, and to have his reasons sometimes approved and hearkened to. Especially in morality, prudence, and breeding, cases should be put to him, and his judgment asked. This opens the understanding better than maxims, how well soever explained, and settles the rules better in the memory for practice. This way lets things into the mind which stick there and retain their evidence with them; whereas words at best are faint representations, being not so much as the true shadows of things, and are much sooner forgotten. He will better comprehend the foundations and measures of decency and justice and have livelier and more lasting impressions of what he ought to do, by giving his opinion on cases proposed and reasoning with his tutor on fit instances than by giving a silent, negligent, sleepy audience to his tutor's lectures and much more than by captious logical disputes, or set declamations of his own upon any question. The one sets the thoughts upon wit and false colors, and not upon truth; the other teaches fallacy, wrangling, and opinionatedness; and they are both of

53. §95.

them things that spoil the judgment and put a man out of the way of right and fair reasoning, and therefore carefully to be avoided by one who would improve himself and be acceptable to others.

99. When, by making your son sensible that he depends on you and     *Reverence.*
is in your power, you have established your authority; and by being inflexibly severe in your carriage to him when obstinately persisting in any illnatured trick which you have forbidden, especially lying, you have imprinted on his mind that awe which is necessary; and on the other side, when (by permitting him the full liberty due to his age and laying no restraint in your presence to those childish actions and gaiety of carriage which, whilst he is very young, is as necessary to him as meat or sleep) you have reconciled him to your company and made him sensible of your care and love of him by indulgence and tenderness, especially caressing him on all occasions wherein he does anything well, and being kind to him after a thousand fashions suitable to his age which nature teaches parents better than I can; when, I say, by these ways of tenderness and affection, which parents never want for their children, you have also planted in him a particular affection for you, he is then in the state you could desire, and you have formed in his mind that true *reverence* which is always afterwards carefully to be continued and maintained in both the parts of it, *love* and *fear*, as the great principle whereby you will always have hold upon him to turn his mind to the ways of virtue and honor.

§100. When this foundation is once well laid, and you find this rever-     *Temper.*
ence begin to work in him, the next thing to be done is carefully to consider his *temper* and the particular constitution of his mind. Stubbornness, lying, and ill-natured actions are not (as has been said) to be permitted in him from the beginning, whatever his temper be; those seeds of vices are not to be suffered to take any root, but must be carefully weeded out as soon as ever they begin to show themselves in him; and your authority is to take place and influence his mind from the very dawning of any knowledge in him that it may operate as a natural principle, whereof he never perceived the beginning, never knew that it was or could be otherwise. By this, if the *reverence* he owes you be established early, it will always be sacred to him, and it will be as hard for him to resist it as the principles of his nature.

§101. Having thus very early set up your authority and by the gentler applications of it shamed him out of what leads towards any immoral habit as soon as you have observed it in him (for I would by no means have chiding used, much less blows, till obstinacy and incorrigibleness make it absolutely necessary), it will be fit to consider which way the natural make of his *mind inclines* him. Some men by the unalterable frame of their constitutions are *stout*, others *timorous*, some *confident*, others *modest, tractable* or *obstinate, curious* or *careless, quick* or *slow*. There are not more differences in men's faces and the outward lineaments of their bodies than there are in the makes and tempers of their minds; only there is this difference, that the distinguishing characters of the face and the lineaments of the body grow more plain and visible with time and age, but the peculiar *physiognomy of the mind* is most discernible in children, before art and cunning has taught them to hide their deformities and conceal their ill inclinations under a dissembled outside.

§102. Begin therefore betimes nicely to observe your son's *temper*, and that when he is under least restraint, in his play and as he thinks out of your sight. See what are his *predominant passions* and *prevailing inclinations*, whether he be fierce or mild, bold or bashful, compassionate or cruel, open or reserved, etc. For as these are different in him, so are your methods to be different, and your authority must hence take measures to apply itself different ways to him. These *native propensities*, these prevalencies of constitution, are not to be cured by rules or a direct contest, especially those of them that are the humbler and meaner sort, which proceed from fear and lowness of spirit, though with art they may be much mended and turned to good purposes. But this, be sure, after all is done, the bias will always hang on that side that nature first placed it; and if you carefully observe the characters of his mind now in the first scenes of his life, you will ever after be able to judge which way his thoughts lean and what he aims at, even hereafter when, as he grows up, the plot thickens, and he puts on several shapes to act it.

*Dominion.* §103. I told you before that children love *liberty* and therefore they should be brought to do the things [that] are fit for them without feeling any restraint laid upon them.[54] I now tell you they love something more: and that is *dominion*; and this is the first origin of most vicious habits that are ordinary and natural. This love of *power* and dominion shows itself very early, and that in these two things:

§104. 1. We see children (as soon almost as they are born, I am sure long before they can speak) cry, grow peevish, sullen, and out of humor, for nothing but to have their *wills*. They would have their desires submitted to by others; they contend for a ready compliance from all about them, especially from those that stand near or beneath them in age or degree, as soon as they come to consider others with those distinctions.

54. §§41, 72–76.

§105. [2.] Another thing wherein they show their love of dominion is their desire to have things to be theirs; they would have *property* and possession, pleasing themselves with the power which that seems to give and the right they thereby have to dispose of them as they please. He that has not observed these two humors working very betimes in children has taken little notice of their actions; and he who thinks that these two roots of almost all the injustice and contention that so disturb human life are not early to be weeded out, and contrary habits introduced, neglects the proper season to lay the foundations of a good and worthy man. To do this, I imagine, these following things may somewhat conduce:

§106. 1. That a child should never be suffered to have what he *craves*, *Craving.* much less what he *cries for*, I would have said *or so much as speaks for*. But that being apt to be misunderstood and interpreted as if I meant a child should never speak to his parents for anything, which will perhaps be thought to lay too great a curb on the minds of children to the prejudice of that love and affection which should be between them and their parents, I shall explain myself a little more particularly. It is fit that they should have liberty to declare their wants to their parents and that with all tenderness they should be hearkened to and supplied at least whilst they are very little. But it is one thing to say, I am hungry; another to say, I would have roast meat. Having declared their wants, their natural wants, the pain they feel from hunger, thirst, cold, or any other necessity of nature, it is the duty of their parents and those about them to relieve them; but children must leave it to the choice and ordering of their parents what they think properest for them and how much, and must not be permitted to choose for themselves and say, I would have wine or white bread; the very naming of it should make them lose it.

§107. That which parents should take care of here is to distinguish between the wants of fancy and those of nature, which Horace has well taught them to do in this verse: *Queis humana sibi doleat natura negatis.*[55]

Those are truly natural wants which reason alone, without some other help, is not able to fence against nor keep from disturbing us. The pains of sickness and hurts, hunger, thirst, and cold, want of sleep and rest or relaxation of the part wearied with labor are what all men feel; and the best disposed minds cannot but be sensible of their uneasiness and therefore ought by fit applications to seek their removal, though not with impatience or overgreat haste upon the first approaches of them where delay does not threaten some irreparable harm. The pains that come from the necessities

55. Horace, *Satires* I i 75, "things which denied, human nature grieves for."

of nature are monitors to us to beware of greater mischiefs, which they are the forerunners of, and therefore they must not be wholly neglected nor strained too far. But yet the more children can be inured to hardships of this kind by a wise care to make them stronger in body and mind, the better it will be for them. I need not here give any caution to keep within the bounds of doing them good and to take care that what children are made to suffer should neither break their spirits nor injure their health, parents being but too apt of themselves to incline, more than they should, to the softer side.

But whatever compliance the necessities of nature may require, the wants of fancy children should never be gratified in nor suffered to *mention*. The very *speaking* for any such thing should make them lose it. Clothes, when they need, they must have; but if they *speak* for this stuff or that color, they should be sure to go without it. Not that I would have parents purposely cross the desires of their children in matters of indifferency: on the contrary, where their carriage deserves it, and one is sure it will not corrupt or effeminate their minds and make them fond of trifles, I think all things should be contrived, as much as could be, to their satisfaction that they might find the ease and pleasure of doing well. The best for children is that they should not place any pleasure in such things at all nor regulate their delight by their fancies, but be indifferent to all that nature has made so. This is what their parents and teachers should chiefly aim at; but till this be obtained, all that I oppose here is the liberty of *asking*, which in these things of conceit ought to be restrained by a constant forfeiture annexed to it.

This may perhaps be thought a little too severe by the natural indulgence of tender parents: but yet it is no more than necessary. For since the method I propose is to banish the rod, this restraint of their tongues will be of great use to settle that awe we have elsewhere spoken of[56] and to keep up in them the respect and reverence due to their parents. Next, it will teach them to keep in and so master their inclinations. By this means they will be brought to learn the art of stifling their desires as soon as they rise up in them, when they are easiest to be subdued. For giving vent gives life and strength to our appetites, and he that has the confidence to turn his wishes into demands will be but a little way from thinking he ought to obtain them. This, I am sure, everyone can more easily bear a denial from himself than from anybody else. They should therefore be accustomed betimes to consult and make use of their reason before they give allowance to their inclinations. 'Tis a great step towards the mastery of our desires to

56. §§40–44.

give this stop to them and shut them up in silence. This habit, got by children, of staying the forwardness of their fancies and deliberating whether it be fit or no before they *speak*, will be of no small advantage to them in matters of greater consequence in the future course of their lives. For that which I cannot too often inculcate is that, whatever the matter be about which it is conversant, whether great or small, the main (I had almost said only) thing to be considered in every action of a child is what influence it will have upon his mind; what habit it tends to and is likely to settle in him; how it will become him when he is bigger; and if it be encouraged, whither it will lead him when he is grown up.

My meaning therefore is not that children should purposely be made uneasy: this would relish too much of inhumanity and ill-nature, and be apt to infect them with it. They should be brought to deny their appetites, and their minds as well as bodies be made vigorous, easy, and strong, by the custom of having their inclinations in subjection and their bodies exercised with hardships; but all this, without giving them any mark or apprehension of ill will towards them. The constant loss of what they *craved* or *carved* to themselves should teach them modesty, submission, and a power to forbear; but the rewarding their modesty and silence by giving them what they liked should also assure them of the love of those who rigorously exacted this obedience. The contenting themselves now in the want of what they wished for is a virtue that another time should be rewarded with what is suited and acceptable to them, which should be bestowed on them as if it were a natural consequence of their good behavior, and not a bargain about it. But you will lose your labor and, what is more, their love and reverence too if they can receive from others what you deny them. This is to be kept very staunchly and carefully to be watched. And here the servants come again in my way.

§108. If this be begun betimes and they accustom themselves early to *Curiosity.* silence their desires, this useful habit will settle in them; and as they come to grow up in age and discretion, they may be allowed greater liberty when reason comes to speak in them and not passion. For whenever reason would speak, it should be hearkened to. But as they should never be heard when they speak for any particular thing they would *have*, unless it be first proposed to them, so they should always be heard and fairly and kindly answered when they ask after anything they would *know* and desire to be informed about. *Curiosity* should be as carefully *cherished* in children as other appetites suppressed.

However strict a hand is to be kept upon all desires of fancy, yet there *Recreation.* is one case wherein fancy must be permitted to speak, and be hearkened to also. *Recreation* is as necessary as labor or food. But because there can be no *recreation* without delight, which depends not always on reason but oftener on fancy, it must be permitted children not only to divert themselves, but to do it after their own fashion provided it be innocently and without prejudice to their health; and therefore in this case they should not be denied if they propose any particular kind of *recreation*. Though, I think, in a well-ordered education they will seldom be brought to the necessity of asking any such liberty. Care should be taken that what is of advantage to them they should always do with delight; and before they are wearied with one, they should be timely *diverted* to some other useful employment. But if they are not yet brought to that degree of perfection that one way of improvement can be made a *recreation* to another, they must be let loose to the childish play they fancy, which they should be weaned from by being made surfeited of it; but from things of use that they are employed in they should always be sent away with an appetite [or] at least be dismissed before they are tired and grow quite sick of it that so they may return to it again as to a pleasure that diverts them. For you must never think them set right till they can find delight in the practice of laudable things; and [till] the useful exercises of the body and mind, taking their turns, make their lives and improvement pleasant in a continued train of *recreations*, wherein the wearied part is constantly relieved and refreshed. Whether this can be done in every temper, or whether tutors and parents will be at the pains and have the discretion and patience to bring them to this, I know not; but that it may be done in most children, if a right course be taken to raise in them the desire of credit, esteem, and reputation, I do not at all doubt. And when they have so much true life put into them, they may freely be talked with about what most *delights* them and be directed or let loose to it so that they may perceive that they are beloved and cherished and that those under whose tuition they are are not enemies to their satisfaction. Such a management will make them in love with the hand that directs them and the virtue they are directed to.

This farther advantage may be made by a free liberty permitted them in their *recreations*, that it will discover their natural tempers, show their inclinations and aptitudes, and thereby direct wise parents in the choice both of the course of life and employment they shall design them for and of fit remedies in the meantime to be applied to whatever bent of nature they may observe most likely to mislead any of their children.

*Complaints.* §109. 2. Children who live together often strive for mastery, whose wills shall carry it over the rest; whoever begins the *contest* should be sure to be crossed in it. But not only that, but they should be taught to have all the *deference, complaisance,* and *civility* one for another imaginable. This, when they see it procures them respect, love, and esteem and that they lose no superiority by it, they will take more pleasure in than in insolent domineering; for so plainly is the other.

The accusations of children one against another, which usually are but the clamors of anger and revenge desiring aid, should not be favorably received nor hearkened to. It weakens and effeminates their minds to suffer them to *complain:* and if they endure sometimes crossing or pain from others without being permitted to think it strange or intolerable, it will do them no harm to learn sufferance and harden them early. But though you give no countenance to the *complaints* of the *querulous,* yet take care to curb the insolence and ill-nature of the injurious. When you observe it yourself, reprove it before the injured party; but if the *complaint* be of something really worth your notice and prevention another time, then reprove the offender by himself alone, out of sight of him that complained, and make him go and ask pardon and make reparation. Which coming thus, as it were, from himself, will be the more cheerfully performed and more kindly received, the love strengthened between them, and a custom of civility grow familiar amongst your children.

§110. 3. As to the having and possessing of things, teach them to part *Liberality.* with what they have easily and freely to their friends; and let them find by experience that the most *liberal* has always most plenty, with esteem and commendation to boot, and they will quickly learn to practice it. This I imagine will make brothers and sisters kinder and civiler to one another, and consequently to others, than twenty rules about good manners, with which children are ordinarily perplexed and cumbered. Covetousness and the desire of having in our possession and under our dominion more than we have need of, being the root of all evil, should be early and carefully weeded out and the contrary quality of a readiness to impart to others implanted. This should be encouraged by great commendation and credit and constantly taking care that he loses nothing by his *liberality.* Let all the instances he gives of such freeness be always repaid, and with interest; and let him sensibly perceive that the kindness he shows to others is no ill husbandry for himself, but that it brings a return of kindness both from those that receive it and those who look on. Make this a contest among children, who shall outdo one another this way; and by this means, by a constant practice, children having made it easy to themselves to part with what they have, good nature may be settled in them into a habit, and they may take pleasure and pique themselves in being *kind, liberal,* and *civil* to others.

*Justice.*　　If liberality ought to be encouraged, certainly great care is to be taken that children transgress not the rules of *justice:* and whenever they do, they should be set right, and if there be occasion for it, severely rebuked.

Our first actions being guided more by self-love than reason or reflection, it is no wonder that in children they should be very apt to deviate from the just measures of right and wrong, which are in the mind the result of improved reason and serious meditation. This the more they are apt to mistake, the more careful guard ought to be kept over them; and every the least slip in this great social virtue taken notice of and rectified, and that in things of the least weight and moment, both to instruct their ignorance and prevent ill habits, which from small beginnings in pins and cherrystones will, if let alone, grow up to higher frauds and be in danger to end at last in a downright hardened dishonesty. The first tendency to any *injustice* that appears must be suppressed with a show of wonder and abhorrence in the parents and governors. But because children cannot well comprehend what *injustice* is till they understand property and how particular persons come by it, the safest way to secure honesty is to lay the foundations of it early in liberality and an easiness to part with to others whatever they have or like themselves. This may be taught them early, before they have language and understanding enough to form distinct notions of property and to know what is theirs by a peculiar right exclusive of others. And since children seldom have anything but by gift, and that for the most part from their parents, they may be at first taught not to take or keep anything but what is given them by those whom they take to have a power over it. And as their capacities enlarge, other rules and cases of *justice* and rights concerning *meum* and *tuum*[57] may be proposed and inculcated. If any act of *injustice* in them appears to proceed not from mistake but a perverseness in their wills, when a gentle rebuke and shame will not reform this irregular and covetous inclination, rougher remedies must be applied: and 'tis but for the father or tutor to take and keep from them something that they value and think their own or order somebody else to do it, and by such instances make them sensible what little advantage they are likely to make by possessing themselves *unjustly* of what is another's whilst there are in the world stronger and more men than they. But if an ingenuous detestation of this shameful vice be but carefully and early instilled into them, as I think it may, that is the true and genuine method to obviate this crime and will be a better guard against *dishonesty* than any considerations drawn from interest; habits working more constantly and with greater facility

57. "Mine" and "yours."

than reason, which when we have most need of it is seldom fairly consulted, and more rarely obeyed.

§111. *Crying* is a fault that should not be tolerated in children not only for the unpleasant and unbecoming noise it fills the house with, but for more considerable reasons in reference to the children themselves, which is to be our aim in education.

Their *crying* is of two sorts: either *stubborn* and *domineering* or *querulous* and *whining*.

1. Their *crying* is very often a striving for mastery and an open declaration of their insolence or obstinacy: when they have not the power to obtain their desire, they will by their *clamor* and *sobbing* maintain their title and right to it. This is an avowed continuing of their claim and a sort of remonstrance against the oppression and injustice of those who deny them what they have a mind to.

§112. 2. Sometimes their *crying* is the effect of pain or true sorrow and a *bemoaning* themselves under it.

These two, if carefully observed, may by the mien, looks, and actions, and particularly by the tone of their crying be easily distinguished; but neither of them must be suffered, much less encouraged.

1. The obstinate or *stomachful crying* should by no means be permitted because it is but another way of flattering their desires and encouraging those passions which it is our main business to subdue; and if it be, as often it is, upon the receiving any correction, it quite defeats all the good effects of it. For any chastisement which leaves them in this declared opposition only serves to make them worse. The restraints and punishments laid on children are all misapplied and lost as far as they do not prevail over their wills, teach them to submit their passions, and make their minds supple and pliant to what their parents' reason advises them now, and so prepare them to obey what their own reason shall advise hereafter. But if in anything wherein they are crossed they may be suffered to go away *crying,* they confirm themselves in their desires and cherish the ill humor with a declaration of their right and a resolution to satisfy their inclination the first opportunity. This therefore is another argument against the frequent use of blows: for whenever you come to that extremity, it is not enough to whip or beat them, you must do it till you find you have subdued their minds, till with submission and patience they yield to the correction, which you shall best discover by their *crying* and their ceasing from it upon your bidding. Without this, the beating of children is but a passionate tyranny over them; and it is mere cruelty and not correction to put their bodies in pain without doing their minds any good. As this gives us a reason

why children should seldom be corrected, so it also prevents their being so. For if, whenever they are chastised, it were done thus without passion, soberly and yet effectually too, laying on the blows and smart not furiously and all at once, but slowly with reasoning between and with observation how it wrought, stopping when it had made them pliant, penitent, and yielding, they would seldom need the like punishment again, being made careful to avoid the fault that deserved it. Besides, by this means, as the punishment would not be lost for being too little and not effectual, so it would be kept from being too much if we gave off as soon as we perceived that it reached the mind and that was bettered. For since the chiding or beating of children should be always the least that possibly may be, that which is laid on in the heat of anger seldom observes that measure, but is commonly more than it should be, though it prove less than enough.

§113. 2. Many children are apt to *cry* upon any little pain they suffer, and the least harm that befalls them puts them into *complaints* and *bawling*. This few children avoid: for it being the first and natural way to declare their sufferings or wants before they can speak, the compassion that is thought due to that tender age foolishly encourages and continues it in them long after they can speak. It is the duty, I confess, of those about children to compassionate them whenever they suffer any hurt; but not to show it in pitying them. Help and ease them the best you can, but by no means bemoan them. This softens their minds and makes them yield to the little harms that happen to them, whereby they sink deeper into that part which alone feels and make larger wounds there than otherwise they would. They should be hardened against all sufferings, especially of the body, and have no tenderness but what rises from an ingenuous shame and a quick sense of reputation. The many inconveniences this life is exposed to require [that] we should not be too sensible of every little hurt. What our minds yield not to makes but a slight impression and does us but very little harm: it is the suffering of our spirits that gives and continues the pain. This brawniness and insensibility of mind is the best armor we can have against the common evils and accidents of life; and being a temper that is to be got by exercise and custom more than any other way, the practice of it should be begun betimes, and happy is he that is taught it early. That effeminacy of spirit which is to be prevented or cured, as nothing that I know so much increases in children as *crying*, so nothing, on the other side, so much checks and restrains [it] as their being hindered from that sort of *complaining*. In the little harms they suffer from knocks and falls, they should not be pitied for falling, but bid do so again; which, besides that it stops their *crying*, is a better way to cure their heedlessness and prevent their tumbling another time than either chiding or bemoaning them. But let the hurts they receive be what they will, stop their *crying*, and that will give them more quiet and ease at present and harden them for the future.

§114. The former sort of *crying* requires severity to silence it, and where a look or a positive command will not do it, blows must. For it proceeding from pride, obstinacy, and stomach, the will, where the fault lies, must be bent and made to comply by a rigor sufficient to master it. But this latter, being ordinarily from softness of mind, a quite contrary cause, ought to be treated with a gentler hand. Persuasion, or diverting the thoughts another way, or laughing at their *whining* may perhaps be at first the proper method. But for this the circumstances of the thing and the particular temper of the child must be considered: no certain invariable rules can be given about it, but it must be left to the prudence of the parents or tutor. But this I think I may say in general, that there should be a constant discountenancing of this sort of *crying* also, and that the father by his authority should always stop it, mixing a greater degree of roughness in his looks or words proportionably as the child is of a greater age or a sturdier temper, but always let it be enough to silence their *whimpering* and put an end to the disorder.

§115. *Cowardice* and *courage* are so nearly related to the aforemen-   *Foolhardiness.* tioned tempers that it may not be amiss here to take notice of them. Fear is a passion that, if rightly governed, has its use. And though self-love seldom fails to keep it watchful and high enough in us, yet there may be an excess on the daring side, *foolhardiness* and insensibility of danger being as little reasonable as trembling and shrinking at the approach of every little evil. Fear was given us as a monitor to quicken our industry and keep us upon our guard against the approaches of evil; and therefore to have no apprehension of mischief at hand, not to make a just estimate of the danger, but heedlessly to run into it, be the hazard what it will, without considering of what use or consequence it may be, is not the resolution of a rational creature but brutish fury. Those who have children of this temper have nothing to do but a little to awaken their reason, which self-preservation will quickly dispose them to hearken to unless (which is usually the case) some other passion hurries them on headlong, without sense, and without consideration. A dislike of evil is so natural to mankind that nobody, I think, can be without fear of it; fear being nothing but an uneasiness under the apprehension of that coming upon us which we dislike. And therefore whenever anyone runs into danger, we may say, it is under the conduct of ignorance or the command of some more imperious passion; nobody being so much an enemy to himself as to come within the reach of evil out of free choice and court danger for danger's sake. If it be therefore pride, vainglory, or rage that silences a child's fear or makes him not hearken to its advice, those are by fit means to be abated that a little consideration may allay his heat and make him bethink himself whether this attempt be worth the venture. But this being a fault that children are not so often guilty of, I shall not be more particular in its cure. Weakness of spirit is the more common defect and therefore will require the greater care.

*Courage.*     *Fortitude* is the guard and support of the other virtues; and without courage a man will scarce keep steady to his duty and fill up the character of a truly worthy man.

*Courage,* that makes us bear up against dangers that we fear and evils that we feel, is of great use in an estate, as ours is in this life, exposed to assaults on all hands; and therefore it is very advisable to get children into this armor as early as we can. Natural temper, I confess, does here a great deal; but even where that is defective and the heart is in itself weak and timorous, it may by a right management be brought to a better resolution. What is to be done to prevent breaking children's spirits by frightful apprehensions instilled into them when young, or bemoaning themselves under every little suffering, I have already taken notice.[58] How to harden their tempers and raise their *courage* if we find them too much subject to fear is farther to be considered.

True fortitude I take to be the quiet possession of a man's self and an undisturbed doing his duty, whatever evil besets or danger lies in his way. This there are so few men attain to that we are not to expect it from children. But yet something may be done, and a wise conduct by insensible degrees may carry them farther than one expects.

The neglect of this great care of them, whilst they are young, is the reason perhaps why there are so few that have this virtue in its full latitude when they are men. I should not say this in a nation so naturally brave as ours is, did I think that true fortitude required nothing but courage in the field and a contempt of life in the face of an enemy. This, I confess, is not the least part of it nor can be denied the laurels and honors always justly due to the valor of those who venture their lives for their country. But yet this is not all. Dangers attack us in other places besides the fields of battle; and though death be the king of terrors, yet pain, disgrace, and poverty have frightful looks able to discompose most men whom they seem ready

58. Preventing breaking children's spirits at §46 and bemoaning at §113, but frightful apprehensions not till later in §115.

to seize on, and there are those who contemn some of these and yet are heartily frighted with the other. True fortitude is prepared for dangers of all kinds and unmoved whatsoever evil it be that threatens. I do not mean unmoved with any fear at all. Where danger shows itself, apprehension cannot, without stupidity, be wanting. Where danger is, sense of danger should be and so much fear as should keep us awake and excite our attention, industry, and vigor but not disturb the calm use of our reason nor hinder the execution of what that dictates.

The first step to get this noble and manly steadiness is what I have above mentioned, carefully to keep children from frights of all kinds when they are young. Let not any fearful apprehensions be talked into them nor terrible objects surprise them. This often so shatters and discomposes *Cowardice.* the spirits that they never recover again, but during their whole life upon the first suggestion or appearance of any terrifying idea are scattered and confounded; the body is enervated, and the mind disturbed, and the man scarce himself or capable of any composed or rational action. Whether this be from a habitual motion of the animal spirits introduced by the first strong impression or from the alteration of the constitution by some more unaccountable way, this is certain, that so it is. Instances of such, who in a weak timorous mind have borne all their whole lives through the effects of a fright when they were young, are everywhere to be seen and therefore as much as may be to be prevented.

The next thing is by gentle degrees to accustom children to those things they are too much afraid of. But here great caution is to be used that you do not make too much haste nor attempt this cure too early, for fear lest you increase the mischief instead of remedying it. Little ones in arms may be easily kept out of the way of terrifying objects and, till they can talk and understand what is said to them, are scarce capable of that reasoning and discourse which should be used to let them know there is no harm in those frightful objects which we would make them familiar with and do, to that purpose, by gentle degrees bring nearer and nearer to them. And therefore it is seldom there is need of any application to them of this kind till after they can run about and talk. But yet, if it should happen that infants should have taken offence at anything which cannot be easily kept out of their way and that they show marks of terror as often as it comes in sight, all the allays of fright by diverting their thoughts or mixing pleasant and agreeable appearances with it must be used till it be grown familiar and inoffensive to them.

I think we may observe that when children are first born all objects of sight that do not hurt the eyes are indifferent to them; and they are no more afraid of a blackamoor or a lion than of their nurse or a cat. What is it then that afterwards in certain mixtures of shape and color comes to affright them? Nothing but the apprehensions of harm that accompany those things. Did a child suck every day a new nurse, I make account it would be no more affrighted with the change of faces at six months old than at sixty. The reason then why it will not come to a stranger is because, having been accustomed to receive its food and kind usage only from one or two that are about it, the child apprehends by coming into the arms of a stranger the being taken from what delights and feeds it and every moment supplies its wants, which it often feels, and therefore fears when the nurse is away.

*Timorousness.*     The only thing we naturally are afraid of is pain or loss of pleasure. And because these are not annexed to any shape, color, or size of visible objects, we are frighted with none of them till either we have felt pain from them or have notions put into us that they will do us harm. The pleasant brightness and lustre of flame and fire so delights children that at first they always desire to be handling of it, but when constant experience has convinced them, by the exquisite pain it has put them to, how cruel and unmerciful it is, they are afraid to touch it and carefully avoid it. This being the ground of fear, it is not hard to find whence it arises and how it is to be cured in all mistaken objects of terror. And when the mind is confirmed against them and has got a mastery over itself and its usual fears in lighter occasions, it is in a good preparation to meet more real dangers. Your child shrieks and runs away at the sight of a frog: let another catch it and lay it down at a good distance from him; at first accustom him to look upon it; when he can do that, then to come nearer to it and see it leap without emotion; then to touch it lightly when it is held fast in another's hand; and so on, till he can come to handle it as confidently as a butterfly or a sparrow. By the same way any other vain terrors may be removed if care be taken that you go not too fast and push not the child on to a new degree of assurance till he be thoroughly confirmed in the former. And thus the young soldier is to be trained on to the warfare of life; wherein care is to be taken that more things be not represented as dangerous than really are so and then that whatever you observe him to be more frighted at than he should you be sure to tole[59] him on to by insensible degrees till he at last, quitting his fears, masters the difficulty and comes off with applause. Successes of this kind often repeated will make him find that evils are not always so certain or so great as our fears represent them and that the way

59. Allure.

to avoid them is not to run away or be discomposed, dejected, and deterred by fear where either our credit or duty requires us to go on.

But since the great foundation of fear in children is pain, the way to *Hardiness.* harden and fortify children against fear and danger is to accustom them to suffer pain. This it is possible will be thought by kind parents a very unnatural thing towards their children, and by most unreasonable to endeavor to reconcile anyone to the sense of pain by bringing it upon him. It will be said it may perhaps give the child an aversion for him that makes him suffer but can never recommend to him suffering itself. This is a strange method. You will not have children whipped and punished for their faults, but you would have them tormented for doing well, or for tormenting's sake. I doubt not but such objections as these will be made, and I shall be thought inconsistent with myself or fantastical in proposing it. I confess it is a thing to be managed with great discretion, and therefore it falls not out amiss that it will not be received or relished but by those who consider well and look into the reason of things. I would not have children much beaten for their faults, because I would not have them think bodily pain the greatest punishment; and I would have them, when they do well, be sometimes put in pain for the same reason, that they might be accustomed to bear it without looking on it as the greatest evil. How much education may reconcile young people to pain and sufferance, the example of Sparta does sufficiently show;[60] and they who have once brought themselves not to think bodily pain the greatest of evils or that which they ought to stand most in fear of have made no small advance towards virtue. But I am not so foolish to propose the Lacedaemonian[61] discipline in our age or constitution, but yet I do say that inuring children gently to suffer some degrees of pain without shrinking is a way to gain firmness to their minds and lay a foundation for courage and resolution in the future parts of their lives.

Not to bemoan them or permit them to bemoan themselves on every little pain they suffer is the first step to be made. But of this I have spoken elsewhere.

The next thing is sometimes designedly to put them in pain; but care must be taken that this be done when the child is in good humor and satisfied of the good will and kindness of him that hurts him at the time that he does it. There must [be] no marks of anger or displeasure, on the one

60. Plutarch, *Lycurgus* 18, *Ancient Customs of the Spartans* 40; Cicero, *Tusculan Disputations* II 34

61. Spartan.

side, nor compassion or repenting, on the other, [to] go along with it; and it must be sure to be no more than the child can bear without repining or taking it amiss or for a punishment. Managed by these degrees and with such circumstances, I have seen a child run away laughing with good smart blows of a wand on his back who would have cried for an unkind word and have been very sensible of the chastisement of a cold look from the same person. Satisfy a child by a constant course of your care and kindness that you perfectly love him, and he may by degrees be accustomed to bear very painful and rough usage from you without flinching or complaining; and this we see children do every day in play one with another. The softer you find your child is, the more you are to seek occasions, at fit times, thus to harden him. The great art in this is to begin with what is but very little painful, and to proceed by insensible degrees, when you are playing and in good humor with him and speaking well of him; and when you have once got him to think himself made amends for his suffering by the praise [that] is given him for his courage, when he can take a pride in giving such marks of his manliness and can prefer the reputation of being brave and stout to the avoiding a little pain or the shrinking under it, you need not despair in time and by the assistance of his growing reason to master his timorousness and mend the weakness of his constitution. As he grows bigger, he is to be set upon bolder attempts than his natural temper carries him to; and whenever he is observed to flinch from what one has reason to think he would come off well in, if he had but courage to undertake, that he should be assisted in at first and by degrees shamed to till at last practice has given more assurance and with it a mastery, which must be rewarded with great praise and the good opinion of others for his performance. When by these steps he has got resolution enough not to be deterred from what he ought to do by the apprehension of danger, when fear does not in sudden or hazardous occurrences discompose his mind, set his body atrembling, and make him unfit for action or run away from it, he has then the courage of a rational creature; and such a hardiness we should endeavor by custom and use to bring children to, as proper occasions come in our way.

*Cruelty.*     §116. One thing I have frequently observed in children, that when they have got possession of any poor creature they are apt to use it ill: they often *torment* and treat very roughly young birds, butterflies, and such other poor animals which fall into their hands, and that with a seeming kind of pleasure. This I think should be watched in them, and if they incline to any such *cruelty*, they should be taught the contrary usage. For the custom of tormenting and killing of beasts will, by degrees, harden their minds even towards men; and they who delight in the suffering and destruction of inferior creatures will not be apt to be very compassionate or benign to those of their own kind. Our practice takes notice of this in the exclusion of *butchers* from juries of life and death. Children should from the beginning be bred up in an abhorrence of *killing* or tormenting any living creature and be taught not to *spoil* or destroy anything, unless it be for the preservation or advantage of some other that is nobler. And truly, if the preservation of all mankind, as much as in him lies, were everyone's persuasion, as indeed it is everyone's duty and the true principle to regulate our religion, politicks, and morality by, the world would be much quieter and better natured than it is. But to return to our present business: I cannot but commend both the kindness and prudence of a mother I knew, who was wont always to indulge her daughters when any of them desired dogs, squirrels, birds, or any such things, as young girls [are] use[d] to be delighted with; but then when they had them, they must be sure to keep them well and look diligently after them, that they wanted nothing, or were not ill used. For if they were negligent in their care of them, it was counted a great fault, which often forfeited their possession, or at least they failed not to be rebuked for it; whereby they were early taught diligence and good nature. And indeed, I think people should be accustomed from their cradles to be tender to all sensible creatures, and to spoil or *waste* nothing at all.

This delight they take in *doing of mischief*, whereby I mean spoiling of anything to no purpose, but more especially the pleasure they take to put anything in pain that is capable of it, I cannot persuade myself to be any other than a foreign and introduced disposition, a habit borrowed from custom and conversation. People teach children to strike, and laugh when they hurt or see harm come to others; and they have the examples of most about them to confirm them in it. All the entertainment and talk of history is of nothing almost but fighting and killing; and the honor and renown that is bestowed on conquerors (who for the most part are but the great butchers of mankind) farther mislead growing youth, who by this means come to think slaughter the laudable business of mankind and the most heroic of virtues. By these steps, unnatural cruelty is planted in us, and what humanity abhors custom reconciles and recommends to us by laying it in the way to honor. Thus, by fashion and opinion, that comes to be a pleasure which in itself neither is nor can be any. This ought carefully to be watched, and early remedied, so as to settle and cherish the contrary and more natural temper of benignity and *compassion* in the room of it: but still by the same gentle methods which are to be applied to the other two faults before mentioned.[62] It may not perhaps be unseasonable here to add this farther caution, viz. that the mischiefs or harms that come by play, inadvertency, or ignorance, and were not known to be harms or designed for mischief's sake, though they may perhaps be sometimes of considerable damage, yet are not at all, or but very gently, to be taken notice of. For this, I think, I cannot too often inculcate, that whatever miscarriage a child is guilty of, and whatever be the consequence of it, the thing to be regarded in taking notice of it is only what root it springs from and what habit it is likely to establish; and to that the correction ought to be directed, and the child not to suffer any punishment for any harm which may have come by his play or inadvertency. The faults to be amended lie in the mind; and if they are such as either age will cure or no ill habits will follow from, the present action, whatever displeasing circumstances it may have, is to be passed by without any animadversion.

§117. Another way to instill sentiments of humanity and to keep them lively in young folks will be to accustom them to civility in their language and deportment towards their inferiors and the meaner sort of people, particularly servants. It is not unusual to observe the children in gentlemen's families treat the servants of the house with domineering words, names of contempt, and an imperious carriage as if they were of another race and species beneath them. Whether ill example, the advantage of fortune, or their natural vanity inspire this haughtiness, it should be prevented or weeded out and a gentle, courteous, affable carriage towards the lower ranks of men placed in the room of it. No part of their superiority will be hereby lost, but the distinction increased and their authority strengthened when love in inferiors is joined to outward respect, and an esteem of the person has a share in their submission; and domestics will pay a more ready and cheerful service, when they find themselves not spurned because fortune has laid them below the level of others at their masters' feet. Children should not be suffered to lose the consideration of human nature in the shufflings of outward conditions. The more they have, the better humored they should be taught to be, and the more compassionate and gentle to those of their brethren who are placed lower and have scantier portions. If they are suffered from their cradles to treat men ill and rudely because, by their father's title, they think they have a little power over them, at best it is ill-bred, and if care be not taken will, by degrees, nurse up their natural pride into a habitual contempt of those beneath them. And where will that probably end, but in oppression and cruelty?

62. Love of dominion at §§103–10 and crying at §§111–15.

§118. Curiosity in children (which I had occasion just to mention §108) is but an appetite after knowledge and therefore ought to be encouraged in them, not only as a good sign, but as the great instrument nature has provided to remove that ignorance they were born with and which, without this busy *inquisitiveness*, will make them dull and useless creatures. The ways to encourage it and keep it active and busy are, I suppose, these following:

1. Not to check or discountenance any *inquiries* he shall make nor suffer them to be laughed at, but to *answer* all his *questions* and *explain* the matters he desires to know, so as to make them as much intelligible to him as suits the capacity of his age and knowledge. But confound not his understanding with explications or notions that are above it or with the variety or number of things that are not to his present purpose. Mark what it is his mind aims at in the *question*, and not what words he expresses it in; and when you have informed and satisfied him in that, you shall see how his thoughts will enlarge themselves, and how by fit answers he may be led on farther than perhaps you could imagine. For knowledge is grateful to the understanding, as light to the eyes; children are pleased and delighted with it exceedingly, especially if they see that their *inquiries* are regarded and that their desire of knowing is encouraged and commended. And I doubt not but one great reason why many children abandon themselves wholly to silly sports and trifle away all their time insipidly is because they have found their *curiosity* balked and their *inquiries* neglected. But had they been treated with more kindness and respect, and their *questions* answered, as they should, to their satisfaction, I doubt not but they would have taken more pleasure in learning and improving their knowledge, wherein there would be still newness and variety, which is what they are delighted with, than in returning over and over to the same play and playthings.

§119. 2. To this serious answering their *questions* and informing their understandings in what they desire, as if it were a matter that needed it, should be added some peculiar ways of *commendation*. Let others whom they esteem be told before their faces of the knowledge they have in such and such things; and since we are all, even from our cradles, vain and proud creatures, let their vanity be flattered with things that will do them good and let their pride set them on work on something which may turn to their advantage. Upon this ground you shall find that there cannot be a greater spur to the attaining what you would have the eldest learn and know himself than to set him upon *teaching* it *his younger brothers* and sisters.

§120. 3. As children's *inquiries* are not to be slighted, so also great care is to be taken that they *never* receive *deceitful* and *eluding answers*. They easily perceive when they are slighted or deceived, and quickly learn the trick of neglect, dissimulation, and falsehood which they observe others to make use of. We are not to entrench upon truth in any conversation, but least of all with children; since if we play false with them, we not only deceive their expectation and hinder their knowledge, but corrupt their innocence and teach them the worst of vices. They are travelers newly arrived in a strange country, of which they know nothing: we should therefore make conscience not to mislead them. And though their *questions* seem sometimes not very material, yet they should be seriously answered: for however they may appear to us (to whom they are long since known) *inquiries* not worth the making, they are of moment to those who are wholly ignorant. Children are strangers to all we are acquainted with, and all the things they meet with are at first unknown to them, as they once were to us; and happy are they who meet with civil people that will comply with their ignorance and help them to get out of it.

If you or I now should be set down in Japan, with all our prudence and knowledge about us, a conceit whereof makes us perhaps so apt to slight the thoughts and *inquiries* of children; should we, I say, be set down in Japan, we should no doubt (if we would inform ourselves of what is there to be known) ask a thousand questions, which to a supercilious or inconsiderate Japanese would seem very idle and impertinent, though to us they would be very material and of importance to be resolved; and we should be glad to find a man so complaisant and courteous as to satisfy our demands, and instruct our ignorance.

When any new thing comes in their way, children usually ask the common *question* of a stranger: *What is it?* Whereby they ordinarily mean nothing but the name; and therefore to tell them how it is called is usually the proper answer to that demand. The next question usually is: *What is it for?* And to this it should be answered truly and directly: the use of the thing should be told, and the way explained how it serves to such a purpose, as far as their capacities can comprehend it. And so of any other circumstances they shall ask about it; not turning them going till you have given them all the satisfaction they are capable of, and so leading them by your answers into farther questions. And perhaps to a grown man such conversation will not be altogether so idle and insignificant as we are apt to imagine. The native and untaught suggestions of inquisitive children do often offer things that may set a considering man's thoughts on work. And I think there is frequently more to be learned from the unexpected questions of a child than the discourses of men, who talk in a road, according to the notions they have borrowed and the prejudices of their education.

§121. 4. Perhaps it may not sometimes be amiss to excite their curiosity by bringing strange and new things in their way, on purpose to engage their inquiry and give them occasion to inform themselves about them; and if by chance their curiosity leads them to ask what they should not know, it is a great deal better to tell them plainly that it is a thing that belongs not to them to know than to pop them off with a falsehood or a frivolous answer.

§122. *Pertness,* that appears sometimes so early, proceeds from a principle that seldom accompanies a strong constitution of body or ripens into a strong judgment of mind. If it were desirable to have a child a more brisk talker, I believe there might be ways found to make him so; but I suppose a wise father had rather that his son should be able and useful when a man than pretty company and a diversion to others whilst a child; though if that too were to be considered, I think I may say there is not so much pleasure to have a child prattle agreeably as to reason well. Encourage therefore his *inquisitiveness* all you can, by satisfying his demands and informing his judgment as far as it is capable. When his reasons are anyway tolerable, let him find the credit and commendation of it; and when they are quite out of the way, let him, without being laughed at for his mistake, be gently put into the right; and if he show a forwardness to be reasoning about things that come in his way, take care as much as you can that nobody check this inclination in him or mislead it by captious or fallacious ways of talking with him. For when all is done, this, as the highest and most important faculty of our minds, deserves the greatest care and attention in cultivating it: the right improvement and exercise of our reason being the highest perfection that a man can attain to in this life.

§123. Contrary to this busy inquisitive temper there is sometimes   *Sauntering.* observable in children a *listless carelessness,* a want of regard to anything, and a sort of *trifling* even at their business. This *sauntering* humor I look on as one of the worst qualities [that] can appear in a child, as well as one of the hardest to be cured where it is natural. But it being liable to be mistaken in some cases, care must be taken to make a right judgment concerning that *trifling* at their books or business which may sometimes be complained of in a child. Upon the first suspicion a father has that his son is of a *sauntering* temper, he must carefully observe him, whether he be *listless* and *indifferent* in all his actions, or whether in some things alone he be slow and sluggish but in others vigorous and eager. For though he find that he does loiter at his book and let a good deal of the time he spends in his chamber or study run idly away, he must not presently conclude that this is from a *sauntering* humor in his temper. It may be childishness and a preferring something to his study which his thoughts run on, and [that] he dislikes his book, as is natural, because it is forced upon him as a task. To know this perfectly, you must watch him at play, when he is out of his place and time of study, following his own inclinations; and see there whether he be stirring and active, whether he designs anything and with labor and eagerness pursues it till he has accomplished what he aimed at, or whether he *lazily* and *listlessly dreams away his time*. If this sloth be only when he is about his book, I think it may be easily cured. If it be in his temper, it will require a little more pains and attention to remedy it.

§124. If you are satisfied by his earnestness at play or anything else he sets his mind on in the intervals between his hours of business, that he is not of himself inclined to *laziness*, but that only want of relish of his book makes him negligent and *sluggish* in his application to it, the first step is to try by talking to him kindly of the folly and inconvenience of it, whereby he loses a good part of his time which he might have for his diversion; but be sure to talk calmly and kindly, and not much at first, but only these plain reasons in short. If this prevails, you have gained the point in the most desirable way, which is that of reason and kindness. If this softer application prevails not, try to shame him out of it by laughing at him for it, asking every day, when he comes to table, if there be no strangers there, how long he was that day about his business; and if he has not done it in the time he might be well supposed to have dispatched it, expose and turn him into ridicule for it; but mix no chiding, only put on a pretty cold brow towards him, and keep it till he reform, and let his mother, tutor, and all about him do so too. If this work not the effect you desire, then tell him he shall be no longer troubled with a tutor to take care of his education, you will not be at the charge to have him spend his time idly with him, but since he prefers this or that (whatever play he delights in) to his book, that only he shall do; and so in earnest set him on [to] work on his beloved play and keep him steadily and in earnest to it morning and afternoon, till he be fully surfeited and would at any rate change it for some hours at his book again. But when you thus set him a task of his play, you must be sure to look after him yourself, or set somebody else to do it that may constantly see him employed in it, and that he be not permitted to be idle at that too. I say, yourself look after him; for it is worth the father's while, whatever business he has, to bestow two or three days upon his son to cure so great a mischief as is *sauntering* at his business.

§125. This is what I propose if it be *idleness* not from his general temper but a peculiar or acquired aversion to learning, which you must be careful to examine and distinguish. But though you have your eyes upon him to watch what he does with the time which he has at his own disposal, yet you must not let him perceive that you or anybody else do so. For that may hinder him from following his own inclination, which he being full of and not daring for fear of you to prosecute what his head and heart are set upon, he may neglect all other things, which then he relishes not, and so may seem to be idle and listless when in truth it is nothing but being intent on that which the fear of your eye or knowledge keeps him from executing. To be clear in this point, the observation must be made when you are out of the way and he not so much as under the restraint of a suspicion that anybody has an eye upon him. In those seasons of perfect freedom, let somebody you can trust mark how he spends his time: whether he inactively loiters it away when without any check he is left to his own inclination. Thus by his employing of such times of liberty, you will easily discern whether it be *listlessness* in his temper or aversion to his book that makes him *saunter* away his time of study.

§126. If some defect in his constitution has cast a damp on his mind, and he be naturally listless and dreaming, this unpromising disposition is none of the easiest to be dealt with because, generally carrying with it an unconcernedness for the future, it wants the two great springs of action: *foresight* and *desire*, which how to plant and increase, where nature has given a cold and contrary temper, will be the question. As soon as you are satisfied that this is the case, you must carefully inquire whether there be nothing he delights in: inform yourself what it is he is most pleased with; and if you can find any particular tendency his mind has, increase it all you can, and make use of that to set him on work and to excite his industry. If he loves praise, or play, or fine clothes, etc., or, on the other side, dreads pain, disgrace, or your displeasure, etc., whatever it be that he loves most, except it be sloth (for that will never set him on work), let that be made use of to quicken him and make him bestir himself. For in this *listless temper*, you are not to fear an excess of appetite (as in all other cases) by cherishing it. It is that which you want and therefore must labor to raise and increase. For where there is no desire, there will be no industry.

§127. If you have not hold enough upon him this way to stir up vigor and activity in him, you must employ him in some constant bodily labor whereby he may get a habit of doing something. The keeping him hard to some study were the better way to get him a habit of exercising and applying his mind. But because this is an invisible attention and nobody can tell when he is or is not idle at it, you must find bodily employments for him, which he must be constantly busied in and kept to; and if they have some little hardship and shame in them, it may not be the worse, that they may the sooner weary him and make him desire to return to his book. But be sure, when you exchange his book for his other labor, set him such a task to be done in such a time as may allow him no opportunity to be idle. Only after you have by this way brought him to be attentive and industrious at his book, you may, upon his dispatching his study within the time set him, give him as a reward some respite from his other labor, which you may diminish as you find him grow more and more steady in his application, and at last wholly take off when his *sauntering* at his book is cured.

*Compulsion.*    §128. We formerly observed that variety and freedom was that that delighted children and recommended their plays to them, and that therefore their book or anything we would have them learn should not be enjoined them *as business.*[63] This their parents, tutors, and teachers are apt to forget, and their impatience to have them busied in what is fit for them to do suffers them not to deceive them into it; but by the repeated injunctions they meet with, children quickly distinguish between what is required of them and what not. When this mistake has once made his book uneasy to him, the cure is to be applied at the other end. And since it will be then too late to endeavor to make it a play to him, you must take the contrary course: observe what play he is most delighted with, enjoin that, and make him play so many hours every day, not as a punishment for playing but as if it were the business required of him. This, if I mistake not, will in a few days make him so weary of his most beloved sport that he will prefer his book or anything to it, especially if it may redeem him from any part of the task of play [that] is set him and he may be suffered to employ some part of the time destined to his *task of play* in his book, or such other exercise as is really useful to him. This I at least think a better cure than that forbidding (which usually increases the desire) or any other punishment should be made use of to remedy it. For when you have once glutted his appetite (which may safely be done in all things but eating and drinking) and made him surfeit of what you would have him avoid, you have put into him a principle of aversion, and you need not so much fear afterwards his longing for the same thing again.

§129. This I think is sufficiently evident: that children generally hate to be idle. All the care then is that their busy humor should be constantly employed in something of use to them; which if you will attain, you must make what you would have them do a recreation to them and not a *business.* The way to do this, so that they may not perceive you have any hand in it, is this proposed here, viz., to make them weary of that which you would

63. §§73–74, 76.

not have them do by enjoining and making them, under some pretence or other, do it till they are surfeited. For example: does your son play at top and scourge[64] too much? Enjoin him to play so many hours every day and look that he do it; and you shall see he will quickly be sick of it and willing to leave it. By this means making the recreations you dislike *a business* to him, he will of himself with delight betake himself to those things you would have him do; especially if they be proposed as rewards for having performed his *task* in that play [which] is commanded him. For if he be ordered every day to whip his top so long as to make him sufficiently weary, do you not think he will apply himself with eagerness to his book and wish for it, if you promise it him as a reward of having whipped his top lustily quite out all the time that is set him? Children, in the things they do, if they comport with their age, find little difference so they may be doing; the esteem they have for one thing above another they borrow from others, so that what those about them make to be a reward to them will really be so. By this art it is in their governor's choice whether *Scotch-hoppers*[65] shall reward their *dancing*, or *dancing* their *Scotch-hoppers;* whether peg top or reading, playing at trap or studying the globes, shall be more acceptable and pleasing to them; all that they desire being to be busy, and busy, as they imagine, in things of their own choice and which they receive as favors from their parents, or others for whom they have respect and with whom they would be in credit. A set of children thus ordered and kept from the ill example of others would all of them, I suppose, with as much earnestness and delight learn to read, write, and what else one would have them, as others do their ordinary plays; and the eldest being thus entered and this made the fashion of the place, it would be as impossible to hinder them from learning the one as it is ordinarily to keep them from the other.

§130. Playthings I think children should have, and of diverse sorts;  *Play-games.* but still to be in the custody of their tutors or somebody else, whereof the child should have in his power but one at once, and should not be suffered to have another but when he restored that. This teaches them betimes to be careful of not losing or spoiling the things they have; whereas plenty and variety in their own keeping makes them wanton and careless and teaches them from the beginning to be squanderers and wasters. These, I confess, are little things and such as will seem beneath the care of a governor: but nothing that may form children's minds is to be overlooked and

64. Whip a top.
65. Hopscotch.

neglected, and whatsoever introduces habits and settles customs in them deserves the care and attention of their governors and is not a small thing in its consequences.

One thing more about children's playthings may be worth their parents' care. Though it be agreed they should have of several sorts, yet, I think, they should have none bought for them. This will hinder that great variety they are often overcharged with, which serves only to teach the mind to wander after change and superfluity, to be unquiet and perpetually stretching itself after something more still, though it knows not what, and never to be satisfied with what it has. The court that is made to people of condition in such kind of presents to their children does the little ones great harm. By it they are taught pride, vanity, and covetousness almost before they can speak; and I have known a young child so distracted with the number and variety of his play-games that he tired his maid every day to look them over and was so accustomed to abundance that he never thought he had enough but was always asking, What more? What more? What new thing shall I have? A good introduction to moderate desires, and the ready way to make a contented happy man!

How then shall they have the play-games you allow them, if none must be bought for them? I answer, they should make them themselves, or at least endeavor it and set themselves about it; till then they should have none, and till then they will want none of any great artifice. A smooth pebble, a piece of paper, the mother's bunch of keys, or anything they cannot hurt themselves with, serves as much to divert little children as those more chargeable and curious toys from the shops, which are presently put out of order and broken. Children are never dull or out of humor for want of such playthings, unless they have been used to them. When they are little, whatever occurs serves the turn; and as they grow bigger, if they are not stored by the expensive folly of others, they will make them themselves. Indeed, when they once begin to set themselves to work about any of their inventions, they should be taught and assisted, but should have nothing whilst they lazily sit still expecting to be furnished from others' hands without employing their own. And if you help them where they are at a stand, it will more endear you to them than any chargeable toys you shall buy for them. Playthings which are above their skill to make, [such] as tops, gigs, battledores,[66] and the like, which are to be used with labor, should indeed be procured them; these it is convenient they should have not for variety but exercise. But these too should be given them as bare as

66. Rackets used for shuttlecock.

might be. If they had a top, the scourge stick and leather strap should be left to their own making and fitting. If they sit gaping to have such things drop into their mouths, they should go without them. This will accustom them to seek for what they want in themselves and in their own endeavors; whereby they will be taught moderation in their desires, application, industry, thought, contrivance, and good husbandry, qualities that will be useful to them when they are men and therefore cannot be learned too soon nor fixed too deep. All the plays and diversions of children should be directed towards good and useful habits, or else they will introduce ill ones. Whatever they do leaves some impression on that tender age, and from thence they receive a tendency to good or evil; and whatever has such an influence ought not to be neglected.

§131. *Lying* is so ready and cheap a cover for any miscarriage and so    *Lying.*
much in fashion amongst all sorts of people that a child can hardly avoid observing the use [that] is made of it on all occasions and so can scarce be kept, without great care, from getting into it. But it is so ill a quality and the mother of so many ill ones that spawn from it and take shelter under it, that a child should be brought up in the greatest abhorrence of it imaginable. It should be always (when occasionally it comes to be mentioned) spoken of before him with the utmost detestation, as a quality so wholly inconsistent with the name and character of a gentleman that nobody of any credit can bear the imputation of a lie, a mark that it is judged the utmost disgrace, which debases a man to the lowest degree of a shameful meanness and ranks him with the most contemptible part of mankind and the abhorred rascality, and is not to be endured in anyone who would converse with people of condition or have any esteem or reputation in the world. The first time he is found in a *lie*, it should rather be wondered at as a monstrous thing in him than reproved as an ordinary fault. If that keeps him not from relapsing, the next time he must be sharply rebuked and fall into the state of great displeasure of his father and mother and all about him who take notice of it. And if this way work not the cure, you must come to blows. For after he has been thus warned, a premeditated *lie* must always be looked upon as obstinacy and never be permitted to escape unpunished.

§132. Children, afraid to have their faults seen in their naked colors,    *Excuses.*
will, like the rest of the sons of Adam, be apt to make *excuses*. This is a fault usually bordering upon and leading to untruth, and is not to be indulged in them; but yet it ought to be cured rather with shame than roughness. If therefore when a child is questioned for anything his first answer be an *excuse*, warn him soberly to tell the truth; and then if he persists to shuffle

it off with a *falsehood,* he must be chastised. But if he directly confess, you must commend his ingenuousness and pardon the fault, be it what it will; and pardon it so that you never so much as reproach him with it or mention it to him again. For if you would have him in love with ingenuousness and by a constant practice make it habitual to him, you must take care that it never procure him the least inconvenience; but on the contrary, his own confession bringing always with it perfect impunity should be besides encouraged by some marks of approbation. If his *excuse* be such at any time that you cannot prove it to have any falsehood in it, let it pass for true and be sure not to show any suspicion of it. Let him keep up his reputation with you as high as is possible; for when once he finds he has lost that, you have lost a great and your best hold upon him. Therefore let him not think he has the character of a liar with you as long as you can avoid it without flattering him in it. Thus some slips in truth may be overlooked. But after he has once been corrected for a *lie*, you must be sure never after to pardon it in him, whenever you find and take notice to him that he is guilty of it. For it being a fault which he has been forbid and may, unless he be willful, avoid, the repeating of it is perfect perverseness and must have the chastisement due to that offence.

§133. This is what I have thought concerning the general method of educating a young gentleman; which though I am apt to suppose may have some influence on the whole course of his education, yet I am far from imagining it contains all those particulars which his growing years or peculiar temper may require. But this being premised in general, we shall in the next place descend to a more particular consideration of the several parts of his education.

§134. That which every gentleman (that takes any care of his education) desires for his son, besides the estate he leaves him, is contained (I suppose) in these four things: *virtue, wisdom, breeding,* and *learning.* I will not trouble myself whether these names do not some of them sometimes stand for the same thing, or really include one another. It serves my turn here to follow the popular use of these words; which, I presume, is clear enough to make me be understood, and I hope there will be no difficulty to comprehend my meaning.

*Virtue.*        §135. I place *virtue* as the first and most necessary of those endowments that belong to a man or a gentleman, as absolutely requisite to make him valued and beloved by others, acceptable or tolerable to himself. Without that, I think, he will be happy neither in this nor the other world.

*God.*        §136. As the foundation of this, there ought very early to be imprinted on his mind a true notion of *God,* as of the independent Supreme Being,

Author and Maker of all things, from whom we receive all our good, who loves us and gives us all things. And consequent to this, instill into him a love and reverence of this Supreme Being. This is enough to begin with, without going to explain this matter any farther; for fear, lest by talking too early to him of spirits, and being unseasonably forward to make him understand the incomprehensible nature of that infinite Being, his head be either filled with false or perplexed with unintelligible notions of him. Let him only be told upon occasion that *God* made and governs all things, hears and sees everything, and does all manner of good to those that love and obey him. You will find that being told of such a *God,* other thoughts will be apt to rise up fast enough in his mind about him; which, as you observe them to have any mistakes, you must set right. And I think it would be better if men generally rested in such an idea of *God* without being too curious in their notions about a Being which all must acknowledge incomprehensible; whereby many who have not strength and clearness of thought to distinguish between what they can and what they cannot know run themselves into superstition or atheism, making *God* like themselves or (because they cannot comprehend anything else) none at all. And I am apt to think, the keeping children constantly morning and evening to acts of devotion to God, as to their Maker, Preserver, and Benefactor, in some plain and short form of prayer, suitable to their age and capacity, will be of much more use to them in religion, knowledge, and virtue than to distract their thoughts with curious inquiries into his inscrutable essence and being.

§137. Having by gentle degrees, as you find him capable of it, settled *Spirits.* such an idea of God in his mind and taught him to *pray* to him and *praise* him as the Author of his being and of all the good he does or can enjoy; forbear any discourse of other *spirits* till the mention of them coming in his way, upon occasion hereafter to be set down[67] and his reading the Scripture history, put him upon that inquiry.

§138. But even then, and always whilst he is young, be sure to preserve *Goblins.* his tender mind from all impressions and notions of *spirits*[68] and *goblins* or any fearful apprehensions in the dark. This he will be in danger of from the indiscretion of servants, whose usual method it is to awe children and keep them in subjection by telling them of *Raw Head* and *Bloody Bones* and such other names as carry with them the ideas of some thing terrible and

---

67. §§190–92.

68. Changed from "sprites" in the fifth edition, which appeared after Locke's death in 1705; see the reference back to this passage in §191.

hurtful which they have reason to be afraid of when alone, especially in the dark. This must be carefully prevented. For though by this foolish way they may keep them from little faults, yet the remedy is much worse than the disease, and there is stamped upon their imaginations ideas that follow them with terror and affrightment. Such *bugbear* thoughts, once gotten into the tender minds of children and being set on with a strong impression from the dread that accompanies such apprehensions, sink deep and fasten themselves so as not easily, if ever, to be got out again, and whilst they are there frequently haunt them with strange visions, making children dastards when alone and afraid of their shadows and darkness all their lives after. I have had those complain to me, when men, who had been thus used when young, that though their reason corrected the wrong ideas they had then taken in, and they were satisfied that there was no cause to fear invisible beings more in the dark than in the light, yet that these notions were apt still upon any occasion to start up first in their prepossessed fancies and not to be removed without some pains. And to let you see how lasting frightful images are that take place in the mind early, I shall here tell you a pretty remarkable but true story. There was in a town in the West a man of a disturbed brain, whom the boys used to tease when he came in their way: this fellow one day seeing in the street one of those lads that used to vex him, stepped into a cutler's shop he was near and there seizing on a naked sword, made after the boy; who seeing him coming so armed, betook himself to his feet and ran for his life and, by good luck, had strength and heels enough to reach his father's house before the madman could get up to him. The door was only latched; and when he had the latch in his hand, he turned about his head to see how near his pursuer was, who was at the entrance of the porch with his sword up ready to strike, and he had just time to get in and clap to the door to avoid the blow, which though his body escaped, his mind did not. This frightening idea made so deep an impression there that it lasted many years, if not all his life after. For, telling this story when he was a man, he said that after that time till then, he never went in at that door (that he could remember) at any time without looking back, whatever business he had in his head or how little soever before he came thither, he thought of this madman.

If children were let alone, they would be no more afraid in the dark than in broad sunshine: they would in their turns as much welcome the one for sleep as the other to play in. There should be no distinction made to them by any discourse of more danger or *terrible things* in the one than the other; but if the folly of anyone about them should do them this harm and make them think there is any difference between being in the dark and winking, you must get it out of their minds as soon as you can and let them know that God, who made all things good for them, made the night that they might sleep the better and the quieter, and that they being under his protection, there is nothing in the dark to hurt them. What is to be known more of God and good spirits is to be deferred till the time we shall hereafter mention;[69] and of evil spirits, it will be well if you can keep him from wrong fancies about them till he is ripe for that sort of knowledge.

§139. Having laid the foundations of virtue in a true notion of a God, *Truth.* such as the Creed wisely teaches, as far as his age is capable, and by accustoming him to pray to him, the next thing to be taken care of is to keep him exactly to speaking of *truth*, and by all the ways imaginable inclining him to be *good-natured*. Let him know that twenty faults are sooner to be forgiven than the *straining of truth* to cover any one *by an excuse*. And to teach him betimes to love and be *good-natured* to others is to lay early the true *Good* foundation of an honest man: all injustice generally springing from too *Nature.* great love of ourselves and too little of others.

This is all I shall say of this matter in general and is enough for laying the first foundations of virtue in a child. As he grows up, the tendency of his natural inclination must be observed, which, as it inclines him more than is convenient on one or the other side from the right path of virtue, ought to have proper remedies applied. For few of Adam's children are so happy as not to be born with some bias in their natural temper, which it is the business of education either to take off or counterbalance; but to enter into the particulars of this would be beyond the design of this short treatise of education. I intend not a discourse of all the virtues and vices and how each virtue is to be attained and every particular vice by its peculiar remedies cured. Though I have mentioned some of the most ordinary faults and the ways to be used in correcting them.

§140. *Wisdom* I take, in the popular acceptation, for a man's managing *Wisdom.* his business ably and with foresight in this world. This is the product of a good natural temper, application of mind, and experience together, and so above the reach of children. The greatest thing that in them can be done towards it is to hinder them, as much as may be, from being *cunning*; which, being the ape of *wisdom*, is the most distant from it that can be, and as an ape for the likeness it has to a man [but] wanting what really should make him so, is by so much the uglier. Cunning is only the want of understanding; which, because it cannot compass its ends by direct ways, would do it by a trick and circumvention; and the mischief of it is, a *cunning* trick

69. §§190–92.

helps but once, but hinders ever after. No cover was ever made either so big or so fine as to hide itself. Nobody was ever so *cunning* as to conceal their being so; and when they are once discovered, everybody is shy, everybody distrustful of *crafty* men, and all the world forwardly join to oppose and defeat them; whilst the open, fair, *wise* man has everybody to make way for him and goes directly to his business. To accustom a child to have true notions of things and not to be satisfied till he has them, to raise his mind to great and worthy thoughts, and to keep him at a distance from falsehood and cunning, which has always a broad mixture of falsehood in it, is the fittest preparation of a child for *wisdom*. The rest, which is to be learned from time, experience and observation, and an acquaintance with men, their tempers, and designs, is not to be expected in the ignorance and inadvertency of childhood or the inconsiderate heats and unwariness of youth; all that can be done towards it during this unripe age is, as I have said, to accustom them to truth and sincerity, to a submission to reason, and as much as may be to reflection on their own actions.

*Breeding.*   §141. The next good quality belonging to a gentleman is *good breeding*. There are two sorts of *ill breeding*: the one a *sheepish bashfulness* and the other a *misbecoming negligence and disrespect* in our carriage; both [of] which are avoided by duly observing this one rule, *not to think meanly of ourselves and not to think meanly of others*.

§142. The first part of this rule must not be understood in opposition to humility, but to assurance. We ought not to think so well of ourselves as to stand upon our own value and assume to ourselves a preference before others because of any advantage we may imagine we have over them, but modestly to take what is offered when it is our due. But yet we ought to think so well of ourselves as to perform those actions which are incumbent on and expected of us without discomposure or disorder, in whose presence soever we are, keeping that respect and distance which is due to everyone's rank and quality. There is often in people, especially children, a clownish shamefacedness before strangers or those above them: they are confounded in their thoughts, words, and looks, and so lose themselves in that confusion as not to be able to do anything, or at least not do it with that freedom and gracefulness which pleases and makes them acceptable. The only cure for this, as for any other miscarriage, is by use to introduce the contrary habit. But since we cannot accustom ourselves to converse with strangers and persons of quality without being in their company, nothing can cure this part of *ill-breeding* but change and variety of company, and that of persons above us.

§143. As the aforementioned consist in too great a concern how to behave ourselves towards others, so the other part of *ill-breeding* lies in the appearance of too *little care* of pleasing or *showing respect* to those we have to do with. To avoid this these two things are requisite: first, a disposition of the mind not to offend others; and, secondly, the most acceptable and agreeable way of expressing that disposition. From the one, men are called *civil*; from the other, *well-fashioned*. The latter of these is that decency and gracefulness of looks, voice, words, motions, gestures, and of all the whole outward demeanor which takes in company and makes those with whom we converse easy and well pleased. This is, as it were, the language whereby that internal civility of the mind is expressed; which, as other languages are, being very much governed by the fashion and custom of every country, must in the rules and practice of it be learned chiefly from observation and the carriage of those who are allowed to be exactly *well-bred*. The other part, which lies deeper than the outside, is that general good will and regard for all people which makes anyone have a care not to show in his carriage any contempt, disrespect, or neglect of them, but to express, according to the fashion and way of that country, a respect and value for them, according to their rank and condition. It is a disposition of the mind that shows itself in the carriage whereby a man avoids making anyone uneasy in conversation.

I shall take notice of four qualities that are most directly opposite to this first and most taking of all the social virtues. And from some one of these four it is that incivility commonly has its rise. I shall set them down that children may be preserved or recovered from their ill influence.

1. The first is a natural *roughness* which makes a man uncomplaisant to others, so that he has no deference for their inclinations, tempers, or conditions. It is the sure badge of a clown not to mind what pleases or displeases those he is with; and yet one may often find a man in fashionable clothes give an unbounded swing to his own humor and suffer it to jostle or overrun anyone that stands in its way with a perfect indifferency how they take it. This is a brutality that everyone sees and abhors, and nobody can be easy with: and therefore this finds no place in anyone who would be thought to have the least tincture of *good breeding*. For the very end and business of *good breeding* is to supple the natural stiffness and so soften men's tempers that they may bend to a compliance and accommodate themselves to those they have to do with. *Roughness.*

2. Contempt or want of due respect discovered either in looks, words, or gesture: this from whomsoever it comes brings always uneasiness with it. For nobody can contentedly bear being slighted. *Contempt.*

*Censoriousness.*        3. *Censoriousness* and finding fault with others has a direct opposition to *civility*. Men, whatever they are or are not guilty of, would not have their faults displayed and set in open view and broad daylight before their own or other people's eyes. Blemishes affixed to anyone always carry shame with them, and the discovery or even bare imputation of any defect *Raillery.*    is not borne without some uneasiness. *Raillery* is the most refined way of exposing the faults of others. But because it is usually done with wit and good language, and gives entertainment to the company, people are led into a mistake that where it keeps within fair bounds there is no incivility in it. And so the pleasantry of this sort of conversation often introduces it amongst people of the better rank; and such talkers are favorably heard and generally applauded by the laughter of the bystanders on their side. But they ought to consider that the entertainment of the rest of the company is at the cost of that one who is set out in their burlesque colors, who therefore is not without uneasiness, unless the subject for which he is rallied be really in itself matter of commendation. For then the pleasant images and representations, which make the *raillery*, carrying praise as well as sport with them, the rallied person also finds his account and takes part in the diversion. But because the right management of so nice and ticklish a business, wherein a little slip may spoil all, is not everybody's talent, I think those who would secure themselves from provoking others, especially all young people, should carefully abstain from *raillery*, which by a small mistake or any wrong turn may leave upon the mind of those who are made uneasy by it the lasting memory of having been piquantly though wittily taunted for something censurable in them.

*Contradiction.*        Besides raillery, *contradiction* is a sort of censoriousness wherein ill breeding often shows itself. Complaisance does not require that we should always admit all the reasonings or relations that the company is entertained with, no nor silently to let pass all that is vented in our hearing. The opposing the opinions and rectifying the mistakes of others is what truth and charity sometimes requires of us, and civility does not oppose if it be done with due caution and care of circumstances. But there are some people that one may observe, possessed as it were with the spirit of contradiction, that steadily and without regard to right or wrong oppose someone or perhaps everyone of the company whatever they say. This is so visible and outrageous a way of *censuring* that nobody can avoid thinking himself injured by it. All opposition to what another man has said is so apt to be suspected of *censoriousness* and is so seldom received without some sort of humiliation that it ought to be made in the gentlest manner and softest words [that] can be found and such as with the whole deportment may express no forwardness to contradict. All marks of respect and good will ought to accompany it, that whilst we gain the argument we may not lose the esteem of those that hear us.

4. *Captiousness* is another fault opposite to *civility*, not only because it often produces misbecoming and provoking expressions and carriage, but because it is a tacit accusation and reproach of some incivility taken notice of in those whom we are angry with. Such a suspicion or intimation cannot be borne by anyone without uneasiness. Besides, one angry body discomposes the whole company, and the harmony ceases upon any such jarring. *Captiousness.*

The happiness that all men so steadily pursue consisting in pleasure, it is easy to see why the *civil* are more acceptable than the useful. The ability, sincerity, and good intention of a man of weight and worth or a real friend seldom atones for the uneasiness that is produced by his grave and solid representations. Power and riches, nay virtue itself, are valued only as conducing to our happiness. And therefore he recommends himself ill to another as aiming at his happiness, who in the services he does him makes him uneasy in the manner of doing them. He that knows how to make those he converses with easy without debasing himself to low and servile flattery has found the true art of living in the world and being both welcome and valued everywhere. *Civility* therefore is what in the first place should with great care be made habitual to children and young people.

§144. There is another fault in good manners, and that is *excess of ceremony* and an obstinate persisting to force upon another what is not his due, and what he cannot take without folly or shame. This seems rather a design to expose than oblige, or at least looks like a contest for mastery, and at best is but troublesome, and so can be no part of *good breeding*, which has no other use or end but to make people easy and satisfied in their conversation with us. This is a fault few young people are apt to fall into; but yet if they are ever guilty of it or are suspected to incline that way, they should be told of it and warned of this *mistaken civility*. The thing they should endeavor and aim at in conversation should be to show respect, esteem, and good will by paying to everyone that common ceremony and regard which is in civility due to them. To do this, without a suspicion of flattery, dissimulation, or meanness, is a great skill, which good sense, reason, and good company can only teach, but is of so much use in civil life that it is well worth the studying. *Breeding.*

§145. Though the managing ourselves well in this part of our behavior has the name of *good breeding*, as if peculiarly the effect of education, yet, as I have said,[70] young children should not be much perplexed about it; I mean about putting off their hats and making legs modishly. Teach them humility and to be good-natured, if you can, and this sort of manners will not be wanting: *civility* being, in truth, nothing but a care not to show any slighting or contempt of anyone in conversation. What are the most allowed and esteemed ways of expressing, this we have above observed. It is as peculiar and different in several countries of the world as their languages; and therefore if it be rightly considered, rules and discourses, made to children about it, are as useless and impertinent as it would be now and then to give a rule or two of the Spanish tongue to one that converses only with Englishmen. Be as busy as you please with discourses of *civility* to your son, such as is his company, such will be his manners. A ploughman of your neighborhood that has never been out of his parish, read what lectures you please to him, will be as soon in his language, as his carriage, a courtier; that is, in neither will be more polite than those he uses to converse with; and therefore of this, no other care can be taken till he be of an age to have a tutor put to him, who must not fail to be a well-bred man. And, in good earnest, if I were to speak my mind freely, so children do nothing out of obstinacy, pride, and ill nature, it is no great matter how they put off their hats or make legs. If you can teach them to love and respect other people, they will, as their age requires it, find ways to express it acceptably to everyone, according to the fashions they have been used to; and as to their motions and carriage of their bodies, a dancing master, as has been said,[71] when it is fit will teach them what is most becoming. In the meantime when they are young, people expect not that children should be overmindful of these ceremonies; carelessness is allowed to that age and becomes them as well as compliments do grown people, or at least, if some very nice people will think it a fault, I am sure it is a fault that should be overlooked and left to time, a tutor, and conversation to cure. And therefore I think it not worth your while to have your son (as I often see children are) molested or chid about it; but where there is *pride* or *ill nature* appearing in his carriage, there he must be persuaded or shamed out of it.

*Interruption.*      Though children, when little, should not be much perplexed with the rules and ceremonious parts of *breeding*, yet there is a sort of unmannerliness very apt to grow up with young people, if not early restrained, and that is a forwardness to *interrupt* others that are speaking and to stop them with some *contradiction*. Whether the custom of disputing and the reputa-

70. §67.
71. §67.

tion of parts and learning usually given to it, as if it were the only standard and evidence of knowledge, make young men so forward to watch occasions to correct others in their discourse and not to slip any opportunity of showing their talents, so it is, that I have found scholars most blamed in this point. There cannot be a greater rudeness than to *interrupt* another in the current of his discourse; for if there be not impertinent folly in answering a man before we know what he will say, yet it is a plain declaration that we are weary to hear him talk any longer and have a disesteem of what he says, which we judging not fit to entertain the company, desire them to give audience to us, who have something to produce worth their attention. This shows a very great disrespect and cannot but be offensive, and yet this is what almost all *interruption* constantly carries with it. To which, if there be added, as is usual, a *correcting* of any mistake or a *contradicting* of what has been said, it is a mark of yet greater pride and self-conceitedness when we thus intrude ourselves for teachers and take upon us either to set another right in his story or show the mistakes of his judgment.

I do not say this, that I think there should be no difference of opinions in conversation, nor opposition in men's discourses: this would be to take away the greatest advantage of society, and the improvements [that] are to be made by ingenious company, where the light [that] is to be got from the opposite arguings of men of parts, showing the different sides of things and their various aspects and probabilities, would be quite lost if everyone were obliged to assent to and say after the first speaker. It is not the owning one's dissent from another that I speak against, but the manner of doing it. Young men should be taught not to be forward to *interpose* their opinions unless asked or when others have done and are silent, and then only by way of inquiry not instruction. The positive asserting and the magisterial air should be avoided; and when a general pause of the whole company affords an opportunity, they may modestly put in their question as learners.

This becoming decency will not cloud their parts nor weaken the strength of their reason, but bespeak the more favorable attention and give what they say the greater advantage. An ill argument or ordinary observation thus introduced, with some civil preface of deference and respect to the opinions of others, will procure them more credit and esteem than the sharpest wit or profoundest science with a rough, insolent, or noisy management, which always shocks the hearers and leaves an ill opinion of the man, though he get the better of it in the argument.

This therefore should be carefully watched in young people, stopped in the beginning, and the contrary habit introduced in all their conversation. And the rather, because forwardness to talk, frequent *interruptions* in arguing, and loud *wrangling,* are too often observable amongst grown people, even of rank amongst us. The Indians, whom we call barbarous, observe much more decency and civility in their discourses and conversation, giving one another a fair silent hearing till they have quite done and then answering them calmly and without noise or passion. And if it be not so in this civilized part of the world, we must impute it to a neglect in education, which has not yet reformed this ancient piece of barbarity amongst us. Was it not, think you, an entertaining spectacle to see two ladies of quality accidentally seated on the opposite sides of a room, set round with company, fall into a dispute and grow so eager in it, that in the heat of their controversy, edging by degrees their chairs forwards, they were in a little time got

*Dispute.* up close to one another in the middle of the room, where they for a good while managed the dispute as fiercely as two gamecocks in the pit, without minding or taking any notice of the circle, which could not all the while forbear smiling? This I was told by a person of quality, who was present at the combat and did not omit to reflect upon the indecencies that warmth in *dispute* often runs people into; which since custom makes too frequent, education should take the more care of. There is nobody but condemns this in others, though they overlook it in themselves: and many who are sensible of it in themselves and resolve against it cannot yet get rid of an ill custom, which neglect in their education has suffered to settle into a habit.

*Company.* §146. What has been said above concerning *company* would perhaps, if it were well reflected on, give us a larger prospect and let us see how much farther its influence reaches. It is not the modes of civility alone that are imprinted by *conversation:* the tincture of company sinks deeper than the outside, and possibly, if a true estimate were made of the morality and religions of the world, we should find that the far greater part of mankind received even those opinions and ceremonies they would die for rather from the fashions of their countries and the constant practice of those about them than from any conviction of their reasons. I mention this only to let you see of what moment I think *company* is to your son in all the parts of his life, and therefore how much that one part is to be weighed and provided for; it being of greater force to work upon him, than all you can do besides.

*Learning.* §147. You will wonder, perhaps, that I put *learning* last, especially if I tell you I think it the least part. This may seem strange in the mouth of a bookish man; and this making usually the chief if not only bustle and stir about children, this being almost that alone which is thought on when people talk of education, makes it the greater paradox. When I consider what ado is made about a little Latin and Greek, how many years are spent in it, and what a noise and business it makes to no purpose, I can hardly forbear thinking that the parents of children still live in fear of the schoolmaster's rod, which they look on as the only instrument of education, as [they do] a language or two to be its whole business. How else is it possible that a child should be chained to the oar seven, eight, or ten of the best years of his life to get a language or two, which I think might be had at a great deal cheaper rate of pains and time and be learned almost in playing?

Forgive me therefore, if I say, I cannot with patience think that a young gentleman should be put into the herd, and be driven with a whip and scourge, as if he were to run the gauntlet through the several classes, *ad capiendum ingenii cultum.*[72] What then, say you, would you not have him write and read? Shall he be more ignorant than the cleric of our parish, who takes Hopkins and Sternhold[73] for the best poets in the world, whom yet he makes worse than they are by his ill reading? Not so, not so fast, I beseech you. Reading, and writing, and *learning,* I allow to be necessary, but yet not the chief business. I imagine you would think him a very foolish fellow that should not value a virtuous or a wise man infinitely before a great scholar. Not but that I think *learning* a great help to both [virtue and wisdom] in well-disposed minds; but yet it must be confessed also that in others not so disposed it helps them only to be the more foolish or worse men. I say this, that when you consider of the breeding of your son and are looking out for a schoolmaster or a tutor, you would not have (as is usual) Latin and *logic* only in your thoughts. *Learning* must be had, but in the second place, as subservient only to greater qualities. Seek out somebody that may know how discreetly to frame his manners: place him in hands where you may, as much as possible, secure his innocence, cherish and nurse up the good and gently correct and weed out any bad inclinations, and settle in him good habits. This is the main point, and this being provided for, *learning* may be had into the bargain, and that, as I think, at a very easy rate, by methods that may be thought on.

§148. When he can talk, it is time he should begin to *learn to read.* But as to this, give me leave here to inculcate again,[74] what is very apt to be forgotten, viz. That a great care is to be taken that it be never made as a business to him, nor he look on it as a task. We naturally, as I said, even from our cradles, love liberty and have therefore an aversion to many things for

*Reading.*

72. "To receive the cultivation of his mind."

73. Authors of a sixteenth-century translation of the Book of Psalms included in the *Book of Common Prayer* used in the Church of England.

74. §§128–29.

no other reason but because they are enjoined us.[75] I have always had a fancy that *learning* might be made a play and recreation to children; and that they might be brought to desire to be taught, if it were proposed to them as a thing of honor, credit, delight and recreation or as a reward for doing something else and if they were never chid or corrected for the neglect of it. That which confirms me in this opinion is that amongst the Portuguese it is so much a fashion and emulation amongst their children to *learn* to *read* and write, that they cannot hinder them from it: they will learn it one from another and are as intent on it as if it were forbidden them. I remember that being at a friend's house, whose younger son, a child in [petti]coats, was not easily *brought* to his book (being taught *to read* at home by his mother); I advised to try another way than requiring it of him as his duty; we therefore, in a discourse on purpose amongst ourselves, in his hearing but without taking any notice of him, declared that it was the privilege and advantage of heirs and elder brothers to be scholars, that this made them fine gentlemen and beloved by everybody, and that for younger brothers it was a favor to admit them to breeding, to be taught to *read* and write was more than came to their share, they might be ignorant bumpkins and clowns if they pleased. This so wrought upon the child, that afterwards he desired to be taught, would come himself to his mother to *learn,* and would not let his maid be quiet till she heard him his lesson. I doubt not but some way like this might be taken with other children; and when their tempers are found, some thoughts be instilled into them that might set them upon desiring of *learning* themselves and make them seek it as another sort of play or recreation. But then, as I said before, it must never be imposed as a task nor made a trouble to them. There may be dice and playthings with the letters on them to teach children the *alphabet* by playing; and twenty other ways may be found, suitable to their particular tempers, to make this kind of *learning a sport* to them.

§149. Thus children may be cozened into a knowledge of the letters, be *taught to read* without perceiving it to be anything but a sport, and play themselves into that which others are whipped for. Children should not have anything like work or serious laid on them; neither their minds nor bodies will bear it. It injures their healths, and their being forced and tied down to their books, in an age at enmity with all such restraint, has, I doubt not, been the reason why a great many have hated books and learning all their lives after: it is like a surfeit that leaves an aversion behind not to be removed.

75. §§41, 73–74.

§150. I have therefore thought that if *playthings* were fitted to this purpose, as they are usually to none, contrivances might be made *to teach children to read* whilst they thought they were only playing. For example, what if an *ivory ball* were made like that of the Royal Oak Lottery with thirty-two sides, or one rather of twenty-four or twenty-five sides; and upon several of those sides pasted on an A, upon several others B, on others C, and on others D. I would have you begin with but these four letters, or perhaps only two at first; and when he is perfect in them, then add another; and so on till each side having one letter, there be on it the whole alphabet. This I would have others play with before him, it being as good a sort of play to lay a stake who shall first throw an A or B, as who upon dice shall throw six or seven. This being a play amongst you, tempt him not to it lest you make it business, for I would not have him understand it is anything but a play of older people, and I doubt not but he will take to it of himself. And that he may have the more reason to think it is a play that he is sometimes in favor admitted to, when the play is done the ball should be laid up safe out of his reach, that so it may not by his having it in his keeping at any time grow stale to him.

§151. To keep up his eagerness to it, let him think it a game belonging to those above him; and when by this means he knows the letters, by changing them into syllables, he may *learn to read* without knowing how he did so, and never have any chiding or trouble about it nor fall out with books because of the hard usage and vexation they have caused him. Children, if you observe them, take abundance of pains to learn several games, which, if they should be enjoined them, they would abhor as a task and business. I know a person of great quality (more yet to be honored for his learning and virtue than for his rank and high place), who by pasting on the six vowels (for in our language Y is one) on the six sides of a die and the remaining eighteen consonants on the sides of three other dice, has made this a play for his children that he shall win who at one cast throws most words on these four dice; whereby his eldest son, yet in [petti]coats, has *played* himself *into spelling* with great eagerness and without once having been chid for it or forced to it.

§152. I have seen little girls exercise whole hours together and take abundance of pains to be expert at dibstones, as they call it; whilst I have been looking on, I have thought it wanted only some good contrivance to make them employ all that industry about something that might be more useful to them; and methinks 'tis only the fault and negligence of elder people that it is not so. Children are much less apt to be idle than men; and men are to be blamed if some part of that busy humor be not turned to useful things, which might be made usually as delightful to them as those they are employed in, if men would be but half so forward to lead the way as these little apes would be to follow. I imagine some wise Portuguese heretofore began this fashion amongst the children of his country, where, I have been told, as I said,[76] it is impossible to hinder the children from *learning to read* and write; and in some parts of France they teach one another to sing and dance from the cradle.

§153. The *letters* pasted upon the sides of the dice or polygon were best to be of the size of those of the folio Bible to begin with, and none of them capital letters; when once he can read what is printed in such letters, he will not long be ignorant of the great ones and in the beginning he should not be perplexed with variety; with this die also, you might have a play just like the Royal Oak, which would be another variety, and play for cherries or apples, etc.

§154. Besides these, twenty other plays might be invented depending on *letters*, which those who like this way may easily contrive and get made to this use if they will. But the four dice mentioned above,[77] I think so easy and useful that it will be hard to find any better, and there will be scarce need of any other.

§155. Thus much for *learning to read*, which let him never be driven to nor chid for: cheat him into it if you can, but make it not a business for him. 'Tis better it be a year later *before he can read*, than that he should this way get an aversion to learning. If you have any contests with him, let it be in matters of moment, of truth and good nature, but lay no task on him about A B C. Use your skill to make his will supple and pliant to reason: teach him to love credit and commendation, to abhor being thought ill or meanly of, especially by you and his mother, and then the rest will come all easily. But I think, if you will do that, you must not shackle and tie him up with rules about indifferent matters nor rebuke him for every little fault or perhaps some that to others would seem great ones; but of this I have said enough already.

§156. When by these gentle ways he begins to be able to *read*, some easy pleasant book suited to his capacity should be put into his hands, wherein the entertainment that he finds might draw him on and reward his pains in reading, and yet not such as should fill his head with perfectly useless trumpery or lay the principles of vice and folly. To this purpose, I think Aesop's *Fables* the best, which being stories apt to delight and entertain a

76.  §148.
77.  §151.

child, may yet afford useful reflections to a grown man. And if his memory retain them all his life after, he will not repent to find them there amongst his manly thoughts and serious business. If his *Aesop has pictures* in it, it will entertain him much the better and encourage him to read, when it carries the increase of knowledge with it. For such visible objects children hear talked of in vain and without any satisfaction, whilst they have no ideas of them; those ideas being not to be had from sounds but from the things themselves or their pictures. And therefore I think, as soon as he begins to spell, as many pictures of animals should be got him as can be found, with the printed names to them, which at the same time will invite him to read and afford him matter of inquiry and knowledge. *Reynard the Fox* is another book, I think, may be made use of to the same purpose. And if those about him will talk to him often about the stories he has read, and hear him tell them, it will, besides other advantages, add encouragement and delight *to* his *reading* when he finds there is some use and pleasure in it. These baits seem wholly neglected in the ordinary method; and it is usually long before learners find any use or pleasure in reading which may tempt them to it, and so take books only for fashionable amusements or impertinent troubles good for nothing.

§157. The Lord's Prayer, the Creeds, and Ten Commandments, it is necessary he should learn perfectly by heart, but I think, not by reading them himself in his primer, but by somebody's repeating them to him even before he can read. But learning by heart and *learning to read* should not, I think, be mixed, and so one made to clog the other. But his *learning to read* should be made as little trouble or business to him as might be.

What other *books* there are in English of the kind of those mentioned above, fit *to engage* the liking of children and tempt them *to read*, I do not know but am apt to think that [because of] children being generally delivered over to the method of schools, where the fear of the rod is to enforce and not any pleasure of the employment to invite them to learn, this sort of useful books amongst the number of silly ones that are of all sorts have yet had the fate to be neglected; and nothing that I know has been considered of this kind out of the ordinary road of the hornbook, primer, Psalter, Testament, and Bible.

§158. As for the *Bible,* which children are usually employed in to exercise and improve their talent *in reading*, I think the promiscuous reading of it through by chapters, as they lie in order, is so far from being of any advantage to children either for the perfecting their *reading* or principling their religion that perhaps a worse could not be found. For what pleasure or encouragement can it be to a child to exercise himself in reading those parts of a book where he understands nothing? And how little are the Law of Moses, the Song of Solomon, the Prophecies in the Old, and the Epistles and Apocalypse in the New Testament, suited to a child's capacity? And though the History of the Evangelists and the Acts have something easier; yet taken altogether, it is very disproportionate to the understanding of childhood. I grant that the principles of religion are to be drawn from thence, and in the words of the Scripture: yet none should be proposed to a child but such as are suited to a child's capacity and notions. But it is far from this to read through *the whole Bible,* and that for reading's sake. And what an odd jumble of thoughts must a child have in his head, if he have any at all, such as he should have concerning religion, who in his tender age reads all the parts of the *Bible* indifferently as the Word of God without any other distinction. I am apt to think that this in some men has been the very reason why they never had clear and distinct thoughts of it all their lifetime.

§159. And now I am by chance fallen on this subject, give me leave to say that there are some parts of the *Scripture* which may be proper to be put into the hands of a child to engage him to read; such as are the story of Joseph and his brethren, of David and Goliath, of David and Jonathan, etc. And others that he should be made to read for his instruction, as that *What you would have others do unto you, do you the same unto them;* and such other easy and plain moral rules, which being fitly chosen, might often be made use of both for reading and instruction together, and so often read till they are thoroughly fixed in the memory; and then afterwards, as he grows ripe for them, may in their turns, on fit occasions, be inculcated as the standing and sacred rules of his life and action. But the reading of the whole Scripture indifferently is what I think very inconvenient for children, till after having been made acquainted with the plainest fundamental parts of it, they have got some kind of general view of what they ought principally to believe and practice, which yet, I think, they ought to receive in the very words of the Scripture, and not in such as men prepossessed by systems and analogies are apt in this case to make use of and force upon them. Dr. Worthington, to avoid this, has made a catechism, which has all its answers in the precise words of the Scripture, a thing of good example and such a sound form of words as no Christian can except against as not fit for his child to learn; of this, as soon as he can say the Lord's Prayer, Creed, and Ten Commandments by heart, it may be fit for him to learn a question every day or every week, as his understanding is able to receive and his memory to retain them. And when he has this catechism perfectly by heart, so as readily and roundly to answer to any question in the whole book, it may be convenient to lodge in his mind the remaining moral rules scattered up and down in the Bible, as the best *exercise of his memory* and that which may be always a rule to him, ready at hand in the whole conduct of his life.

§160. When he can read English well, it will be seasonable to enter him *Writing.* in *writing*; and here the first thing should be taught him is to *hold his pen right*, and this he should be perfect in before he should be suffered to put it to paper. For not only children, but anybody else that would do anything well, should never be put upon too much of it at once or be set to perfect themselves in two parts of an action at the same time, if they can possibly be separated. I think the Italian way of holding the pen between the thumb and the forefinger alone may be best: but in this, you should consult some good writing master or any other person who writes well and quick. When he has learned to hold his pen right, in the next place he should learn how to *lay his paper and place his arm and body to it*. These practices being got over, the way to teach him to write without much trouble is to get a plate engraved with the characters of such a hand as you like best: but you must remember to have them a pretty deal bigger than he should ordinarily write, for everyone naturally comes by degrees to write a less hand than he at first was taught but never a bigger. Such a plate being engraved, let several sheets of good writing paper be printed off with red ink, which he has nothing to do but to go over with a good pen filled with black ink, which will quickly bring his hand to the formation of those characters, being at first showed where to begin and how to form every letter. And when he can do that well, he must then exercise on fair paper; and so may easily be brought *to write* the hand you desire.

§161. When he can write well and quick, I think it may be convenient *Drawing.* not only to continue the exercise of his hand in writing, but also to improve the use of it farther in *drawing*, a thing very useful to a gentleman in several occasions, but especially if he travel, as that which helps a man often to express in a few lines well put together what a whole sheet of paper in writing would not be able to represent and make intelligible. How many buildings may a man see, how many machines and habits meet with, the ideas whereof would be easily retained and communicated by a little skill in *drawing*, which being committed to words are in danger to be lost or at best but ill retained in the most exact descriptions? I do not mean that I would have your son a *perfect painter*; to be that to any tolerable degree will require more time than a young gentleman can spare from his other improvements of greater moment. But so much insight into *perspective* and skill in *drawing* as will enable him to represent tolerably on paper anything he sees, except faces, may, I think, be got in a little time, especially if he have a genius to it; but where that is wanting, unless it be in things absolutely necessary, it is better to let him pass them by quietly than to vex him about them to no purpose; and therefore in this, as in all other things not absolutely necessary, the rule holds, *Nihil invita Minerva.*[78]

*Shorthand.*    ¶1. *Shorthand,* an art, as I have been told, known only in England, may perhaps be thought worth the learning both for dispatch in what men write for their own memory and concealment of what they would not have lie open to every eye. For he that has once learned any sort of character may easily vary it to his own private use or fancy and with more contraction suited to the business he would employ it in. Mr. Rich's, the best contrived of any I have seen, may, as I think, by one who knows and considers grammar well be made much easier and shorter. But for the learning this compendious way of writing, there will be no need hastily to look out a master; it will be early enough when any convenient opportunity offers itself at any time after his hand is well settled in fair and quick writing. For boys have but little use of *shorthand* and should by no means practice it till they write perfectly well and have thoroughly fixed the habit of doing so.

*French.*    §162. As soon as he can speak English, it is time for him to learn some other language; this nobody doubts of when *French* is proposed. And the reason is because people are accustomed to the right way of teaching that language, which is by talking it into children in constant conversation, and not by grammatical rules. The Latin tongue would easily be taught the same way if his tutor, being constantly with him, would talk nothing else to him and make him answer still in the same language. But because *French* is a living language and to be used more in speaking, that should be first learned, that the yet pliant organs of speech might be accustomed to a due formation of those sounds and he get the habit of pronouncing *French* well, which is the harder to be done the longer it is delayed.

*Latin.*    §163. When he can speak and read French well, which in this method is usually in a year or two, he should proceed to *Latin,* which it is a wonder parents, when they have had the experiment in French, should not think ought to be learned the same way, by talking and reading. Only care is to be taken whilst he is learning these foreign languages by speaking and reading nothing else with his tutor, that he do not forget to read *English,* which may be preserved by his mother or somebody else hearing him read some chosen parts of the Scripture or other English book every day.

78. "Do nothing against the will of Minerva" (natural talent), Horace *De Arte Poetica* 385.

§164. *Latin* I look upon as absolutely necessary to a gentleman; and indeed, custom, which prevails over everything, has made it so much a part of education that even those children are whipped to it and made [to] spend many hours of their precious time uneasily in *Latin* who, after they are once gone from school, are never to have more to do with it as long as they live. Can there be anything more ridiculous than that a father should waste his own money and his son's time in setting him to learn the *Roman language,* when at the same time he designs him for a trade, wherein he having no use of *Latin* fails not to forget that little which he brought from school and which it is ten to one he abhors for the ill usage it procured him? Could it be believed, unless we had everywhere amongst us examples of it, that a child should be forced to learn the rudiments of a language which he is never to use in the course of life that he is designed to and neglect all the while the writing a good hand and casting accounts, which are of great advantage in all conditions of life and to most trades indispensably necessary? But though these qualifications, requisite to trade and commerce and the business of the world, are seldom or never to be had at grammar schools, yet thither not only gentlemen send their younger sons, intended for trades, but even tradesmen and farmers fail not to send their children, though they have neither intention nor ability to make them scholars. If you ask them why they do this, they think it as strange a question, as if you should ask them why they go to church. Custom serves for reason and has, to those who take it for reason, so consecrated this method that it is almost religiously observed by them, and they stick to it as if their children had scarce an orthodox education, unless they learned Lily's Grammar.[79]

§165. But how necessary soever *Latin* be to some and is thought to be to others to whom it is of no manner of use or service; yet the ordinary way of learning it in a grammar school is that which, having had thoughts about, I cannot be forward to encourage. The reasons against it are so evident and cogent that they have prevailed with some intelligent persons to quit the ordinary road, not without success, though the method made use of was not exactly that which I imagine the easiest, and in short is this. To trouble the child with no *grammar* at all, but to have *Latin,* as English has been, without the perplexity of rules, talked into him; for if you will consider it, *Latin* is no more unknown to a child when he comes into the world than English; and yet he learns English without master, rule, or grammar and so might he *Latin* too, as Tully[80] did, if he had somebody always to talk

79. A sixteenth-century Latin grammar textbook.
80. Cicero.

to him in this language. And when we so often see a Frenchwoman teach an English girl to speak and read French perfectly in a year or two, without any rule of grammar or anything else but prattling to her, I cannot but wonder how gentlemen have overseen[81] this way for their sons and thought them more dull or incapable than their daughters.

§166. If therefore a man could be got, who himself speaking good *Latin* would always be about your son, talk constantly to him, and suffer him to speak or read nothing else, this would be the true and genuine way and that which I would propose not only as the easiest and best, wherein a child might without pains or chiding get a language which others are wont to be whipped for at school six or seven years together, but also as that wherein at the same time he might have his mind and manners formed, and he be instructed to boot in several sciences, such as are a good part of *geography, astronomy, chronology, anatomy,* besides some parts of *history,* and all other parts of knowledge of things that fall under the senses and require little more than memory. For there, if we would take the true way, our knowledge should begin, and in those things be laid the foundation, and not in the abstract notions of *logic* and *metaphysics,* which are fitter to amuse[82] than inform the understanding in its first setting out towards knowledge. When young men have had their heads employed a while in those abstract speculations without finding the success and improvement or that use of them which they expected, they are apt to have mean thoughts either of learning or themselves: they are tempted to quit their studies and throw away their books as containing nothing but hard words and empty sounds or else to conclude that if there be any real knowledge in them, they themselves have not understandings capable of it. That this is so, perhaps I could assure you upon my own experience. Amongst other things to be learned by a young man in this method, whilst others of his age are wholly taken up with Latin and languages, I may also set down *geometry* for one, having known a young gentleman, bred something after this way, able to demonstrate several propositions in Euclid before he was thirteen.

§167. But if such a man cannot be got, who speaks good *Latin* and, being able to instruct your son in all these parts of knowledge, will undertake it by this method, the next best is to have him taught as near this way as may be, which is by taking some easy and pleasant book, such as Aesop's *Fables,* and writing the English translation (made as literal as it can be) in

81. Overlooked.
82. Bewilder.

one line and the *Latin* words which answer each of them just over it in another. These let him read every day over and over again, till he perfectly understands the *Latin*, and then go on to another fable, till he be also perfect in that, not omitting what he is already perfect in but sometimes reviewing that to keep it in his memory. And when he comes to write, let these be set him for copies, which with the exercise of his hand will also advance him in *Latin*. This being a more imperfect way than by *talking Latin* unto him; the formation of the verbs first, and afterwards the declensions of the nouns and pronouns perfectly learned by heart, may facilitate his acquaintance with the genius and manner of the *Latin tongue,* which varies the signification of verbs and nouns not as the modern languages do by particles prefixed but by changing the last syllables. More than this of grammar, I think he need not have till he can read himself Sanctii Minerva with Scioppius and Perizonius's notes.[83]

In teaching of children this too, I think, is to be observed, that in most cases where they stick they are not to be farther puzzled by putting them upon finding it out themselves, as by asking such questions as these, viz. which is the nominative case in the sentence they are to construe, or demanding what *aufero* signifies to lead them to the knowledge what *abstulere* signifies etc.[84] when they cannot readily tell. This wastes time only in disturbing them: for whilst they are learning and apply themselves with attention they are to be kept in good humor and everything made easy to them and as pleasant as possible. Therefore wherever they are at a stand and are willing to go forwards, help them presently over the difficulty without any rebuke or chiding, remembering that where harsher ways are taken they are the effect only of pride or peevishness in the teacher, who expects children should instantly be masters of as much as he knows; whereas he should rather consider that his business is to settle in them habits, not angrily to inculcate rules which serve for little in the conduct of our lives [or] at least are of no use to children, who forget them as soon as given. In sciences where their reason is to be exercised, I will not deny but this method may sometimes be varied and difficulties proposed on purpose to excite industry and accustom the mind to employ its own strength and sagacity in reasoning. But yet, I guess, this is not to be done to children whilst very young nor at their entrance upon any sort of knowledge: then everything of itself is difficult, and the great use and skill of a teacher is to make all as easy as he can. But particularly in learning of languages there

83. A sixteenth-century grammar with notes by seventeenth-century scholars.

84. Two declensions of the verb for "carry off" or "steal."

is least occasion for posing[85] of children. For languages, being to be learned by rote, custom, and memory, are then spoken in greatest perfection when all rules of grammar are utterly forgotten. I grant the grammar of a language is sometimes very carefully to be studied; but it is only to be studied by a grown man, when he applies himself to the understanding of any language critically, which is seldom the business of any but professed scholars. This I think will be agreed to, that if a gentleman be to study any language, it ought to be that of his own country, that he may understand the language which he has constant use of with the utmost accuracy.

There is yet a farther reason why masters and teachers should raise no difficulties to their scholars but on the contrary should smooth their way and readily help them forwards where they find them stop. Children's minds are narrow and weak and usually susceptible but of one thought at once. Whatever is in a child's head fills it for the time, especially if set on with any passion. It should therefore be the skill and art of the teacher to clear their heads of all other thoughts whilst they are learning of anything, the better to make room for what he would instill into them, that it may be received with attention and application, without which it leaves no impression. The natural temper of children disposes their minds to wander. Novelty alone takes them; whatever that presents, they are presently eager to have a taste of, and are as soon satiated with it. They quickly grow weary of the same thing, and so have almost their whole delight in change and variety. It is a contradiction to the natural state of childhood for them to fix their fleeting thoughts. Whether this be owing to the temper of their brains or the quickness or instability of their animal spirits, over which the mind has not yet got a full command, this is visible, that it is a pain to children to keep their thoughts steady to anything. A lasting continued attention is one of the hardest tasks [that] can be imposed on them; and therefore he that requires their application should endeavor to make what he proposes as grateful and agreeable as possible; at least, he ought to take care not to join any displeasing or frightful idea with it. If they come not to their books with some kind of liking and relish, it is no wonder their thoughts should be perpetually shifting from what disgusts them and seek better entertainment in more pleasing objects, after which they will unavoidably be gadding.

It is, I know, the usual method of tutors to endeavor to procure attention in their scholars and to fix their minds to the business in hand by rebukes and corrections if they find them ever so little wandering. But

85. Questioning or puzzling.

such treatment is sure to produce the quite contrary effect. Passionate words or blows from the tutor fill the child's mind with terror and affrightment, which immediately takes it wholly up and leaves no room for other impressions. I believe there is nobody that reads this but may recollect what disorder hasty or imperious words from his parents or teachers have caused in his thoughts, how for the time it has turned his brains so that he scarce knew what was said by or to him. He presently lost the sight of what he was upon, his mind was filled with disorder and confusion, and in that state was no longer capable of attention to anything else.

'Tis true, parents and governors ought to settle and establish their authority by an awe over the minds of those under their tuition, and to rule them by that; but when they have got an ascendant over them, they should use it with great moderation and not make themselves such scarecrows that their scholars should always tremble in their sight. Such an austerity may make their government easy to themselves, but of very little use to their pupils. 'Tis impossible children should learn anything whilst their thoughts are possessed and disturbed with any passion, especially fear, which makes the strongest impression on their yet tender and weak spirits. Keep the mind in an easy calm temper when you would have it receive your instructions or any increase of knowledge. It is as impossible to draw fair and regular characters on a trembling mind as on a shaking paper.

The great skill of a teacher is to get and keep the attention of his scholar; whilst he has that, he is sure to advance as fast as the learner's abilities will carry him; and without that, all his bustle and pother will be to little or no purpose. To attain this, he should make the child comprehend (as much as may be) the usefulness of what he teaches him and let him see by what he has learned that he can do something which he could not do before, something which gives him some power and real advantage above others who are ignorant of it. To this he should add sweetness in all his instructions and by a certain tenderness in his whole carriage make the child sensible that he loves him and designs nothing but his good, the only way to beget love in the child, which will make him hearken to his lessons and relish what he teaches him.

Nothing but obstinacy should meet with any imperiousness or rough usage. All other faults should be corrected with a gentle hand, and kind encouraging words will work better and more effectually upon a willing mind and even prevent a good deal of that perverseness which rough and imperious usage often produces in well-disposed and generous minds. 'Tis true, obstinacy and willful neglects must be mastered, even though it cost blows to do it; but I am apt to think perverseness in the pupils is often the effect of frowardness in the *tutor* and that most children would seldom have deserved blows if needless and misapplied roughness had not taught them ill nature and given them an aversion for their teacher and all that comes from him.

Inadvertency, forgetfulness, unsteadiness, and wandering of thought, are the natural faults of childhood and therefore, where they are not observed to be willful, are to be mentioned softly and gained upon by time. If every slip of this kind produces anger and berating, the occasions of rebuke and corrections will return so often that the tutor will be a constant terror and uneasiness to his pupils. Which one thing is enough to hinder their profiting by his lessons and to defeat all his methods of instruction.

Let the awe he has got upon their minds be so tempered with the constant marks of tenderness and good will, that affection may spur them to their duty and make them find a pleasure in complying with his dictates. This will bring them with satisfaction to their tutor, make them hearken to him, as to one who is their friend that cherishes them and takes pains for their good; this will keep their thoughts easy and free, whilst they are with him, the only temper wherein the mind is capable of receiving new information and of admitting into itself those impressions which, if not taken and retained, all that they and their teacher do together is lost labor: there is much uneasiness and little learning.

§168. When by this way of interlining *Latin* and English one with another, he has got a moderate knowledge of the *Latin tongue*, he may then be advanced a little farther to the reading of some other easy *Latin* book, such as Justin or Eutropius, and to make the reading and understanding of it the less tedious and difficult to him, let him help himself if he please with the English translation. Nor let the objection, that he will then know it only by rote, frighten anyone. This when well considered is not of any moment against but plainly for this way of learning a language. For languages are only to be learned by rote; and a man who does not speak English or *Latin* perfectly by rote, so that having thought of the thing he would speak of, his tongue of course without thought of rule or grammar falls into the proper expression and idiom of that language, does not speak it well nor is master of it. And I would fain[86] have anyone name to me that tongue that anyone can learn or speak as he should do by the rules of grammar. Languages were made not by rules or art, but by accident and the common use of the people. And he that will speak them well has no other rule but that nor anything to trust to but his memory and the habit of

86. Gladly.

speaking after the fashion learned from those that are allowed to speak properly, which in other words is only to speak by rote.

It will possibly be asked here, is *grammar* then of no use? And have those who have taken so much pains in reducing several languages to rules and observations, who have written so much about *declensions* and *conjugations*, about *concords* and *syntaxes*, lost their labor and been learned to no purpose? I say not so, *grammar* has its place too. But this I think I may say, there is more stir a great deal made with it than there needs, and those are tormented about it to whom it does not at all belong. I mean children at the age wherein they are usually perplexed with it in grammar schools. *Grammar.*

There is nothing more evident than that languages learned by rote serve well enough for the common affairs of life and ordinary commerce. Nay, persons of quality of the softer sex and such of them as have spent their time in well-bred company show us that this plain natural way, without the least study or knowledge of *grammar,* can carry them to a great degree of elegance and politeness in their language: and there are ladies who, without knowing what *tenses* and *participles, adverbs* and *prepositions* are, speak as properly and as correctly (they might take it for an ill compliment if I said as any country schoolmaster) as most gentlemen who have been bred up in the ordinary methods of grammar schools. Grammar therefore we see may be spared in some cases. The question then will be, to whom should it be taught, and when? To this I answer:

1. Men learn languages for the ordinary intercourse of society and communication of thoughts in common life without any farther design in their use of them. And for this purpose, the original way of learning a language by conversation not only serves well enough, but is to be preferred as the most expeditious, proper, and natural. Therefore, to this use of language one may answer that grammar is not necessary. This so many of my readers must be forced to allow as understand what I here say and who, conversing with others, understand them without having ever been taught the grammar of the English tongue. Which I suppose is the case of incomparably the greatest part of English men, of whom I have never yet known anyone who learned his mother tongue by rules.

2. Others there are the greatest part of whose business in this world is to be done with their tongues and with their pens, and to those it is convenient if not necessary that they should speak properly and correctly, whereby they may let their thoughts into other men's minds the more easily and with the greater impression. Upon this account it is, that any sort of speaking, so as will make him be understood, is not thought enough for a gentleman. He ought to study grammar amongst the other helps of

speaking well, but it must be the grammar of his own tongue, of the language he uses, that he may understand his own country speech nicely and speak it properly without shocking the ears of those it is addressed to with solecisms and offensive irregularities. And to this purpose grammar is necessary. But it is the grammar only of their own proper tongues, and to those only who would take pains in cultivating their language and in perfecting their styles. Whether all gentlemen should not do this I leave to be considered, since the want of propriety and grammatical exactness is thought very misbecoming one of that rank and usually draws on one guilty of such faults the censure of having had a lower breeding and worse company than suits with his quality. If this be so (as I suppose it is), it will be matter of wonder why young gentlemen are forced to learn the grammars of foreign and dead languages and are never once told of the grammar of their own tongues: they do not so much as know there is any such thing, much less is it made their business to be instructed in it. Nor is their own language ever proposed to them as worthy their care and cultivating, though they have daily use of it and are not seldom in the future course of their lives judged of by their handsome or awkward way of expressing themselves in it. Whereas the languages whose grammars they have been so much employed in are such as probably they shall scarce ever speak or write; or if upon occasion this should happen, they shall be excused for the mistakes and faults they make in it. Would not a Chinese who took notice of this way of breeding be apt to imagine that all our young gentlemen were designed to be teachers and professors of the dead languages of foreign countries, and not to be men of business in their own?

3. There is a third sort of men, who apply themselves to two or three foreign, dead, and (which amongst us are called the) learned languages, make them their study, and pique themselves upon their skill in them. No doubt those who propose to themselves the learning of any language with this view and would be critically exact in it ought carefully to study the grammar of it. I would not be mistaken here, as if this were to undervalue Greek and Latin: I grant these are languages of great use and excellency, and a man can have no place amongst the learned in this part of the world who is a stranger to them. But the knowledge a gentleman would ordinarily draw for his use out of the Roman and Greek writers, I think he may attain without studying the grammars of those tongues and by bare reading may come to understand them sufficiently for all his purposes. How much farther he shall at any time be concerned to look into the grammar and critical niceties of either of these tongues, he himself will be able to determine when he comes to propose to himself the study of anything that

shall require it. Which brings me to the other part of the inquiry, viz. *when grammar should be taught.* To which upon the premised grounds the answer is obvious, viz:.

That if grammar ought to be taught at any time, it must be to one that can speak the language already; how else can he be taught the grammar of it? This at least is evident from the practice of the wise and learned nations amongst the ancients. They made it a part of education to cultivate their own, not foreign tongues. The Greeks counted all other nations barbarous, and had a contempt for their languages. And though the Greek learning grew in credit amongst the Romans towards the end of their commonwealth, yet it was the Roman tongue that was made the study of their youth: their own language they were to make use of, and therefore it was their own language they were instructed and exercised in.

But more particularly to determine the proper season for grammar, I do not see how it can reasonably be made anyone's study but as an introduction to rhetoric; when it is thought time to put anyone upon the care of polishing his tongue, and of speaking better than the illiterate, then is the time for him to be instructed in the rules of grammar and not before. For grammar being to teach men not to speak, but to speak correctly and according to the exact rules of the tongue, which is one part of elegance, there is little use of the one to him that has no need of the other: where rhetoric is not necessary, grammar may be spared. I know not why anyone should waste his time and beat his head about the Latin grammar who does not intend to be a critic or make speeches and write dispatches in it. When anyone finds in himself a necessity or disposition to study any foreign language to the bottom and to be nicely exact in the knowledge of it, it will be time enough to take a grammatical survey of it. If his use of it be only to understand some books written in it, without a critical knowledge of the tongue itself, reading alone, as I have said, will attain this end without charging the mind with the multiplied rules and intricacies of grammar.

§169. For the exercise of his writing, let him sometimes *translate Latin* into English; but the learning of *Latin,* being nothing but the learning of words, a very unpleasant business both to young and old, join as much other real knowledge with it as you can, beginning still with that which lies most obvious to the senses, such as is the knowledge of *minerals, plants,* and *animals,* and particularly timber and fruit trees, their parts and ways of propagation, wherein a great deal may be taught a child which will not be useless to the man. But more especially *geography, astronomy,* and *anatomy.* But whatever you are teaching him, have a care still that you do not clog him with too much at once, or make anything his business but down-

*Latin.*

right virtue, or reprove him for anything but vice or some apparent tendency to it.

§170. But if, after all, his fate be to go to school to get the *Latin tongue*, it will be in vain to talk to you concerning the method I think best to be observed in schools; you must submit to that you find there nor expect to have it changed for your son; but yet by all means obtain, if you can, that *Themes.* he be not employed in making *Latin themes* and *declamations*, and least of all *verses* of any kind. You may insist on it, if it will do any good, that you have no design to make him either a *Latin* orator or a poet, but barely would have him understand perfectly a *Latin* author, and that you observe that those who teach any of the modern languages, and that with success, never amuse their scholars to make speeches or verses either in French or Italian, their business being *language barely* and not invention.

§171. But to tell you a little more fully why I would not have him exercised in making of *themes and verses*: 1. As to *themes*, they have, I confess, the pretence of something useful, which is to teach people to speak handsomely and well on any subject; which, if it could be attained this way, I own would be a great advantage, there being nothing more becoming a gentleman nor more useful in all the occurrences of life than to be able, on any occasion, to speak well and to the purpose. But this I say, that the making of *themes*, as is usual in schools, helps not one jot toward it. For do but consider what it is, in making a *theme*, that a young lad is employed about: it is to make a speech on some Latin saying, as *Omnia vincit amor* or *Non licet in bello bis peccare*, etc.[87] And here the poor lad, who wants knowledge of those things he is to speak of, which is to be had only from time and observation, must set his invention on the rack to say something, where he knows nothing; which is a sort of Egyptian tyranny, to bid them make bricks who have not yet any of the materials.[88] And therefore it is usual in such cases for the poor children to go to those of higher forms with this petition, *pray give me a little sense*; which whether it be more reasonable or more ridiculous is not easy to determine. Before a man can be in any capacity to speak on any subject, it is necessary he be acquainted with it, or else it is as foolish to set him to discourse of it as to set a blind man to talk of colors or a deaf man of music. And would you not think him a little cracked who would require another to make an argument on a moot point who understands nothing of our laws? And what, I pray, do schoolboys understand concerning those matters which are used to be proposed

87. "Love conquers all" and "It is not permitted in war to err twice."
88. Exodus 5:7.

to them in their *themes* as subjects to discourse on to whet and exercise their fancies?

§172. In the next place consider the language that their *themes* are made in: 'tis Latin, a language foreign in their country, and long since dead everywhere; a language which your son, 'tis a thousand to one, shall never have an occasion once to make a speech in as long as he lives after he comes to be a man; and a language wherein the manner of expressing oneself is so far different from ours, that to be perfect in that would very little improve the purity and facility of his English style. Besides that, there is now so little room or use for set speeches in our own language in any part of our English business, that I can see no pretence for this sort of exercise in our schools, unless it can be supposed that the making of set Latin speeches should be the way to teach men to speak well in English *extempore*. The way to that, I should think rather to be this: that there should be proposed to young gentleman rational and useful questions, suited to their age and capacities, and on subjects not wholly unknown to them nor out of their way; such as these, when they are ripe for exercises of this nature, they should *extempore*, or after a little meditation upon the spot, speak to without penning of anything. For, I ask, if we will examine the effects of this way of learning to speak well, who speak best in any business when occasion calls them to it, upon any debate, either those who have accustomed themselves to compose and write down beforehand what they would say or those who, thinking only of the matter to understand that as well as they can, use themselves only to speak *extempore*? And he that shall judge by this, will be little apt to think that the accustoming him to studied speeches and set compositions is the way to fit a young gentleman for business.

§173. But perhaps, we shall be told, it is to improve and perfect them in the Latin tongue. 'Tis true, that is their proper business at school, but the making of *themes* is not the way to it: that perplexes their brains about invention of things to be said, not about the signification of words to be learned; and when they are making a *theme*, it is thoughts they search and sweat for, and not language. But the learning and mastery of a tongue, being uneasy and unpleasant enough in itself, should not be cumbered with any other difficulties, as is done in this way of proceeding. In fine, if boys' invention be to be quickened by such exercise, let them make *themes* in English, where they have facility and a command of words, and will better see what kind of thoughts they have, when put into their own language; and if the Latin tongue be to be learned, let it be done the easiest way without toiling and disgusting the mind by so uneasy an employment as that of making speeches joined to it.

*Verses.*        §174. If these may be any reasons against children's making Latin themes at school, I have much more to say and of more weight against their making *verses*, verses of any sort. For if he has no *genius* to *poetry*, it is the most unreasonable thing in the world to torment a child and waste his time about that which can never succeed; and if he have a poetic vein, it is to me the strangest thing in the world that the father should desire or suffer it to be cherished or improved. Methinks the parents should labor to have it stifled and suppressed, as much as may be; and I know not what reason a father can have to wish his son a poet who does not desire to have him bid defiance to all other callings and business; which is not yet the worst of the case. For if he proves a successful rhymer and get once the reputation of a wit, I desire it may be considered what company and places he is likely to spend his time in, nay, and estate too: for it is very seldom seen that anyone discovers mines of gold or silver in Parnassus.[89] 'Tis a pleasant air, but a barren soil; and there are very few instances of those who have added to their patrimony by anything they have reaped from thence. Poetry and gaming, which usually go together, are alike in this too, that they seldom bring any advantage but to those who have nothing else to live on. Men of estates almost constantly go away losers; and it is well if they escape at a cheaper rate than their whole estates or the greatest part of them. If therefore you would not have your son the fiddle to every jovial company, without whom the sparks could not relish their wine nor know how to pass an afternoon idly, if you would not have him waste his time and estate to divert others and contemn the dirty acres left him by his ancestors, I do not think you will much care he should be a *poet* or that his schoolmaster should enter him in versifying. But yet, if anyone will think poetry a desirable quality in his son, and that the study of it would raise his fancy and parts, he must needs yet confess that to that end reading the excellent Greek and Roman poets is of more use than making bad verses of his own in a language that is not his own. And he whose design it is to excel in English poetry would not, I guess, think the way to it were to make his first essays in Latin verses.

*Memoriter.*     §175. Another thing very ordinary in the vulgar method of grammar schools there is of which I see no use at all, unless it be to balk young lads in the way to learning languages, which, in my opinion, should be made as easy and pleasant as may be and that which was painful in it as much as possible quite removed. That which I mean and here complain of is their being forced to learn by heart great parcels of the authors which are taught

---

89. The Greek mountain sacred to the muses.

them; wherein I can discover no advantage at all, especially to the business they are upon. Languages are to be learned only by reading and talking and not by scraps of authors got by heart; which when a man's head is stuffed with, he has got the just furniture of a pedant, and 'tis the ready way to make him one, than which there is nothing less becoming a gentleman. For what can be more ridiculous than to mix the rich and handsome thoughts and sayings of others with a deal of poor stuff of his own; which is thereby the more exposed and has no other grace in it nor will otherwise recommend the speaker than a threadbare russet coat would that was set off with large patches of scarlet and glittering brocade. Indeed, where a passage comes in the way whose matter is worth remembrance and the expression of it very close and excellent (as there are many such in the ancient authors), it may not be amiss to lodge it in the mind of young scholars and with such admirable strokes of those great masters sometimes exercise the memory of schoolboys. But their learning of their lessons by heart as they happen to fall out in their books, without choice or distinction, I know not what it serves for but to misspend their time and pains and give them a disgust and aversion to their books, wherein they find nothing but useless trouble.

§176. I hear it's said that children should be employed in getting things by heart to exercise and improve their memories. I could wish this were said with as much authority of reason as it is with forwardness of assurance, and that this practice were established upon good observation more than old custom. For it is evident that strength of memory is owing to a happy constitution and not to any habitual improvement got by exercise. 'Tis true, what the mind is intent upon and, for fear of letting it slip, often imprints afresh on itself by frequent reflection, that it is apt to retain, but still according to its own natural strength of retention. An impression made on beeswax or lead will not last so long as on brass or steel. Indeed, if it be renewed often, it may last the longer; but every new reflecting on it is a new impression, and it is from thence one is to reckon if one would know how long the mind retains it. But the learning pages of Latin by heart no more fits the memory for retention of anything else than the graving of one sentence in lead makes it the more capable of retaining firmly any other characters. If such a sort of exercise of the memory were able to give it strength and improve our parts, players of all other people must needs have the best memories, and be the best company. But whether the scraps they have got into their head this way make them remember other things the better, and whether their parts be improved proportionably to the pains they have taken in getting by heart others' sayings, experience will show. Memory is so necessary to all parts and conditions of life and so little is to be done without it, that we are not to fear it should grow dull and useless for want of exercise, if exercise would make it grow stronger. But I fear this faculty of the mind is not capable of much help and amendment in general by any exercise or endeavor of ours, at least not by that used upon this pretence in grammar schools. And if Xerxes was able to call every common soldier by name in his army that consisted of no less than a hundred thousand men, I think it may be guessed he got not this wonderful ability by learning his lessons by heart when he was a boy. This method of exercising and improving the memory by toilsome repetitions without book of what they read is, I think, little used in the education of princes, which if it had that advantage [that] is talked of should be as little neglected in them as in the meanest schoolboys: princes having as much need of good memories as any men living and having generally an equal share in this faculty with other men, though it has never been taken care of this way. What the mind is intent upon and careful of, that it remembers best and for the reason mentioned above; to which, if method and order be joined, all is done, I think, that can be for the help of a weak memory; and he that will take any other way to do it, especially that of charging it with a train of other people's words, which he that learns cares not for, will, I guess, scarce find the profit answer half the time and pains employed in it.

I do not mean hereby that there should be no exercise given to children's memories. I think their memories should be employed, but not in learning by rote whole pages out of books, which the lesson being once said and that task over, are delivered up again to oblivion and neglected forever. This mends neither the memory nor the mind. What they should learn by heart out of authors, I have above mentioned;[90] and such wise and useful sentences being once given in charge to their memories, they should never be suffered to forget again but be often called to an account for them; whereby, besides the use those sayings may be to them in their future life, as so many good rules and observations, they will be taught to reflect often and bethink themselves what they have to remember, which is the only way to make the memory quick and useful. The custom of frequent reflection will keep their minds from running adrift and call their thoughts home from useless inattentive roving, and therefore, I think, it may do well, to give them something every day to remember, but something still that is in itself worth the remembering and what you would never have out

90. §175.

of mind whenever you call or they themselves search for it. This will oblige them often to turn their thoughts inward, than which you cannot wish them a better intellectual habit.

§177. But under whose care soever a child is put to be taught during the *Latin.* tender and flexible years of his life, this is certain: it should be one who thinks *Latin* and *language* the least part of education; one who, knowing how much virtue and a well-tempered soul is to be preferred to any sort of *learning* or *language,* makes it his chief business to form the mind of his scholars and give that a right disposition, which if once got, though all the rest should be neglected, would in due time produce all the rest and which, if it be not got and settled so as to keep out ill and vicious habits, *languages* and *sciences* and all the other accomplishments of education will be to no purpose but to make the worse or more dangerous man. And, indeed, whatever stir there is made about getting of *Latin* as the great and difficult business, his mother may teach it him herself if she will but spend two or three hours in a day with him and make him read the Evangelists in *Latin* to her: for she need but buy a *Latin* Testament and, having got somebody to mark the last syllable but one, where it is long, in words above two syllables (which is enough to regulate her pronunciation and accenting the words), read daily in the *Gospels,* and then let her avoid understanding them in *Latin* if she can. And when she understands the Evangelists in *Latin,* let her in the same manner read Aesop's *Fables,* and so proceed on to Eutropius, Justin, and other such books. I do not mention this as an imagination of what I fancy [one] may do, but as of a thing I have known done and the *Latin* tongue with ease got this way.

But to return to what I was saying: he that takes on him the charge of bringing up young men, especially young gentlemen, should have something more in him than *Latin,* more than even a knowledge in the liberal sciences; he should be a person of eminent virtue and prudence, and with good sense, have good humor, and the skill to carry himself with gravity, ease, and kindness in a constant conversation with his pupils. But of this I have spoken at large in another place.[91]

§178. At the same time that he is learning French and Latin, a child, *Geography.* as has been said,[92] may also be entered in *arithmetic, geography, chronology, history,* and *geometry* too. For if these be taught him in French or Latin when he begins once to understand either of these tongues, he will get a knowledge in these sciences and the language to boot.

91. §§88–94.
92. §166.

*Geography,* I think, should be begun with: for the learning of the figure of the *globe,* the situation and boundaries of the four parts of the world, and that of particular kingdoms and countries, being only an exercise of the eyes and memory, a child with pleasure will learn and retain them; and this is so certain, that I now live in the house with a child whom his mother[93] has so well instructed this way in *geography* that he knew the limits of the four parts of the world, could readily point, being asked, to any country upon the globe or any county[94] in the map of England, knew all the great rivers, promontories, straits, and bays in the world, and could find the longitude and latitude of any place before he was six years old. These things, that he will thus learn by sight and have by rote in his memory, is not all, I confess, that he is to learn upon the *globes.* But yet it is a good step and preparation to it and will make the remainder much easier when his judgment is grown ripe enough for it; besides, that it gets so much time now and by the pleasure of knowing things leads him on insensibly to the gaining of languages.

§179. When he has the natural parts of the globe well fixed in his memory, it may then be time to begin *arithmetic.* By the natural parts of the globe, I mean the several positions of the parts of the earth and sea under different names and distinctions of countries, not coming yet to those artificial and imaginary Lines which have been invented and are only supposed for the better improvement of that science.

*Arithmetic.*  §180. *Arithmetic* is the easiest and consequently the first sort of abstract reasoning which the mind commonly bears or accustoms itself to, and is of so general use in all parts of life and business that scarce anything is to be done without it. This is certain, a man cannot have too much of it nor too perfectly: he should therefore begin to be exercised in *counting* as soon and as far as he is capable of it and do something in it every day till he is master of the art of *numbers.* When he understands *addition* and *substraction,* he may then be advanced farther in *geography,* and after he is acquainted with the *poles, zones, parallel circles,* and *meridians,* be taught *longitude* and *latitude* and by them be made to understand the use of maps and by the numbers placed on their sides to know the respective situation of countries and *Astronomy.*  how to find them out on the terrestrial globe. Which when he can readily do, he may then be entered in the celestial; and there going over all the circles again, with a more particular observation of the ecliptic or zodiac to fix

93. Damaris Masham.

94. Accepting the Yoltons' emendation of "county" for "country" in their 1989 edition.

them all very clearly and distinctly in his mind, he may be taught the figure
and position of the several constellations, which may be showed him first
upon the globe and then in the heavens.

When that is done, and he knows pretty well the constellations of this
our hemisphere, it may be time to give him some notion of this our planetary world, and to that purpose it may not be amiss to make him a draft of
the Copernican system, and therein explain to him the situation of the
planets, their respective distances from the sun, the center of their revolu-
tions. This will prepare him to understand the motion and theory of the
planets the most easy and natural way. For since astronomers no longer
doubt of the motion of the planets about the sun, it is fit he should proceed
upon that hypothesis, which is not only the simplest and least perplexed
for a learner, but also the likeliest to be true in itself. But in this as in all
other parts of instruction, great care must be taken with children to begin
with that which is plain and simple, and to teach them as little as can be at
once and settle that well in their heads before you proceed to the next or
anything new in that science. Give them first one simple idea, and see that
they take it right and perfectly comprehend it before you go any farther,
and then add some other simple idea which lies next in your way to what
you aim at; and so proceeding by gentle and insensible steps, children
without confusion and amazement will have their understandings opened
and their thoughts extended farther than could have been expected. And
when anyone has learned anything himself, there is no such way to fix it in
his memory and to encourage him to go on as to set him to teach it others.

§181. When he has once got such an acquaintance with the globes as is *Geometry.*
above mentioned, he may be fit to be tried a little in *geometry*, wherein I
think the six first books of Euclid enough for him to be taught. For I am in
some doubt whether more to a man of business be necessary or useful. At
least if he have a genius and inclination to it, being entered so far by his
tutor, he will be able to go on of himself without a teacher.

The *globes* therefore must be studied, and that diligently, and I think
may be begun betimes if the tutor will but be careful to distinguish what
the child is capable of knowing and what not; for which this may be a rule
that perhaps will go a pretty way, viz. that children may be taught anything
that falls under their senses, especially their sight, as far as their memories
only are exercised; and thus a child very young may learn which is the *equa-
tor*, which the *meridian*, etc., which Europe, and which England upon the
globes as soon almost as he knows the rooms of the house he lives in if care
be taken not to teach him too much at once nor to set him upon a new part
till that which he is upon be perfectly learned and fixed in his memory.

*Chronology.*　§182. With geography, *chronology* ought to go hand in hand. I mean the general part of it, so that he may have in his mind a view of the whole current of time and the several considerable *epochs* that are made use of in history. Without these two, history, which is the great mistress of prudence and civil knowledge and ought to be the proper study of a gentleman or man of business in the world, without geography and *chronology*, I say, history will be very ill retained and very little useful, but be only a jumble of matters of fact confusedly heaped together without order or instruction. It is by these two that the actions of mankind are ranked into their proper places of times and countries, under which circumstances they are not only much easier kept in the memory, but in that natural order are only capable to afford those observations which make a man the better and the abler for reading them.

§183. When I speak of *chronology* as a science he should be perfect in, I do not mean the little controversies that are in it. These are endless, and most of them of so little importance to a gentleman as not to deserve to be inquired into were they capable of an easy decision. And therefore all that learned noise and dust of the chronologist is wholly to be avoided. The most useful book I have seen in that part of learning is a small treatise of Strauchius, which is printed in twelves, under the title of *Breviarum Chronologium*, out of which may be selected all that is necessary to be taught a young gentleman concerning *chronology;* for all that is in that treatise a learner need not be cumbered with. He has in him the most remarkable or usual *epochs* reduced all to that of the *Julian Period,* which is the easiest and plainest and surest method that can be made use of in *chronology.* To this treatise of Strauchius, Helvicus's tables may be added as a book to be turned to on all occasions.

*History.*　§184. As nothing teaches, so nothing delights more than history. The first of these recommends it to the study of grown men; the latter makes me think it the fittest for a young lad, who as soon as he is instructed in chronology and acquainted with the several *epochs* in use in this part of the world, and can reduce them to the *Julian Period,* should then have some *Latin history* put into his hand. The choice should be directed by the easiness of the style; for wherever he begins, chronology will keep it from confusion; and the pleasantness of the subject inviting him to read, the language will insensibly be got without that terrible vexation and uneasiness which children suffer where they are put into books beyond their capacity, such as are the Roman orators and poets, only to learn the Roman language. When he has by reading mastered the easier, such perhaps as Justin, Eutropius, Quintus Curtius etc., the next degree to these will give him no great trouble: and thus by a gradual progress from the plainest and easiest *historians* he may at last come to read the most difficult and sublime of the *Latin* authors, such as are Tully, Virgil, and Horace.

§185. The knowledge of *virtue*, all along from the beginning, in all the instances he is capable of, being taught him more by practice than rules; and the love of reputation instead of satisfying his appetite being made habitual in him, I know not whether he should read any other discourses of morality but what he finds in the Bible or have any system of *ethics* put into his hand till he can read Tully's *Offices*,[95] not as a schoolboy to learn Latin, but as one that would be informed in the principles and precepts of virtue for the conduct of his life. *Ethics.*

§186. When he has pretty well digested Tully's *Offices* and added to it Pufendorf's *De officio hominis & civis*, it may be seasonable to set him upon Grotius's *De jure belli & pacis*, or which perhaps is the better of the two, Pufendorf's *De jure naturali & gentium;* wherein he will be instructed in the natural rights of men, and the origin and foundations of society, and the duties resulting from thence. This *general part of civil law* and history are studies which a gentleman should not barely touch at, but constantly dwell upon and never have done with. A virtuous and well behaved young man that is well versed in the *general part of the civil law* (which concerns not the chicane of private cases, but the affairs and intercourse of civilized nations in general grounded upon principles of reason), understands Latin well, and can write a good hand, one may turn loose into the world with great assurance that he will find employment and esteem everywhere. *Civil Law.*

§187. It would be strange to suppose an English gentleman should be ignorant of the *law* of his country. This, whatever station he is in, is so requisite that from a justice of the peace to a minister of state I know no place he can well fill without it. I do not mean the chicane or wrangling and captious part of the *law*; a gentleman, whose business it is to seek the true measures of right and wrong and not the arts how to avoid doing the one and secure himself in doing the other, ought to be as far from such a study of the *law* as he is concerned diligently to apply himself to that wherein he may be serviceable to his country. And to that purpose, I think the right way for a gentleman to study *our law*, which he does not design for his calling, is to take a view of our English constitution and government in the ancient books of the *common law* and some more modern writers, who out of them have given an account of this government. And having got a true idea of that, then to read our history and with it join in every king's reign *Law.*

95. Cicero's *De Officiis*, *Of Duties.*

the *laws* then made. This will give an insight into the reason of our *statutes*, and show the true ground upon which they came to be made and what weight they ought to have.

Rhetoric.
Logic.

§188. *Rhetoric* and *logic* being the arts that in the ordinary method usually follow immediately after grammar, it may perhaps be wondered that I have said so little of them. The reason is because of the little advantage young people receive by them. For I have seldom or never observed anyone to get the skill of reasoning well or speaking handsomely by studying those rules which pretend to teach it; and therefore I would have a young gentleman take a view of them in the shortest systems could be found without dwelling long on the contemplation and study of those formalities. Right reasoning is founded on something else than the *predicaments* and *predicables*, and does not consist in talking in *mode* and *figure* itself. But it is besides my present business to enlarge upon this speculation. To come therefore to what we have in hand: if you would have your son *reason well*, let him read Chillingworth;[96] and if you would have him speak well, let him be conversant in Tully to give him the true *idea* of *eloquence*, and let him read those things that are well written in English to perfect his style in the purity of our language.

§189. If the use and end of right reasoning be to have right notions and a right judgment of things, to distinguish between truth and falsehood, right and wrong, and to act accordingly, be sure not to let your son be bred up in the art and formality of disputing, either practicing it himself or admiring it in others; unless instead of an able man, you desire to have him an insignificant wrangler, opiniated in discourse, and priding himself in contradicting others or, which is worse, questioning everything and thinking there is no such thing as truth to be sought but only victory in disputing. There cannot be anything so disingenuous, so misbecoming a gentleman or anyone who pretends to be a rational creature, as not to yield to plain reason and the conviction of clear arguments. Is there anything more inconsistent with civil conversation and the end of all debate than not to take an answer, though ever so full and satisfactory, but still to go on with the dispute as long as equivocal sounds can furnish (a *medius terminus*[97]) a term to wrangle with on the one side, or a distinction on the other? Whether pertinent or impertinent, sense or nonsense, agreeing with or contrary to what he had said before, it matters not. For this in short is the way and perfection of logical disputes: that the opponent never take any

96. William Chillingworth's *The Religion of Protestants* (1638).
97. "Middle boundary" or "intermediate limit."

answer, nor the respondent ever yield to any argument. This neither of them must do, whatever becomes of truth or knowledge, unless he will pass for a poor baffled wretch and lie under the disgrace of not being able to maintain whatever he has once affirmed, which is the great aim and glory in disputing. Truth is to be found and supported by a mature and due consideration of things themselves, and not by artificial terms and ways of arguing: these lead not men so much into the discovery of truth as into a captious and fallacious use of doubtful words, which is the most useless and most offensive way of talking, and such as least suits a gentleman or a lover of truth of anything in the world.

There can scarce be a greater defect in a gentleman than not to express *Style.* himself well either in writing or speaking. But yet, I think, I may ask my reader whether he does not know a great many who live upon their estates and so, with the name, should have the qualities of gentlemen, who cannot so much as tell a story as they should, much less speak clearly and persuasively in any business. This I think not to be so much their fault as the fault of their education. For I must without partiality do my countrymen this right, that where they apply themselves, I see none of their neighbors outgo them. They have been taught *rhetoric* but yet never taught how to express themselves handsomely with their tongues or pens in the language they are always to use: as if the names of the figures that embellished the discourses of those who understood the art of speaking were the very art and skill of speaking well. This, as all other things of practice, is to be learned not by a few, or a great many rules given, but by exercise and application according to good rules, or rather patterns, till habits are got and a facility of doing it well.

Agreeable hereunto, perhaps it might not be amiss to make children, as soon as they are capable of it, often to tell a story of anything they know, and to correct at first the most remarkable fault they are guilty of in their way of putting it together. When that fault is cured, then to show them the next, and so on, till one after another all, at least the gross ones, are mended. When they can tell tales pretty well, then it may be time to make them write them. The *Fables* of Aesop, the only book almost that I know fit for children, may afford them matter for this exercise of writing English, as well as for reading and translating to enter them in the Latin tongue. When they are got past the faults of grammar and can join in a continued coherent discourse the several parts of a story without bald and unhandsome forms of transition (as is usual) often repeated, he that desires to perfect them yet farther in this, which is the first step to speaking well and needs no invention, may have recourse to Tully and, by putting in practice those rules which that master of eloquence gives in his First Book *De Inventione* §20, make them know wherein the skill and graces of a handsome narrative, according to the several subjects and designs of it, lie. Of each of which rules fit examples may be found out, and therein they may be shown how others have practiced them. The ancient classic authors afford plenty of such examples, which they should be made not only to translate but have set before them as patterns for their daily imitation.

*Letters.*   When they understand how to write English with due connection, propriety, and order, and are pretty well masters of a tolerable narrative style, they may be advanced to writing of letters. Wherein they should not be put upon any strains of wit or compliment, but taught to express their own plain easy sense without any incoherence, confusion or roughness. And when they are perfect in this, they may, to raise their thoughts, have set before them the example of *Voiture*[98] for the entertainment of their friends at a distance with letters of compliment, mirth, raillery, or diversion; and Tully's *Epistles* as the best pattern whether for business or conversation. The writing of letters has so much to do in all the occurrences of human life that no gentleman can avoid showing himself in this kind of writing. Occasions will daily force him to make this use of his pen, which, besides the consequences that in his affairs his well or ill managing of it often draws after it, always lays him open to a severer examination of his breeding, sense, and abilities than oral discourses, whose transient faults, dying for the most part with the sound that gives them life and so not subject to a strict review, more easily escape observation and censure.

Had the methods of education been directed to their right ends, one would have thought this so necessary a part could not have been neglected, whilst themes and verses in Latin, of no use at all, were so constantly everywhere pressed, to the racking of children's inventions beyond their strength and hindering their cheerful progress in learning the tongues by unnatural difficulties. But custom has so ordained it, and who dares disobey? And would it not be very unreasonable to require of a learned country schoolmaster (who has all the tropes and figures in Farnaby's *Rhetoric*[99] at his fingers' ends) to teach his scholar to express himself handsomely in *English.*   English, when it appears to be so little his business or thought that the boy's mother (despised, it is likely, as illiterate for not having read a system of *logic* and *rhetoric*) outdoes him in it?

98. *Les Lettres de Monsieur de Voiture* (1657).

99. A seventeenth-century Latin textbook.

To write and speak correctly gives a grace and gains a favorable attention to what one has to say; and since it is *English* that an *English* gentleman
will have constant use of, that is the language he should chiefly cultivate
and wherein most care should be taken to polish and perfect his style. To
speak or write better Latin than *English* may make a man be talked of, but
he would find it more to his purpose to express himself well in his own
tongue, that he uses every moment, than to have the vain commendation
of others for a very insignificant quality. This I find universally neglected,
and no care taken anywhere to improve young men in their own language
that they may thoroughly understand and be masters of it. If anyone
among us have a facility or purity more than ordinary in his mother
tongue, it is owing to chance, or his genius, or anything rather than to his
education or any care of his teacher. To mind what *English* his pupil speaks
or writes is below the dignity of one bred up amongst Greek and Latin,
though he have but little of them himself. These are the learned languages
fit only for learned men to meddle with and teach: *English* is the language
of the illiterate vulgar. Though yet we see the policy of some of our neighbors has not thought it beneath the public care to promote and reward the
improvement of their own language; polishing and enriching their tongue
is no small business amongst them, it has colleges and stipends appointed
it, and there is raised amongst them a great ambition and emulation of
writing correctly; and we see what they are come to by it, and how far they
have spread one of the worst languages possibly in this part of the world,
if we look upon it as it was in some few reigns backwards, whatever it be
now.[100] The great men amongst the Romans were daily exercising themselves in their own language, and we find yet upon record the names of
orators who taught some of their emperors Latin, though it were their
mother tongue.

'Tis plain, the Greeks were yet more nice[101] in theirs, all other speech
was barbarous to them but their own, and no foreign language appears to
have been studied or valued amongst that learned and acute people,
though it be past doubt that they borrowed their learning and philosophy
from abroad.

I am not here speaking against Greek and Latin: I think they ought to
be studied, and the Latin at least understood well by every gentleman. But
whatever foreign languages a young man meddles with (and the more he
knows the better), that which he should critically study and labor to get a

100.  A reference to the activities of the French Academy.

101.  Fastidious.

facility, clearness, and elegance to express himself in should be his own, and to this purpose he should daily be exercised in it.

*Natural*
*Philosophy.* §190. *Natural philosophy,* as a speculative science, I imagine we have none, and perhaps, I may think I have reason to say, we never shall be able to make a science of it. The works of nature are contrived by a wisdom and operate by ways too far surpassing our faculties to discover or capacities to conceive for us ever to be able to reduce them into a science. *Natural philosophy* being the knowledge of the principles, properties, and operations of things as they are in themselves, I imagine there are two parts of it, one comprehending spirits with their nature and qualities, and the other *bodies.* The first of these is usually referred to *metaphysics;* but under what title soever the consideration of *spirits* comes, I think it ought to go before the study of matter and body, not as a science that can be methodized into a system and treated of upon principles of knowledge, but as an enlargement of our minds towards a truer and fuller comprehension of the intellectual world, to which we are led both by reason and revelation. And since the clearest and largest discoveries we have of other *spirits,* besides God and our own souls, is imparted to us from heaven by revelation, I think the information that at least young people should have of them should be taken from that revelation. To this purpose, I conclude, it would be well if there were made a good history of the Bible for young people to read: wherein if everything that is fit to be put into it were laid down in its due order of time, and several things omitted which are suited only to riper age, that confusion which is usually produced by promiscuous reading of the Scripture, as it lies now bound up in our Bibles, would be avoided. And also this other good obtained, that by reading of it constantly there would be instilled into the minds of children a notion and belief of *spirits,* they having so much to do in all the transactions of that history, which will be a good preparation to the study of *bodies.* For without the notion and allowance of *spirits* our philosophy will be lame and defective in one main part of it, when it leaves out the contemplation of the most excellent and powerful part of the creation.

§191. Of this *history of the Bible* I think too it would be well if there were a short and plain epitome made, containing the chief and most material heads, for children to be conversant in as soon as they can read. This, though it will lead them early into some notion of *spirits,* yet is not contrary to what I said above,[102] that I would not have children troubled whilst young with notions of *spirits;* whereby my meaning was that I think it

102. §§136–38.

inconvenient that their yet tender minds should receive early impressions of *goblins, specters,* and *apparitions,* wherewith their maids and those about them are apt to frighten them into a compliance with their orders, which often proves a great inconvenience to them all their lives after by subjecting their minds to frights, fearful apprehensions, weakness, and superstition; which, when coming abroad into the world and conversation they grow weary and ashamed of, it not seldom happens that to make as they think a thorough cure and ease themselves of a load which has sat so heavy on them, they throw away the thoughts of all *spirits* together and so run into the other but worse extreme.

§192. The reason why I would have this premised to *the study of bodies,* and the doctrine of the scriptures well imbibed before young men be entered in *natural philosophy,* is because matter being a thing that all our senses are constantly conversant with, it is so apt to possess the mind and exclude all other beings but matter, that prejudice, grounded on such principles, often leaves no room for the admittance of spirits or the allowing any such things as *immaterial beings in rerum natura;*[103] when yet it is evident that by mere matter and motion none of the great phenomena of nature can be resolved, to instance but in that common one of gravity, which I think impossible to be explained by any natural operation of matter or any other law of motion but the positive will of a Superior Being so ordering it. And therefore since the Deluge cannot be well explained without admitting something out of the ordinary course of nature, I propose it to be considered whether God's altering the center of gravity in the Earth for a time (a thing as intelligible as gravity itself, which perhaps a little variation of causes unknown to us would produce) will not more easily account for Noah's Flood than any *hypothesis* yet made use of to solve it. I hear the great objection to this is that it would produce but a partial Deluge. But the alteration of the center of gravity once allowed, it is no hard matter to conceive that the Divine Power might make the center of gravity placed at a due distance from the center of the Earth move round it in a convenient space of time, whereby the Flood would become universal and, as I think, answer all the phenomena of the Deluge as delivered by Moses at an easier rate than those many hard suppositions that are made use of to explain it. But this is not a place for that argument, which is here only mentioned by the bye to show the necessity of having recourse to something beyond bare matter and its motion in the explication of nature; to which the notions of spirits and their power, as delivered in the Bible,

103. "In the things of nature," or "in the universe."

where so much is attributed to their operation, may be a fit preparative, reserving to a fitter opportunity a fuller explication of this *hypothesis* and the application of it to all the parts of the Deluge and any difficulties [that] can be supposed in the history of the Flood as recorded in the Scripture.

§193. But to return to the study of *natural philosophy*, though the world be full of systems of it, yet I cannot say I know any one which can be taught a young man as a science, wherein he may be sure to find truth and certainty, which is what all sciences give an expectation of.[104] I do not hence conclude that none of them are to be read: it is necessary for a gentleman in this learned age to look into some of them to fit himself for conversation. But whether that of Descartes be put into his hands as that which is most in fashion, or it be thought fit to give him a short view of that and several others also, I think the systems of *natural philosophy* that have obtained in this part of the world are to be read more to know the *hypotheses* and to understand the terms and ways of talking of the several sects than with hopes to gain thereby a comprehensive, scientific, and satisfactory knowledge of the works of nature; only this may be said, that the modern *Corpuscularians*[105] talk, in most things, more intelligibly than the Peripatetics, who possessed the Schools immediately before them. He that would look farther back and acquaint himself with the several opinions of the ancients, may consult Dr. Cudworth's *Intellectual System*,[106] wherein that very learned author has with such accurateness and judgment collected and explained the opinions of the Greek philosophers that what principles they built on and what were the chief *hypotheses* that divided them is better to be seen in him than anywhere else that I know. But I would not deter anyone from the study of nature because all the knowledge we have, or possibly can have, of it cannot be brought into a science. There are very many things in it that are convenient and necessary to be known to a gentleman, and a great many other that will abundantly reward the pains of the curious with delight and advantage. But these, I think, are rather to be found amongst such writers as have employed themselves in making rational

104. By science Locke means certain and demonstrative knowledge such as geometry, as distinguished from experimental knowledge; see *Essay Concerning Human Understanding* (hereafter cited as *Essay*) IV iii 26–29, vi 7–13, xii 9–13.

105. Advocates such as Robert Boyle of the view that matter was composed of atoms or corpuscles.

106. *A True Intellectual System of the Universe* (1678) by Ralph Cudworth, the Cambridge Platonist and father of Damaris Masham, Locke's friend in whose house he spent his last years.

experiments and observations than in starting barely speculative systems. Such writings therefore, as many of Mr. Boyle's[107] are, with others that have written of *husbandry, planting, gardening,* and the like, may be fit for a gentleman when he has a little acquainted himself with some of the systems of the *natural philosophy* in fashion.

§194. Though the systems of *physics* that I have met with afford little encouragement to look for certainty or science in any treatise which shall pretend to give us a body of *natural philosophy* from the first principles of bodies in general, yet the incomparable Mr. Newton has shown how far mathematics, applied to some parts of nature, may, upon principles that matter of fact justify, carry us in the knowledge of some, as I may so call them, particular provinces of the incomprehensible universe. And if others could give us so good and clear an account of other parts of *nature* as he has of this our planetary world and the most considerable *phenomena* observable in it in his admirable book, *Philosophiae naturalis principia Mathematica,* we might in time hope to be furnished with more true and certain knowledge in several parts of this stupendous machine than hitherto we could have expected. And though there are very few that have mathematics enough to understand his demonstrations, yet the most accurate mathematicians who have examined them allowing them to be such, his book will deserve to be read and give no small light and pleasure to those who, willing to understand the motions, properties, and operations of the great masses of matter in this our solar system, will but carefully mind his conclusions, which may be depended on as propositions well proved.

§195. This is, in short, what I have thought concerning a young gentle- *Greek.* man's studies; wherein it will possibly be wondered that I should omit *Greek,* since amongst the Grecians is to be found the origin, as it were, and foundation of all that learning which we have in this part of the world. I grant it so, and will add that no man can pass for a scholar that is ignorant of the *Greek* tongue. But I am not here considering of the education of a professed scholar, but of a gentleman, to whom Latin and French, as the world now goes, is by everyone acknowledged to be necessary. When he comes to be a man, if he has a mind to carry his studies farther and look into the *Greek* learning, he will then easily get that tongue himself; and if he has not that inclination, his learning of it under a tutor will be but lost labor, and much of his time and pains spent in that which will be neglected and thrown away as soon as he is at liberty. For how many are there of a

107. Robert Boyle, Locke's friend and mentor in natural science.

hundred, even amongst scholars themselves, who retain the *Greek* they carried from school, or ever improve it to a familiar reading and perfect understanding of *Greek* authors?

To conclude this part which concerns a young gentleman's studies, his tutor should remember that his business is not so much to teach him all that is knowable, as to raise in him a love and esteem of knowledge and to put him in the right way of knowing, and improving himself, when he has a mind to it.

The thoughts of a judicious author on the subject of languages, I shall here give the reader, as near as I can, in his own way of expressing them. He says,[108] "One can scarce burden children too much with the knowledge of languages. They are useful to men of all conditions, and they equally open them the entrance either to the most profound or the more easy and entertaining parts of learning. If this irksome study be put off to a little more advanced age, young men either have not resolution enough to apply to it out of choice or steadiness to carry it on. And if anyone has the gift of perseverance, it is not without the inconvenience of spending that time upon languages which is destined to other uses; and he confines to the study of words that age of his life that is above it and requires things; at least it is the losing the best and beautifullest season of one's life. This large foundation of languages cannot be well laid but when everything makes an easy and deep impression on the mind: when the memory is fresh, ready, and tenacious; when the head and heart are as yet free from cares, passions, and designs; and those on whom the child depends have authority enough to keep him close to a long continued application. I am persuaded that the small number of truly learned and the multitude of superficial pretenders is owing to the neglect of this."

I think everybody will agree with this observing gentleman that languages are the proper study of our first years. But it is to be considered by the parents and tutors, what tongues it is fit the child should learn. For it must be confessed that it is fruitless pains and loss of time to learn a language which, in the course of life that he is designed to, he is never likely to make use of, or which one may guess by his temper he will wholly neglect and lose again as soon as an approach to manhood, setting him free from a governor, shall put him into the hands of his own inclination, which is not likely to allot any of his time to the cultivating the learned tongues

---

108. *La Bruyere, Moeurs de ce siecle* (1696) p. 577 [Locke's note and presumably his translation].

or dispose him to mind any other language but what daily use or some particular necessity shall force upon him.

But yet for the sake of those who are designed to be scholars, I will add
what the same author subjoins to make good his foregoing remark. It will
deserve to be considered by all who desire to be truly learned, and therefore may be a fit rule for tutors to inculcate and leave with their pupils to
guide their future studies.

"The study," says he, "of the original text can never be sufficiently recommended. It is the shortest, surest, and most agreeable way to all sorts of
learning. Draw from the springhead, and take not things at secondhand.
Let the writings of the great masters be never laid aside; dwell upon them,
settle them in your mind, and cite them upon occasion; make it your business thoroughly to understand them in their full extent and all their circumstances; acquaint yourself fully with the principles of original authors;
bring them to a consistency, and then do you yourself make your deductions. In this state were the first commentators, and do not you rest till you
bring yourself to the same. Content not yourself with those borrowed
lights, nor guide yourself by their views but where your own fails you and
leaves you in the dark. Their explications are not yours, and will give you
the slip. On the contrary, your own observations are the product of your
own mind, where they will abide and be ready at hand upon all occasions
in conversation, consultation, and dispute. Lose not the pleasure it is to see
that you were not stopped in your reading but by difficulties that are invin-
cible, where the commentators and scholiasts themselves are at a stand and
have nothing to say, those copious expositors of other places, who, with a
vain and pompous overflow of learning poured out on passages plain and
easy in themselves, are very free of their words and pains where there is no
need. Convince yourself fully by thus ordering your studies that it is nothing but men's laziness which has encouraged pedantry to cram rather than
enrich libraries and to bury good authors under heaps of notes and com-
mentaries, and you will perceive that sloth herein has acted against itself
and its own interest by multiplying reading and inquiries and increasing
the pains it endeavored to avoid."

This, though it may seem to concern none but direct scholars, is of so
great moment for the right ordering of their education and studies that I
hope I shall not be blamed for inserting of it here, especially if it be considered that it may be of use to gentlemen too, when at any time they have
a mind to go deeper than the surface and get to themselves a solid satisfactory and masterly insight in any part of learning.

*Method.*       Order and constancy are said to make the great difference between one man and another: this I am sure, nothing so much clears a learner's way, helps him so much on in it, and makes him go so easy and so far in any inquiry as a good *method*. His governor should take pains to make him sensible of this, accustom him to order, and teach him *method* in all the application of his thoughts; show him wherein it lies, and the advantages of it; acquaint him with the several sorts of it, either from general to particulars, or from particulars to what is more general; exercise him in both of them; and make him see in what cases each different *method* is most proper and to what ends it best serves.

In history the order of time should govern, in philosophical inquiries that of nature, which in all progression is to go from the place one is then in to that which joins and lies next to it; and so it is in the mind, from the knowledge it stands possessed of already, to that which lies next and is coherent to it, and so on to what it aims at, by the simplest and most uncompounded parts it can divide the matter into. To this purpose, it will be of great use to his pupil to accustom him to distinguish well, that is, to have distinct notions wherever the mind can find any real difference, but as carefully to avoid distinctions in terms where he has not distinct and different clear ideas.

§196. Besides what is to be had from study and books, there are other *accomplishments* necessary for a gentleman to be got by exercise, and to which time is to be allowed, and for which masters must be had.

*Dancing.*       *Dancing* being that which gives *graceful motions* all the life, and above all things manliness and a becoming confidence to young children, I think it cannot be learned too early, after they are once of an age and strength capable of it. But you must be sure to have a good master that knows and can teach what is graceful and becoming and what gives a freedom and easiness to all the motions of the body. One that teaches not this is worse than none at all, natural unfashionableness being much better than apish, affected postures; and I think it much more passable to put off the hat and make a leg like an honest country gentleman than like an ill-fashioned dancing master. For as for the jigging part and the figures of dances, I count that little or nothing farther than as it tends to perfect *graceful carriage*.

*Music.*       §197. *Music* is thought to have some affinity with dancing, and a good hand upon some instruments is by many people mightily valued. But it wastes so much of a young man's time to gain but a moderate skill in it and engages often in such odd company that many think it much better spared; and I have, amongst men of parts and business, so seldom heard anyone commended or esteemed for having an excellency in *music*, that amongst

all those things that ever came into the list of accomplishments I think I
may give it the last place. Our short lives will not serve us for the attainment of all things; nor can our minds be always intent on something to be
learned. The weakness of our constitutions, both of mind and body,
requires that we should be often unbent; and he that will make a good use
of any part of his life must allow a large portion of it to recreation. At least
this must not be denied to young people, unless whilst you with too much
haste make them old, you have the displeasure to see them in their graves
or a second childhood sooner than you could wish. And therefore, I think,
that the time and pains allotted to serious improvements should be
employed about things of most use and consequence, and that too in the
methods the most easy and short that could be at any rate obtained; and
perhaps, as I have above said, it would be none of the least secrets in education to make the exercises of the body and the mind the *recreation* one to
another.[109] I doubt not but that something might be done in it by a prudent
man that would well consider the temper and inclination of his pupil. For
he that is wearied either with study or dancing does not desire presently to
go to sleep, but to do something else which may divert and delight him.
But this must be always remembered, that nothing can come into the
account of *recreation* that is not done with delight.

§198. *Fencing* and *riding* the *great horse*[110] are looked upon as so necessary parts of breeding that it would be thought a great *omission* to neglect
them; the latter of the two, being for the most part to be learned only in
great towns, is one of the best exercises for health which is to be had in
those places of ease and luxury, and upon that account makes a fit part of
a young gentleman's employment during his abode there. And as far as it
conduces to give a man a firm and graceful seat on horseback and to make
him able to teach his horse to stop and turn quick and to rest on his
haunches, is of use to a gentleman both in peace and war. But whether it
be of moment enough to be made a business of and deserve to take up more
of his time than should barely for his health be employed at due intervals
in some such vigorous exercise, I shall leave to the discretion of parents
and tutors, who will do well to remember, in all the parts of education, that
most time and application is to be bestowed on that which is likely to be of
greatest consequence and frequentest use in the ordinary course and
occurrences of that life the young man is designed for.

109. §108.
110. Warhorse or charger.

*Fencing.*    §199. As for *fencing*, it seems to me a good exercise for health, but dangerous to the life. The confidence of their skill being apt to engage in quarrels those that think they have learned to use their swords, this presumption makes them often more touchy than needs on points of honor and slight or no provocations. Young men in their warm blood are forward to think they have in vain learned to fence if they never show their skill and courage in a duel; and they seem to have reason. But how many sad tragedies that reason has been the occasion of, the tears of many a mother can witness. A man that cannot *fence* will be more careful to keep out of bullies' and gamesters' company, and will not be half so apt to stand upon punctilios, nor to give affronts or fiercely justify them when given, which is that which usually makes the quarrel. And when a man is in the field, a moderate skill in fencing rather exposes him to the sword of his enemy than secures him from it. And certainly a man of courage who cannot *fence* at all, and therefore will put all upon one thrust and not stand parrying, has the odds against a moderate fencer, especially if he has skill in *wrestling*. And therefore, if any provision be to be made against such accidents, and a man be to prepare his son for duels, I had much rather mine should be a good *wrestler* than an ordinary *fencer*, which is the most a gentleman can attain to in it, unless he will be constantly in the fencing school and every day exercising. But since fencing and riding the great horse are so generally looked upon as necessary qualifications in the breeding of a gentleman, it will be hard wholly to deny anyone of that rank these marks of distinction. I shall leave it therefore to the father to consider how far the temper of his son and the station he is likely to be in will allow or encourage him to comply with fashions which, having very little to do with civil life, were yet formerly unknown to the most warlike nations and seem to have added little of force or courage to those who have received them, unless we will think martial skill or prowess have been improved by *duelling*, with which fencing came into and with which, I presume, it will go out of the world.

§200. These are my present thoughts concerning *learning* and *accomplishments*. The great business of all is *virtue* and *wisdom*.

> *Nullum numen abest si sit prudentia.*[111]

Teach him to get a mastery over his inclinations and *submit his appetite to reason*. This being obtained, and by constant practice settled into habit, the hardest part of the task is over. To bring a young man to this, I know nothing which so much contributes as the love of praise and commenda-

111. "No deity is lacking where there is prudence," Juvenal *Satires* x 365, xiv 315.

tion, which should therefore be instilled into him by all arts imaginable. Make his mind as sensible of credit and shame as may be; and when you have done that, you have put a principle into him which will influence his actions when you are not by, to which the fear of a little smart of a rod is not comparable, and which will be the proper stock whereon afterwards to graft the true principles of morality and religion.

§201. I have one thing more to add, which as soon as I mention, I shall *Trade.* run the danger of being suspected to have forgot what I am about and what I have above written concerning education, all tending towards a gentleman's calling, with which a *trade* seems wholly to be inconsistent. And yet, I cannot forbear to say, I would have him *learn a trade, a manual trade*, nay, two or three, but one more particularly.

§202. The busy inclination of children being always to be directed to something that may be useful to them, the advantages proposed from what they are set about may be considered of two kinds: 1. Where the skill itself, that is got by exercise, is worth the having. Thus skill not only in languages and learned sciences, but in painting, turning,[112] gardening, tempering and working in iron, and all other useful arts, is worth the having. 2. Where the exercise itself, without any other consideration, is necessary or useful for health. Knowledge in some things is so necessary to be got by children whilst they are young, that some part of their time is to be allotted to their improvement in them, though those employments contribute nothing at all to their health: such are reading and writing and all other sedentary studies for the cultivating of the mind, which unavoidably take up a great part of gentlemen's time quite from their cradles. Other *manual arts*, which are both got and exercised by labor, do many of them, by that exercise, not only increase our dexterity and skill, but contribute to our health too, especially such as employ us in the open air. In these, then, health and improvement may be joined together, and of these should some fit ones be chosen to be made the recreations of one whose chief business is with books and study. In this choice, the age and inclination of the person is to be considered, and constraint always to be avoided in bringing him to it. For command and force may often create but can never cure an aversion; and whatever anyone is brought to by compulsion, he will leave as soon as he can and be little profited and less recreated by [it], whilst he is at it.

§203. That which of all others would please me best would be a *painter*, *Painting.* were there not an argument or two against it not easy to be answered. First,

112. Lathe work.

ill painting is one of the worst things in the world; and to attain a tolerable degree of skill in it requires too much of a man's time. If he has a natural inclination to it, it will endanger the neglect of all other more useful studies to give way to that; and if he have no inclination to it, all the time, pains, and money [that] shall be employed in it will be thrown away to no purpose. Another reason why I am not for *painting* in a gentleman is because it is a sedentary recreation which more employs the mind than the body. A gentleman's more serious employment I look on to be study; and when that demands relaxation and refreshment, it should be in some exercise of the body, which unbends the thought and confirms the health and strength. For these two reasons I am not for *painting*.

*Gardening.* §204. In the next place, for a country gentleman I should propose one
*Joiner.* or rather both these: viz. *gardening* or *husbandry* in general and working in wood, as a *carpenter, joiner,* or *turner,* these being fit and healthy recreations for a man of study or business. For since the mind endures not to be constantly employed in the same thing or way, and sedentary or studious men should have some exercise that at the same time might divert their minds and employ their bodies, I know none that could do it better for a country gentleman than these two, the one of them affording him exercise when the weather or season keeps him from the other. Besides that, by being skilled in the one of them he will be able to govern and teach his gardener; by the other contrive and make a great many things both of delight and use; though these I propose not as the chief end of his labor, but as temptations to it; diversion from his other more serious thoughts and employments, by useful and healthy manual exercise, being what I chiefly aim at in it.

§205. The great men among the ancients understood very well how to reconcile manual labor with affairs of state, and thought it no lessening to their dignity to make the one the recreation to the other. That indeed which seems most generally to have employed and diverted their spare hours was agriculture. Gideon amongst the Jews was taken from threshing, as well as Cincinnatus amongst the Romans from the plough, to command the armies of their countries against their enemies, and it is plain their dexterous handling of the flail or the plough and being good workmen with these tools did not hinder their skill in arms nor make them less able in the arts of war or government.[113] They were great captains and statesmen as well as husbandmen. Cato major, who had with great reputation borne all the great offices of the commonwealth, has left us an evidence under his

113. Judges 6:11 and Livy III 26.

own hand,[114] how much he was versed in country affairs, and as I remember, Cyrus when possessed of the Persian throne thought *gardening* so little beneath the dignity and grandeur of a throne that he showed Xenophon a large field of fruit trees all of his own planting.[115] The records of antiquity both amongst Jews and Gentiles are full of instances of this kind, if it were necessary to recommend useful recreations by examples.

§206. Nor let it be thought that I mistake when I call these or the like exercises of manual arts *diversions* or *recreations*, for *recreation* is not being idle (as everyone may observe) but easing the wearied part by change of business; and he that thinks *diversion* may not lie in hard and painful labor forgets the early rising, hard riding, heat, cold and hunger of huntsmen, which is yet known to be the constant recreation of men of the greatest condition. *Delving, planting, inoculating,* or any the like profitable employments would be no less a *diversion* than any of the idle sports in fashion if men could but be brought to delight in them, which custom and skill in a trade will quickly bring anyone to do. And I doubt not but there are to be found those who, being frequently called to cards or any other play by those they could not refuse, have been more tired with these *recreations* than with any the most serious employment of life, though the play has been such as they have naturally had no aversion to and with which they could willingly sometimes divert themselves.

§207. Play, wherein persons of condition, especially ladies, waste so much of their time, is a plain instance to me that men cannot be perfectly idle; they must be doing something. For how else could they sit so many hours toiling at that which generally gives more vexation than delight to people whilst they are actually engaged in it? 'Tis certain, gaming leaves no satisfaction behind it to those who reflect when it is over, and it no way profits either body or mind; as to their estates, if it strike so deep as to concern them, it is a *trade* then, and not a *recreation,* wherein few that have anything else to live on thrive, and, at best, a thriving gamester has but a poor trade on it, who fills his pockets at the price of his reputation.

Recreation belongs not to people who are strangers to business and are not wasted and wearied with the employment of their calling. The skill should be so to order their time of recreation that it may relax and refresh the part that has been exercised and is tired, and yet do something which, besides the present delight and ease, may produce what will afterwards be profitable. It has been nothing but the vanity and pride of greatness and

*Recreation.*

114. His work *De re rustica, Of Country Affairs.*
115. Xenophon *Oeconomicus* iv 20–25.

riches that has brought unprofitable and dangerous *pastimes* (as they are called) into fashion and persuaded people into a belief that the learning or putting their hands to anything that was useful could not be a *diversion* fit for a gentleman. This has been that which has given *cards, dice,* and *drinking* so much credit in the world; and a great many throw away their spare hours in them through the prevalency of custom and want of some better employment to fill up the vacancy of leisure more than from any real delight [that] is to be found in them. They cannot bear the dead weight of unemployed time lying upon their hands nor the uneasiness it is to do nothing at all; and having never learned any laudable manual art wherewith to divert themselves, they have recourse to those foolish or ill ways in use to help off their time, which a rational man, till corrupted by custom, could find very little pleasure in.

§208. I say not this, that I would never have a young gentleman accommodate himself to the innocent *diversions* in fashion amongst those of his age and condition. I am so far from having him austere and morose to that degree that I would persuade him to more than ordinary complaisance for all the gaieties and *diversions* of those he converses with and [to] be averse or restive in nothing they should desire of him that might become a gentleman and an honest man. Though as to *cards* and *dice,* I think the safest and best way is never to learn any play upon them, and so to be incapacitated for those dangerous temptations and encroaching wasters of useful time. But allowance being made for *idle and jovial conversation* and all fashionable becoming recreations; I say a young man will have time enough,

*Trade.*    from his serious and main business, to learn almost any *trade.* 'Tis [from] want of application, and not of leisure, that men are not skilful in more *arts* than one; and an hour in a day, constantly employed in such a way of *diversion,* will carry a man in a short time a great deal farther than he can imagine; which, if it were of no other use but to drive the common, vicious, useless, and dangerous pastimes out of fashion and to show there was no need of them, would deserve to be encouraged. If men from their youth were weaned from that sauntering humor, wherein some out of custom let a good part of their lives run uselessly away without either business or recreation, they would find time enough to acquire *dexterity and skill in hundreds of things,* which though remote from their proper callings would not at all interfere with them. And therefore, I think, for this as well as other reasons before mentioned,[116] a lazy listless humor that idly dreams away the days is of all others the least to be indulged or permitted in young peo-

116. §§123, 126.

ple. It is the proper state of one sick and out of order in his health, and is tolerable in nobody else, of what age or condition soever.

§209. To the arts above mentioned,[117] may be added *perfuming, varnishing, engraving,* and several sorts of working in *iron, brass,* and *silver*; and if, as it happens to most young gentlemen, that a considerable part of his time be spent in a great town, he may learn to cut, polish, and set *precious stones* or employ himself in grinding and polishing *optical glasses.* Amongst the great variety there is of ingenious *manual arts,* it will be impossible that none should be found to please and delight him unless he be either idle or debauched, which is not to be supposed in a right way of education. And since he cannot be always employed in study, reading, and conversation, there will be many an hour, besides what his exercises will take up, which, if not spent this way, will be spent worse. For, I conclude, a young man will seldom desire to sit perfectly still and idle; or if he does, it is a fault that ought to be mended.

§210. But if his mistaken parents, affrighted with the disgraceful names of *mechanic* and *trade,* shall have an aversion to anything of this kind in their children, yet there is one thing relating to trade, which when they consider, they will think absolutely necessary for their sons to learn.

*Merchants' accounts,* though a science not likely to help a gentleman to get an estate, yet possibly there is not anything of more use and efficacy to make him preserve the estate he has. 'Tis seldom observed that he who keeps an account of his income and expenses, and thereby has constantly under view the course of his domestic affairs, lets them run to ruin; and I doubt not but many a man gets behindhand before he is aware, or runs further on when he is once in, for want of this care or the skill to do it. I would therefore advise all gentlemen to learn perfectly *merchants' accounts* and not to think it is a skill that belongs not to them because it has received its name [from] and has been chiefly practiced by men of traffic.

*Merchants' Accounts.*

§211. When my young master has once got the skill of *keeping accounts* (which is a business of reason more than arithmetic), perhaps it will not be amiss that his father from thenceforth require him to do it in all his concernments. Not that I would have him set down every pint of wine or play that costs him money; the general name of expenses will serve for such things well enough; nor would I have his father look so narrowly into these accounts as to take occasion from thence to criticize on his expenses. He must remember that he himself was once a young man, and not forget the thoughts he had then, nor the right his son has to have the same and to

117. §204.

have allowance made for them. If therefore I would have the young gentleman obliged to keep an account, it is not at all to have that way a check
upon his expenses (for what the father allows him, he ought to let him be
fully master of), but only that he might be brought early into the custom
of doing it, and that that might be made familiar and habitual to him
betimes which will be so useful and necessary to be constantly practiced
the whole course of his life. A noble Venetian whose son wallowed in the
plenty of his father's riches, finding his son's expenses grow very high and
extravagant, ordered by his cashier to let him have for the future no more
money than what he should count when he received it. This one would
think no great restraint to a young gentleman's expenses, who could freely
have as much money as he would tell.[118] But yet this, to one who was used
to nothing but the pursuit of his pleasures, proved a very great trouble,
which at last ended in this sober and advantageous reflection. If it be so
much pains to me barely to count the money I would spend, what labor
and pains did it cost my ancestors not only to count but get it? This rational thought, suggested by this little pains imposed upon him, wrought so
effectually upon his mind that it made him take up,[119] and from that time
forwards, prove a good husband.[120] This at least everybody must allow,
that nothing is likelier to keep a man within compass than the having constantly before his eyes the state of his affairs in a regular course of *accounts*.

*Travel.*          §212. The last part usually in education is *travel*, which is commonly
thought to finish the work and complete the gentleman. I confess *travel*
into foreign countries has great advantages, but the time usually chosen to
send young men abroad is, I think, of all other, that which renders them
least capable of reaping those advantages. Those which are proposed, as to
the main of them, may be reduced to these two: first, language; secondly,
an improvement in wisdom and prudence by seeing men and conversing
with people of tempers, customs, and ways of living different from one
another and especially from those of his parish and neighborhood. But
from sixteen to one-and-twenty, which is the ordinary *time of travel*, men
are of all their lives the least suited to these improvements. The first season to get foreign languages and form the tongue to their true accents, I
should think, should be from seven to fourteen or sixteen; and then too a
tutor with them is useful and necessary, who may with those languages

118. Count.
119. Check oneself, mend one's ways.
120. Frugal manager.

teach them other things. But to put them out of their parents' view at a great distance under a governor, when they think themselves too much men to be governed by others, and yet have not prudence and experience enough to govern themselves, what is it but to expose them to all the greatest dangers of their whole life when they have the least fence and guard against them? Till that boiling boisterous part of life comes in, it may be hoped the tutor may have some authority; neither the stubbornness of age nor the temptation or examples of others can take him from his tutor's conduct till fifteen or sixteen; but then, when he begins to consort himself with men and think himself one, when he comes to relish and pride himself in manly vices and thinks it a shame to be any longer under the control and conduct of another, what can be hoped from even the most careful and discreet governor, when neither he has power to compel nor his pupil a disposition to be persuaded but on the contrary has the advice of warm blood and prevailing fashion to hearken to the temptations of his companions, just as wise as himself, rather than to the persuasions of his tutor, who is now looked on as the enemy to his freedom? And when is a man so likely to miscarry as when at the same time he is both raw and unruly? This is the season of all his life that most requires the eye and authority of his parents and friends to govern it. The flexibleness of the former part of a man's age, not yet grown up to be headstrong, makes it more governable and safe; and in the after-part, reason and foresight begin a little to take place and mind a man of his safety and improvement. The time therefore I should think the fittest for a young gentleman to be *sent abroad* would be either when he is younger under a tutor, whom he might be the better for, or when he is some years older without a governor, when he is of age to govern himself and make observations of what he finds in other countries worthy his notice and that might be of use to him after his return; and when too, being thoroughly acquainted with the laws and fashions, the natural and moral advantages and defects of his own country, he has something to exchange with those abroad from whose conversation he hoped to reap any knowledge.

§213. The ordering of *travel* otherwise is that, I imagine, which makes so many young gentlemen come back so little improved by it. And if they do bring home with them any knowledge of the places and people they have seen, it is often an admiration of the worst and vainest practices they met with abroad, retaining a relish and memory of those things wherein their liberty took its first swing rather than of what should make them better and wiser after their return. And indeed how can it be otherwise, going abroad at the age they do under the care of another who is to provide their

necessaries and make their observations for them? Thus under the shelter
and pretence of a governor, thinking themselves excused from standing
upon their own legs or being accountable for their own conduct, they very
seldom trouble themselves with inquiries or making useful observations of
their own. Their thoughts run after play and pleasure, wherein they take
it as a lessening to be controlled, but seldom trouble themselves to examine
the designs, observe the address, and consider the arts, tempers, and inclinations of men they meet with that so they may know how to comport
themselves towards them. Here he that travels with them is to screen
them, get them out when they have run themselves into the briars, and in
all their miscarriages be answerable for them.

§214. I confess the knowledge of men is so great a skill that it is not to
be expected a young man should presently be perfect in it. But yet his *going
abroad* is to little purpose if *travel* does not somewhat open his eyes, make
him cautious and wary, and accustom him to look beyond the outside and,
under the inoffensive guard of a civil and obliging carriage, keep himself
free and safe in his conversation with strangers and all sorts of people without forfeiting their good opinion. He that is sent out to *travel* at the age and
with the thoughts of a man designing to improve himself may get into the
conversation and acquaintance of persons of condition where he comes;
which though a thing of most advantage to a gentleman that travels, yet I
ask, amongst our young men that go abroad under tutors, what one is there
of a hundred that ever visits any person of quality? Much less makes an
acquaintance with such from whose conversation he may learn what is
good breeding in that country and what is worth observation in it; though
from such persons it is one may learn more in one day than in a year's ram-
bling from one inn to another. Nor indeed is it to be wondered. For men
of worth and parts will not easily admit the familiarity of boys, who yet
need the care of a tutor; though a young gentleman and stranger, appearing like a man and showing a desire to inform himself in the customs, manners, laws, and government of the country he is in, will find welcome,
assistance, and entertainment amongst the best and most knowing persons
everywhere, who will be ready to receive, encourage, and countenance an
ingenuous and inquisitive foreigner.

§215. This, how true soever it be, will not, I fear, alter the custom which
has cast the time of travel upon the worst part of a man's life but for reasons not taken from their improvement. The young lad must not be ventured abroad at eight or ten, for fear [of] what may happen to the tender
child, though he then runs ten times less risk than at sixteen or eighteen.
Nor must he stay at home till that dangerous heady age be over, because

he must be back again by one-and-twenty to marry and propagate. The father cannot stay any longer for the portion,[121] nor the mother for a new set of babies to play with, and so my young master, whatever comes of it, must have a wife looked out for him by that time he is of age; though it would be no prejudice to his strength, his parts, or his issue, if it were respited for some time, and he had leave to get, in years and knowledge, the start a little of his children, who are often found to tread too near upon the heels of their fathers, to the no great satisfaction either of son or father. But the young gentleman being got within view of matrimony, 'tis time to leave him to his mistress.

§216. Though I am now come to a conclusion of what obvious *Conclusion.* remarks have suggested [themselves] to me concerning education, I would not have it thought that I look on it as a just treatise on this subject. There are a thousand other things that may need consideration, especially if one should take in the various tempers, different inclinations, and particular defaults that are to be found in children and prescribe proper remedies. The variety is so great that it would require a volume; nor would that reach it. Each man's mind has some peculiarity, as well as his face, that distinguishes him from all others; and there are possibly scarce two children who can be conducted by exactly the same method. Besides that I think a prince, a nobleman, and an ordinary gentleman's son should have different ways of breeding. But having had here only some general views in reference to the main end and aims in education, and those designed for a gentleman's son who, being then very little, I considered only as white paper or wax to be molded and fashioned as one pleases; I have touched little more than those heads which I judged necessary for the breeding of a young gentleman of his condition in general; and have now published these my occasional thoughts with this hope, that though this be far from being a complete treatise on this subject or such as that everyone may find what will just fit his child in it, yet it may give some small light to those whose concern for their dear little ones makes them so irregularly bold that they dare venture to consult their own reason in the education of their children rather than wholly to rely upon old custom.

121. Dowry.

# Of the Conduct of the Understanding

Quid tam temerarium tamque indignum sapientis
gravitate atque constantia, quam aut falsum
sentire aut quod non satis explorate perceptum sit
et cognitum sine ulla dubitatione defendere?

Cicero, *De Natura Deorum*, B. I C. I.[1]

John Locke

1.  "What is so unrash and so unworthy of the dignity and firmness of the wise as either to believe falsely or to maintain without any doubt what is perceived and conceived without enough investigation?"

# Contents of
## *Of the Conduct of the Understanding*

§1. The last resort a man has recourse to in the conduct of himself is his understanding; for though we distinguish the faculties of the mind, and give the supreme command to the will as to an agent, yet the truth is, the man which is the agent determines himself to this or that voluntary action upon some precedent knowledge, or appearance of knowledge, in the understanding. No man ever sets himself about anything but upon some view or other which serves him for a reason for what he does: and whatsoever faculties he employs, the understanding, with such light as it has, well or ill informed, constantly leads; and by that light, true or false, all his operative powers are directed. The will itself, how absolute and uncontrollable soever it may be thought, never fails in its obedience to the dictates of the understanding. Temples have their sacred images, and we see what influence they have always had over a great part of mankind. But in truth the ideas and images in men's minds are the invisible powers that constantly govern them, and to these they all universally pay a ready submission. It is therefore of the highest concernment that great care should be taken of the understanding, to conduct it right in the search of knowledge and in the judgments it makes.

The logic now in use has so long possessed the chair, as the only art taught in the Schools for the direction of the mind in the study of the arts and sciences, that it would perhaps be thought an affectation of novelty to suspect that rules that have served the learned world these two or three thousand years, and which, without any complaint of defects, the learned have rested in, are not sufficient to guide the understanding.[2] And I should not doubt but this attempt would be censured as vanity or presumption, did not the great Lord Verulam's authority justify it;[3] who, not servilely thinking learning could not be advanced beyond what it was, because for many ages it had not been, did not rest in the lazy approbation and applause of what was, because it was, but enlarged his mind to what might be. In his preface to his *Novum Organum*,[4] concerning logic he pronounces

2.  The logic Locke refers to was central to the educational program of the ecclesiastical Schools throughout the Middle Ages and was derived from Aristotle's philosophy. Locke criticizes the logic associated with the Schools throughout this work and offers his own approach as an alternative to it. See, for example, section 7. Mathematics.

3.  Locke refers here to Francis Bacon (1561–1626), who was made Baron Verulam in 1618.

4.  The passage is actually to be found in the preface to Bacon's *Instauratio Magna*, an unfinished work of which the *Novum Organum* was originally meant to be a part.

thus: *Qui summas dialecticae partes tribuerunt atque inde fidissima scientiis praesidia comparari putarunt, verissime et optime viderunt intellectum humanum sibi permissum merito suspectum esse debere. Verum infirmior omnino est malo medicina; nec ipsa mali expers. Siquidem dialectica quae recepta est, licet ad civilia et artes quae in sermone et opinione positae sunt rectissime adhibeatur, naturae tamen subtilitatem longo intervallo non attingit; et prensando quod non capit, ad errores potius stabiliendos et quasi figendos quam ad viam veritati aperiendam valuit.*

'They,' says he, 'who attributed so much to logic, perceived very well and truly, that it was not safe to trust the understanding to itself, without the guard of any rules. But the remedy reached not the evil; but became a part of it: for the logic which took place, though it might do well enough in civil affairs and the arts which consisted in talk and opinion, yet comes very far short of subtlety in the real performances of nature, and, catching at what it cannot reach, has served to confirm and establish errors, rather than to open a way to truth.' And therefore a little after he says, 'That it is absolutely necessary that a better and perfecter use and employment of the mind and understanding should be introduced.' *Necessario requiritur ut melior et perfectior mentis et intellectus humani usus et adoperatio introducatur.*

*Parts.*[5]    §2. There is, it is visible, great variety in men's understandings, and their natural constitutions put so wide a difference between some men in this respect, that art and industry would never be able to master; and their very natures seem to want a foundation to raise on it that which other men easily attain unto. Amongst men of equal education there is great inequality of parts. And the woods of America, as well as the schools of Athens, produce men of several abilities in the same kind. Though this be so, yet I imagine most men come very short of what they might attain unto in their several degrees by a neglect of their understandings. A few rules of logic are thought sufficient in this case for those who pretend to the highest improvement; whereas I think there are a great many natural defects in the understanding capable of amendment, which are overlooked and wholly neglected. And it is easy to perceive that men are guilty of a great many faults in the exercise and improvement of this faculty of the mind, which hinder them in their progress and keep them in ignorance and error all their lives. Some of them I shall take notice of, and endeavor to point out proper remedies for in the following discourse.

*Reasoning.*    §3. Besides the want of determined ideas, and of sagacity and exercise in finding out and laying in order intermediate ideas, there are three mis-

5.  Talents, or abilities.

carriages that men are guilty of in reference to their reason, whereby this faculty is hindered in them from that service it might do and was designed for. And he that reflects upon the actions and discourses of mankind, will find their defects in this kind very frequent and very observable.

1. The first is of those who seldom reason at all, but do and think according to the example of others, whether parents, neighbors, ministers, or who else they are pleased to make choice of to have an implicit faith in, for the saving of themselves the pains and trouble of thinking and examining for themselves.

2. The second is of those who put passion in the place of reason, and, being resolved that shall govern their actions and arguments, neither use their own nor hearken to other people's reason, any farther than it suits their humor, interest, or party; and these one may observe commonly content themselves with words which have no distinct ideas to them, though, in other matters, that they come with an unbiased indifferency to, they want not abilities to talk and hear reason, where they have no secret inclination that hinders them from being tractable[6] to it.

3. The third sort is of those who readily and sincerely follow reason, but, for want of having that which one may call *large, sound, round-about sense,* have not a full view of all that relates to the question and may be of moment to decide it. We are all short sighted, and very often see but one side of a matter; our views are not extended to all that has a connection with it. From this defect I think no man is free. We see but in part, and we know but in part, and therefore it is no wonder we conclude not right from our partial views. This might instruct the proudest esteemer of his own parts, how useful it is to talk and consult with others, even such as come short of him in capacity, quickness and penetration: for since no one sees all, and we generally have different prospects of the same thing, according to our different, as I may say, positions to it, it is not incongruous to think nor beneath any man to try, whether another may not have notions of things which have escaped him, and which his reason would make use of if they came into his mind. The faculty of reasoning seldom or never deceives those who trust to it; its consequences from what it builds on are evident and certain, but that which it oftenest, if not only, misleads us in is that the principles from which we conclude, the grounds upon which we bottom our reasoning, are but a part, something is left out which should go into the reckoning to make it just and exact. Here we may imagine a vast and almost infinite advantage that angels and separate spirits may have

6. Locke's original reads "untractable."

over us; who, in their several degrees of elevation above us, may be endowed with more comprehensive faculties, and some of them perhaps have perfect and exact views of all finite beings that come under their consideration, can, as it were, in the twinkling of an eye, collect together all their scattered and almost boundless relations. A mind so furnished, what reason has it to acquiesce in the certainty of its conclusions!

In this we may see the reason why some men of study and thought, that reason right and are lovers of truth, do make no great advances in their discoveries of it. Error and truth are uncertainly blended in their minds; their decisions are lame and defective, and they are very often mistaken in their judgments: the reason whereof is, they converse but with one sort of men, they read but one sort of books, they will not come in the hearing but of one sort of notions; the truth is, they canton out to themselves a little Goshen[7] in the intellectual world, where light shines, and, as they conclude, day blesses them; but the rest of that vast firmament[8] they give up to night and darkness, and so avoid coming near it. They have a pretty traffick with known correspondents in some little creek; within that they confine themselves, and are dexterous managers enough of the wares and products of that corner with which they content themselves, but will not venture out into the great ocean of knowledge, to survey the riches that nature has stored other parts with, no less genuine, no less solid, no less useful, than what has fallen to their lot in the admired plenty and sufficiency of their own little spot, which to them contains whatsoever is good in the universe. Those who live thus mued up within their own contracted territories, and will not look abroad beyond the boundaries that chance, conceit, or laziness has set to their enquiries, but live separate from the notions, discourses and attainments of the rest of mankind, may not amiss be represented by the inhabitants of the Marian islands; who, being separated by a large tract of sea from all communion with the habitable parts of the earth, thought themselves the only people of the world. And though the straitness of the conveniences of life amongst them had never reached so far as to the use of fire, until the Spaniards, not many years since, in their voyages from Acapulco to Manilia brought it amongst them; yet in the want and ignorance of almost all things, they looked upon themselves, even after that the Spaniards had brought amongst them the notice of variety of nations abounding in sciences, arts and conveniences of life, of which they knew nothing, they looked upon themselves, I say, as the hap-

---

7. The fertile land assigned to the Israelites in Egypt; Gen. 45:10.
8. Locke uses the Latin word, *Expansum*, here.

piest and wisest people of the universe. But for all that, nobody, I think, will imagine them deep naturalists, or solid metaphysicians; nobody will deem the quickest sighted amongst them to have very enlarged views in ethics or politics, nor can anyone allow the most capable amongst them to be advanced so far in his understanding as to have any other knowledge but of the few little things of his and the neighboring islands within his commerce, but far enough from that comprehensive enlargement of mind which adorns a soul devoted to truth, assisted with letters, and a free consideration of the several views and sentiments of thinking men of all sides. Let not men therefore that would have a sight of, what everyone pretends to be desirous to have a sight of, truth in its full extent, narrow and blind their own prospect. Let not men think there is no truth but in the sciences that they study, or the books that they read. To prejudge other men's notions before we have looked into them is not to show their darkness, but to put out our own eyes. *Try all things, hold fast that which is good,*[9] is a divine rule coming from the Father of Light and Truth; and it is hard to know what other way men can come at truth, to lay hold of it, if they do not dig and search for it as for gold and hid treasure; but he that does so must have much earth and rubbish before he gets the pure metal; sand, and pebbles, and dross usually lie blended with it, but the gold is nevertheless gold, and will enrich the man that employs his pains to seek and separate it. Neither is there any danger he should be deceived by the mixture. Every man carries about him a touchstone, if he will make use of it, to distinguish substantial gold from superficial glitterings, truth from appearances. And indeed the use and benefit of this touchstone, which is natural reason, is spoiled and lost only by assumed prejudices, overweening presumption, and narrowing our minds. The want of exercising it in the full extent of things intelligible, is that which weakens and extinguishes this noble faculty in us. Trace it, and see whether it be not so. The day laborer in a country village has commonly but a small pittance of knowledge, because his ideas and notions have been confined to the narrow bounds of a poor conversation[10] and employment; the low mechanic of a country town does somewhat outdo him; porters and cobblers of great cities surpass them. A country gentleman, who, leaving Latin and learning in the University, removes thence to his mansion house, and associates with neighbors of the

9. I Thess. 5:21. From a 1611 English version of I Thess. 5:19–22; "Quench not the spirit: Despise not prophecyings: Prove all things: hold fast that which is good. Abstaine from all appearance of evill."

10. Social interaction generally.

same strain, who relish nothing but hunting and a bottle; with those alone he spends his time, with these alone he converses, and can away with no company whose discourse goes beyond what claret and dissoluteness inspire. Such a patriot, formed in this happy way of improvement, cannot fail, as we see, to give notable decisions upon the bench at quarter sessions,[11] and eminent proofs of his skill in politics, when the strength of his purse and party have advanced him to a more conspicuous station. To such a one, truly an ordinary coffee-house gleaner of the City[12] is an errant statesman, and as much superior to [him], as a man conversant about Whitehall[13] and the Court is to an ordinary shopkeeper. To carry this a little farther: here is one muffled up in the zeal and infallibility of his own sect, and will not touch a book or enter into debate with a person that will question any of those things which to him are sacred; another surveys our differences in religion with an equitable and fair indifference, and so finds probably that none of them are in everything unexceptionable. These divisions and systems were made by men, and carry the mark of fallibility on them; and in those whom he differs from, and, until he opened his eyes, had a general prejudice against, he meets with more to be said for a great many things than before he was aware of, or could have imagined. Which of these two now is most likely to judge right in our religious controversies, and to be most stored with truth, the mark all pretend to aim at? All these men that I have instanced in, thus unequally furnished with truth and advanced in knowledge, I suppose of equal natural parts; all the odds between them has been the different scope that has been given to their understandings to range in, for the gathering up of information, and furnishing their heads with ideas, notions and observations, whereon to employ their minds and form their understandings.

It will possibly be objected, who is sufficient for all this? I answer, more than can be imagined. Everyone knows what his proper business is, and what, according to the character he makes of himself, the world may justly expect of him; and to answer that, he will find he will have time and opportunity enough to furnish himself, if he will not deprive himself by a narrowness of spirit of those helps that are at hand. I do not say to be a good geographer that a man should visit every mountain, river, promontory and

11.  A criminal court whose sessions were held quarterly.

12.  The financial area of London.

13.  An area of London, still synonymous with the British government's executive branch, which included Whitehall Palace, built in the reign of Henry III and largely destroyed by fire in 1698.

creek upon the face of the earth, view the buildings, and survey the land everywhere, as if he were going to make a purchase. But yet everyone must allow that he shall know a country better that makes often sallies into it, and traverses it up and down, than he that like a mill horse goes still round in the same track, or keeps within the narrow bounds of a field or two that delight him. He that will enquire out the best books in every science, and inform himself of the most material authors of the several sects of philosophy and religion, will not find it an infinite work to acquaint himself with the sentiments of mankind concerning the most weighty and comprehensive subjects. Let him exercise the freedom of his reason and understanding in such a latitude as this, and his mind will be strengthened, his capacity enlarged, his faculties improved; and the light, which the remote and scattered parts of truth will give to one another, will so assist his judgment, that he will seldom be widely out, or miss giving proof of a clear head and a comprehensive knowledge. At least, this is the only way I know to give the understanding its due improvement to the full extent of its capacity, and to distinguish the two most different things I know in the world, a logical chicaner from a man of reason. Only, he that would thus give the mind its flight, and send abroad his enquiries into all parts after truth, must be sure to settle in his head determined ideas of all that he employs his thoughts about, and never fail to judge himself, and judge unbiasedly of all that he receives from others, either in their writings or discourses. Reverence or prejudice must not be suffered to give beauty or deformity to any of their opinions.

§4. We are born with faculties and powers capable almost of anything, such at least as would carry us farther than can easily be imagined: but it is only the exercise of those powers which gives us ability and skill in anything, and leads us towards perfection.

*Of Practice and Habits.*

A middle-aged ploughman will scarce ever be brought to the carriage and language of a gentleman, though his body be as well proportioned, and his joints as supple, and his natural parts not any way inferior. The legs of a dancing master and the fingers of a musician fall as it were naturally, without thought or pains, into regular and admirable motions. Bid them change their parts, and they will in vain endeavor to produce like motions in the members not used to them, and it will require length of time and long practice to attain but some degrees of a like ability. What incredible and astonishing actions do we find rope dancers and tumblers bring their bodies to; not but that sundry in almost all manual arts are as wonderful; but I name those which the world takes notice of for such, because on that very account they give money to see them. All these admired motions beyond the reach, and almost the conception, of unpracticed spectators are nothing but the mere effects of use and industry in men, whose bodies have nothing peculiar in them from those of the amazed lookers on.

As it is in the body, so it is in the mind; practice makes it what it is, and most even of those excellences which are looked on as natural endowments will be found, when examined into more narrowly, to be the product of exercise, and to be raised to that pitch only by repeated actions. Some men are remarked for pleasantness in raillery; others for apologues and apposite diverting stories. This is apt to be taken for the effect of pure nature, and that the rather, because it is not got by rules, and those who excel in either of them never purposely set themselves to the study of it as an art to be learned. But yet it is true that at first some lucky hit, which took with some-body and gained him commendation, encouraged him to try again, inclined his thoughts and endeavors that way, until at last he insensibly got a facility in it without perceiving how; and that is attributed wholly to nature which was much more the effect of use and practice. I do not deny that natural disposition may often give the first rise to it; but that never carries a man far without use and exercise, and it is practice alone that brings the powers of the mind as well as those of the body to their perfection. Many a good poetic vein is buried under a trade, and never produces anything for want of improvement. We see the ways of discourse and reasoning are very dif-ferent, even concerning the same matter, at Court and in the University. And he that will go but from Westminster-Hall to the Exchange,[14] will find a different genius and turn in their ways of talking, and yet one cannot think that all whose lot fell in the City were born with different parts from those who were bred at the University or Inns of Court.[15]

To what purpose all this, but to show that the difference, so observable in men's understandings and parts, does not arise so much from their nat-ural faculties as acquired habits. He would be laughed at that should go about to make a fine dancer out of a country hedger, at past fifty. And he will not have much better success, who shall endeavor at that age to make a man reason well, or speak handsomely, who has never been used to it, though you should lay before him a collection of all the best precepts of

14. Westminster Hall was the seat of the chief law court of England. The Exchange was the center of trade.

15. The Inns of Court were a group of four voluntary legal societies responsible for legal education and admission to the bar. They were established to provide training in English law, rather than Roman law, which was taught in the Univer-sities.

logic or oratory. Nobody is made anything by hearing of rules, or laying them up in his memory; practice must settle the habit of doing without reflecting on the rule, and you may as well hope to make a good painter or musician extempore by a lecture and instruction in the arts of music and painting, as a coherent thinker or strict reasoner by a set of rules, showing him wherein right reasoning consists.

This being so, that defects and weakness in men's understandings, as well as other faculties, come from want of a right use of their own minds, I am apt to think the fault is generally mislaid upon nature, and there is often a complaint of want of parts, when the fault lies in want of a due improvement of them. We see men frequently dexterous and sharp enough in making a bargain, who, if you reason with them about matters of religion, appear perfectly stupid.

§5. I will not here, in what relates to the right conduct and improvement *Ideas.* of the understanding, repeat again the getting clear and determined ideas, and the employing our thoughts rather about them than about sounds put for them, nor of settling the signification of words which we use with ourselves in the search of truth or with others in discoursing about it. Those hindrances of our understandings in the pursuit of knowledge, I have sufficiently enlarged upon in another place; so that nothing more needs here to be said of those matters.[16]

§6. There is another fault that stops or misleads men in their knowl- *Principles.* edge, which I have also spoken something of, but yet is necessary to mention here again, that we may examine it to the bottom and see the root it springs from, and that is a custom of taking up with principles that are not self-evident and very often not so much as true. It is not unusual to see men rest their opinions upon foundations that have no more certainty and solidity than the propositions built on them and embraced for their sake. Such foundations are these and the like, viz. the founders or leaders of my party are good men, and therefore their tenets are true; it is the opinion of a sect that is erroneous, therefore it is false; it has been long received in the world, therefore it is true; or it is new, and therefore false.

These, and many the like, which are by no means the measures of truths and falsehood, the generality of men make the standards by which they accustom their understanding to judge. And thus they, falling into a habit of determining truth and falsehood by such wrong measures, it is no wonder they should embrace error for certainty, and be very positive in things they have no ground for.

16. *Essay* II xxix; III ix, x, xi.

There is not any who pretends to the least reason, but, when any of these his false maxims are brought to the test, must acknowledge them to be fallible,[17] and such as he will not allow in those that differ from him; and yet, after he is convinced of this, you shall see him go on in the use of them, and the very next occasion that offers argue again upon the same grounds. Would one not be ready to think that men are willing to impose upon themselves and mislead their own understandings, who conduct them by such wrong measures, even after they see they cannot be relied on? But yet they will not appear so blameable as may be thought at first sight; for I think there are a great many that argue thus in earnest, and do it not to impose on themselves or others. They are persuaded of what they say, and think there is weight in it, though in a like case they have been convinced there is none; but men would be intolerable to themselves, and contemptible to others, if they should embrace opinions without any ground, and hold what they could give no manner of reason for. True or false, solid or sandy, the mind must have some foundation to rest itself upon, and, as I have remarked in another place, it no sooner entertains any proposition, but it presently hastens to some hypothesis to bottom it on; until then it is unquiet and unsettled. So much do our own very tempers dispose us to a right use of our understandings, if we would follow as we should the inclinations of our nature.

In some matters of concernment, especially those of religion, men are not permitted to be always wavering and uncertain, they must embrace and profess some tenets or other; and it would be a shame, nay, a contradiction too heavy for anyone's mind to lie constantly under, for him to pretend seriously to be persuaded of the truth of any religion, and yet not to be able to give any reason of his belief, or to say anything for his preference of this to any other opinion. And therefore they must make use of some principles or other, and those can be no other than such as they have and can manage; and to say they are not in earnest persuaded by them, and do not rest upon those they make use of, is contrary to experience, and to allege that they are not misled when we complain they are.

If this be so, it will be urged, why then do they not make use of sure and unquestionable principles,[18] rather than rest on such grounds as may deceive them, and will, as is visible, serve to support error as well as truth?

To this I answer, the reason why they do not make use of better and surer principles, is because they cannot; but this inability proceeds not

---

17.  The word "but" appears before "must" in this phrase in the original text.

18.  The word "rather" appears before "make" in this phrase in the original text.

from want of natural parts (for those few whose case that is are to be excused) but for want of use and exercise. Few men are from their youth accustomed to strict reasoning, and to trace the dependence of any truth in a long train of consequences to its remote principles, and to observe its connection; and he that by frequent practice has not been used to this employment of his understanding, it is no more wonder that he should not, when he is grown into years, be able to bring his mind to it, than that he should not be on a sudden able to grave or design, dance on the ropes, or write a good hand, who has never practiced either of them.

Nay, the most of men are so wholly strangers to this, that they do not so much as perceive their want of it. They dispatch the ordinary business of their callings by rote, as we say, as they have learned it, and, if at any time they miss success, they impute it to anything rather than want of thought or skill; that they conclude (because they know no better) they have in perfection. Or if there be any subject that interest or fancy has recommended to their thoughts, their reasoning about it is still after their own fashion; be it better or worse, it serves their turns, and is the best they are acquainted with: and therefore when they are led by it into mistakes, and their business succeeds accordingly, they impute it to any cross accident, or default of others, rather than to their own want of understanding; that is what nobody discovers or complains of in himself. Whatsoever made his business to miscarry, it was not want of right thought and judgment in himself: he sees no such defect in himself, but is satisfied that he carries on his designs well enough by his own reasoning, or at least should have done, had it not been for unlucky traverses not in his power. Thus being content with this short and very imperfect use of his understanding, he never troubles himself to seek out methods of improving his mind, and lives all his life without any notion of close reasoning in a continued connection of a long train of consequences from sure foundations, such as is requisite for the making out and clearing most of the speculative truths most men own to believe and are most concerned in. Not to mention here what I shall have occasion to insist on by and by more fully, viz. that in many cases it is not one series of consequences will serve the turn, but many different and opposite deductions must be examined and laid together, before a man can come to make a right judgment of the point in question. What then can be expected from men that neither see the want of any such kind of reasoning as this, nor, if they do, know they how to set about it, or could perform it? You may as well set a countryman who scarce knows the figures, and never cast up a sum of three particulars, to state a merchant's long account, and find the true balance of it.

What then should be done in the case? I answer, we should always remember what I said above, that the faculties of our souls are improved and made useful to us just after the same manner as our bodies are. Would you have a man write or paint, dance or fence well, or perform any other manual operation dexterously and with ease, let him have ever so much vigor and activity, suppleness and address naturally, yet nobody expects this from him unless he has been used to it, and has employed time and pains in fashioning and forming his hand or outward parts to these motions. Just so it is in the mind; would you have a man reason well, you must use him to it betimes, exercise his mind in observing the connection of ideas and following them in train. Nothing does this better than mathematics, which therefore I think should be taught all those who have the time and opportunity, not so much to make them mathematicians as to make them reasonable creatures; for though we all call ourselves so, because we are born to it if we please, yet we may truly say nature gives us but the seeds of it; we are born to be, if we please, rational creatures, but it is use and exercise only that makes us so, and we are indeed so no farther than industry and application has carried us. And therefore, in ways of reasoning which men have not been used to, he that will observe the conclusions they take up must be satisfied they are not at all rational.

This has been the less taken notice of, because everyone, in his private affairs, uses some sort of reasoning or other, enough to denominate him reasonable. But the mistake is, that he that is found reasonable in one thing is concluded to be so in all, and to think or say otherwise is thought so unjust an affront, and so senseless a censure, that nobody ventures to do it. It looks like the degradation of a man below the dignity of his nature. It is true that he that reasons well in any one thing has a mind naturally capable of reasoning well in others, and to the same degree of strength and clearness, and possibly much greater, had his understanding been so employed. But it is as true that he, who can reason well today about one sort of matters, cannot at all reason today about others, though perhaps a year hence he may. But wherever a man's rational faculty fails him, and will not serve him to reason, there we cannot say he is rational, how capable soever he may be by time and exercise to become so.

Try in men of low and mean education, who have never elevated their thoughts above the spade and the plough, nor looked beyond the ordinary drudgery of a day laborer. Take the thoughts of such an one, used for many years to one track, out of that narrow compass he has been all his life confined to, you will find him no more capable of reasoning than almost a perfect natural. Some one or two rules, on which their conclusions immediately depend, you will find in most men have governed all their thoughts; these, true or false, have been the maxims they have been guided by: take these from them, and they are perfectly at a loss, their compass and pole star then are gone, and their understanding is perfectly at a nonplus, and therefore they either immediately return to their old maxims again as the foundations of all truth to them, notwithstanding all that can be said to show their weakness, or, if they give them up to their reasons, they with them give up all truth and further enquiry, and think there is no such thing as certainty. For if you would enlarge their thoughts, and settle them upon more remote and surer principles, they either cannot easily apprehend them, or, if they can, know not what use to make of them; for long deductions from remote principles is what they have not been used to, and cannot manage.

What then, can grown men never be improved or enlarged in their understandings? I say not so, but this I think I may say, that it will not be done without industry and application, which will require more time and pains than grown men, settled in their course of life, will allow to it, and therefore very seldom is done. And this very capacity of attaining it by use and exercise only brings us back to that which I laid down before, that it is only practice that improves our minds as well as bodies, and we must expect nothing from our understandings any farther than they are perfected by habits.

The Americans are not all born with worse understandings than the Europeans, though we see none of them have such reaches in the arts and sciences. And among the children of a poor countryman, the lucky chance of education and getting into the world gives one infinitely the superiority in parts over the rest, who, continuing at home, had continued also just of the same size with his brethren.

He that has to do with young scholars, especially in mathematics, may perceive how their minds open by degrees, and how it is exercise alone that opens them. Sometimes they will stick a long time at a part of a demonstration, not for want of will and application, but really for want of perceiving the connection of two ideas that, to one whose understanding is more exercised, is as visible as anything can be. The same would be with a grown man beginning to study mathematics; the understanding, for want of use, often sticks in very plain way, and he himself that is so puzzled, when he comes to see the connection, wonders what it was he stuck at in a case so plain.

§7. I have mentioned mathematics as a way to settle in the mind a *Mathematics.* habit of reasoning closely and in train; not that I think it necessary that all men should be deep mathematicians, but that having got the way of reasoning, which that study necessarily brings the mind to, they might be able to transfer it to other parts of knowledge as they shall have occasion. For, in all sorts of reasoning, every single argument should be managed as a mathematical demonstration, the connection and dependence of ideas should be followed until the mind is brought to the source on which it bottoms and observes the coherence all along, though, in proofs of probability, one such train is not enough to settle the judgment as in demonstrative knowledge.

Where a truth is made out by one demonstration, there needs no farther enquiry, but in probabilities where there wants demonstration to establish the truth beyond doubt, there it is not enough to trace one argument to its source, and observe its strength and weakness, but all the arguments, after having been so examined on both sides, must be laid in balance one against another, and upon the whole the understanding determine its assent.

This is a way of reasoning the understanding should be accustomed to, which is so different from what the illiterate are used to, that even learned men oftentimes seem to have very little or no notion of it. Nor is it to be wondered, since the way of disputing in the Schools leads them quite away from it, by insisting on one topical argument, by the success of which the truth or falsehood of the question is to be determined and victory adjudged to the opponent or defendant; which is all one as if one should balance an account by one sum charged and discharged, when there are a hundred others to be taken into consideration.

This therefore it would be well if men's minds were accustomed to, and that early, that they might not erect their opinions upon one single view, when so many other are requisite to make up the account, and must come into the reckoning before a man can form a right judgment. This would enlarge their minds, and give a due freedom to their understandings, that they might not be led into error by presumption, laziness or precipitancy; for I think nobody can approve such a conduct of the understanding as should mislead it from truth, though it be ever so much in fashion to make use of it.

To this perhaps it will be objected, that to manage the understanding, as I propose, would require every man to be a scholar, and to be furnished with all the materials of knowledge, and exercised in all the ways of reasoning. To which I answer, that it is a shame for those that have time and the means to attain knowledge, to want any helps or assistance for the improvement of their understandings that are to be got, and to such I would be thought here chiefly to speak. Those methinks, who by the industry and parts of their ancestors have been set free from a constant drudgery to their backs and their bellies, should bestow some of their spare time on their heads, and open their minds by some trials and essays in all the sorts and matters of reasoning. I have before mentioned mathematics, wherein algebra gives new helps and views to the understanding. If I propose these, it is not, as I said, to make every man a thorough mathematician, or a deep algebraist; but yet I think the study of them is of infinite use even to grown men; first, by experimentally convincing them that, to make anyone reason well, it is not enough to have parts wherewith he is satisfied and that serve him well enough in his ordinary course. A man in those studies will see that, however good he may think his understanding, yet in many things, and those very visible, it may fail him. This would take off that presumption that most men have of themselves in this part; and they would not be so apt to think their minds wanted no helps to enlarge them, that there could be nothing added to the acuteness and penetration of their understandings.

Secondly, the study of mathematics would show them the necessity there is, in reasoning, to separate all the distinct ideas, and see the habitudes that all those concerned in the present enquiry have to one another, and to lay by those which relate not to the proposition in hand and wholly to leave them out of the reckoning. This is that which in other subjects, besides quantity, is what is absolutely requisite to just reasoning, though in them it is not so easily observed nor so carefully practiced. In those parts of knowledge where it is thought demonstration has nothing to do, men reason as it were in the lump: and, if, upon a summary and confused view or upon a partial consideration, they can raise the appearance of a probability, they usually rest content; especially if it be in a dispute where every little straw is laid hold on, and everything that can but be drawn in any way to give color to the argument is advanced with ostentation. But that mind is not in a posture to find the truth, that does not distinctly take all the parts asunder, and, omitting what is not at all to the point, draw a conclusion from the result of all the particulars which any way influence it. There is another no less useful habit to be got by an application to mathematical demonstrations, and that is, of using the mind to a long train of consequences; but, having mentioned that already, I shall not again here repeat it.

As to men whose fortunes and time is narrower, what may suffice them is not of that vast extent as may be imagined, and so comes not within the objection.

Nobody is under an obligation to know everything. Knowledge and science in general is the business only of those who are at ease and leisure. Those who have particular callings ought to understand them; and it is no unreasonable proposal, nor impossible to be compassed, that they should think and reason right about what is their daily employment. This one cannot think them incapable of, without levelling them with the brutes, and charging them with a stupidity below the rank of rational creatures.

*Religion.*     §8. Besides his particular calling for the support of this life, everyone has a concern in a future life, which he is bound to look after. This engages his thoughts in religion; and here it mightily lies upon him to understand and reason right. Men therefore cannot be excused from understanding the words, and framing the general notions, relating to religion right. The one day of seven, besides other days of rest, allows in the Christian world time enough for this (had they no other idle hours), if they would but make use of these vacancies from their daily labor, and apply themselves to an improvement of knowledge, with as much diligence as they often do to a great many other things that are useless, and had but those that would enter them according to their several capacities in a right way to this knowledge. The original make of their minds is like that of other men, and they would be found not to want understanding fit to receive the knowledge of religion, if they were a little encouraged and helped in it as they should be. For there are instances of very mean people, who have raised their minds to a great sense and understanding of religion. And though these have not been so frequent as could be wished, yet they are enough to clear that condition of life from a necessity of gross ignorance, and to show that more might be brought to be rational creatures and Christians (for they can hardly be thought really to be so, who, wearing the name, know not so much as the very principles of that religion) if due care were taken of them. For, if I mistake not, the peasantry lately in France (a rank of people under a much heavier pressure of want and poverty than the day laborers in England) of the Reformed religion understood it much better, and could say more for it, than those of a higher condition among us.

But if it shall be concluded that the meaner sort of people must give themselves up to a brutish stupidity in the things of their nearest concernment, which I see no reason for, this excuses not those of a freer fortune and education, if they neglect their understandings, and take no care to employ them as they ought and set them right in the knowledge of those things for which principally they were given them. At least those whose plentiful fortunes allow them the opportunities and helps of improvements are not so few, but that it might be hoped great advancements might be made in knowledge of all kinds, especially in that of the greatest concern and largest views, if men would make a right use of their faculties and study their own understandings.

§9. Outward corporeal objects that constantly importune our senses, *Ideas.* and captivate our appetites, fail not to fill our heads with lively and lasting ideas of that kind. Here the mind needs not be set upon getting greater store; they offer themselves fast enough, and are usually entertained in such plenty and lodged so carefully, that the mind wants room or attention for others that it has more use and need of. To fit the understanding therefore for such reasoning as I have been above speaking of, care should be taken to fill it with moral and more abstract ideas; for these not offering themselves to the senses, but being to be framed to the understanding, people are generally so neglectful of a faculty they are apt to think wants nothing, that I fear most men's minds are more unfurnished with such ideas than is imagined. They often use the words, and how can they be suspected to want the ideas? What I have said in the third book of my Essay, will excuse me from any other answer to this question.[19] But to convince people of what moment it is to their understandings to be furnished with such abstract ideas steady and settled in them, give me leave to ask how anyone shall be able to know whether he be obliged to be just, if he has not established ideas in his mind of obligation and of justice, since knowledge consists in nothing but the perceived agreement or disagreement of those ideas;[20] and so of all others the like which concern our lives and manners. And if men do find a difficulty to see the agreement or disagreement of two angles which lie before their eyes, unalterable in a diagram, how utterly impossible will it be to perceive it in ideas that have no other sensible objects to represent them to the mind but sounds with which they have no manner of conformity, and therefore had need to be clearly settled in the mind themselves, if we would make any clear judgment about them. This therefore is one of the first things the mind should be employed about in the right conduct of the understanding, without which it is impossible it should be capable of reasoning right about those matters. But in these and all other ideas, care must be taken that they harbor no inconsistencies, and that they have a real existence where real existence is supposed, and are not mere chimeras with a supposed existence.[21]

19. See especially chapter v.
20. See *Essay*, IV i.
21. See *Essay*, II xxx.

*Prejudices.*     §10. Everyone is forward to complain of the prejudices that mislead other men or parties, as if he were free, and had none of his own. This being objected on all sides, it is agreed that it is a fault and a hindrance to knowledge. What now is the cure? No other but this, that every man should let alone others' prejudices and examine his own. Nobody is convinced of his by the accusation of another; he recriminates by the same rule, and is clear. The only way to remove this great cause of ignorance and error out of the world is for everyone impartially to examine himself. If others will not deal fairly with their own minds, does that make my errors truths, or ought it to make me in love with them and willing to impose on myself? If others love cataracts on their eyes, should that hinder me from couching of mine as soon as I could? Everyone declares against blindness, and yet who almost is not fond of that which dims his sight, and keeps the clear light out of his mind, which should lead him into truth and knowledge? False or doubtful positions, relied upon as unquestionable maxims, keep those in the dark from truth, who build on them. Such are usually the prejudices imbibed from education, party, reverence, fashion, interest, etc. This is the mote which everyone sees in his brother's eye, but never regards the beam in his own. For who is there almost that is ever brought fairly to examine his own principles, and see whether they are such as will bear the trial; but yet this should be one of the first things everyone should set about, and be scrupulous in, who would rightly conduct his understanding in the search of truth and knowledge.

To those who are willing to get rid of this great hindrance of knowledge (for to such only I write) to those who would shake off this great and dangerous impostor prejudice, who dresses up falsehood in the likeness of truth, and so dexterously hoodwinks men's minds as to keep them in the dark with a belief that they are more in the light than any that do not see with their eyes, I shall offer this one mark whereby prejudice may be known. He that is strongly of any opinion, must suppose (unless he be self-condemned) that his persuasion is built upon good grounds, and that his assent is no greater than what the evidence of the truth he holds forces him to, and that they are arguments and not inclination or fancy that make him so confident and positive in his tenets. Now if, after all his profession, he cannot bear any opposition to his opinion, if he cannot so much as give a patient hearing, much less examine and weigh the arguments on the other side, does he not plainly confess it is prejudice governs him? And it is not the evidence of truth, but some lazy anticipation, some beloved presumption that he desires to rest undisturbed in. For if what he holds be, as he gives out, well fenced with evidence, and he sees it to be true, what need he fear to put it to the proof? If his opinion be settled upon a firm foundation, if the arguments that support it and have obtained his assent be clear, good, and convincing, why should he be shy to have it tried whether they be proof or not? He whose assent goes beyond his evidence owes this excess of his adherence only to prejudice, and does, in effect, own it, when he refuses to hear what is offered against it; declaring thereby that it is not evidence he seeks, but the quiet enjoyment of the opinion he is fond of, with a forward condemnation of all that may stand in opposition to it, unheard and unexamined; which, what is it but prejudice? *Qui aequum statuerit parte inauditā alterā, etiam si aequum statuerit, haud aequus fuerit.*[22] He that would acquit himself in this case as a lover of truth, not giving way to any preoccupation or bias that may mislead him, must do two things that are not very common nor very easy.

§11. First, he must not be in love with any opinion, or wish it to be   *Indifferency.* true, until he knows it to be so, and then he will not need to wish it: for nothing that is false can deserve our good wishes, nor a desire that it should have the place and force of truth; and yet nothing is more frequent than this. Men are fond of certain tenets upon no other evidence but respect and custom, and think they must maintain them, or all is gone, though they have never examined the ground they stand on, nor have ever made them out to themselves, or can make them out to others. We should contend earnestly for the truth, but we should first be sure that it is truth, or else we fight against God, who is the God of Truth, and do the work of the devil, who is the father and propagator of lies; and our zeal, though ever so warm, will not excuse us; for this is plainly prejudice.

§12. Secondly, he must do that which he will find himself very averse   *Examine.* to, as judging the thing unnecessary or himself incapable of doing it. He must try whether his principles be certainly true or not, and how far he may safely rely upon them. This, whether fewer have the heart or the skill to do, I shall not determine; but this I am sure, this is that which everyone ought to do, who professes to love truth and would not impose upon himself which is a surer way to be made a fool of than by being exposed to the sophistry of others. The disposition to put any cheat upon ourselves works constantly, and we are pleased with it, but are impatient of being bantered or misled by others. The inability I here speak of is not any natural defect that makes men incapable of examining their own principles. To such, rules of conducting their understandings are useless, and that is the case of

22. "Whoever decides the right with the other side unheard, even if it is decided rightly, is not at all right."

very few. The great number is of those whom the ill habit of never exerting their thoughts has disabled: the powers of their minds are starved by disuse, and have lost that reach and strength which nature fitted them to receive from exercise. Those who are in a condition to learn the first rules of plain arithmetic, and could be brought to cast up an ordinary sum, are capable of this, if they had but accustomed their minds to reasoning: but they that have wholly neglected the exercise of their understandings in this way will be very far at first from being able to do it, and as unfit for it as one unpracticed in figures to cast up a shopbook, and perhaps think it as strange to be set about it. And yet it must nevertheless be confessed to be a wrong use of our understandings to build our tenets (in things where we are concerned to hold the truth) upon principles that may lead us into error. We take our principles at haphazard upon trust, and without ever having examined them, and then believe a whole system, upon a presumption that they are true and solid; and what is all this but childish, shameful, senseless credulity?

In these two things, viz. an equal indifferency for all truth, I mean the receiving it in the love of it as truth, but not loving it for any other reason before we know it to be true, and in the examination of our principles, and not receiving any for such nor building on them until we are fully convinced, as rational creatures, of their solidity, truth, and certainty, consists that freedom of the understanding which is necessary to a rational creature, and without which it is not truly an understanding. It is conceit, fancy, extravagance, anything rather than understanding, if it must be under the constraint of receiving and holding opinions by the authority of anything but their own, not fancied, but perceived, evidence. This was rightly called imposition, and is of all others the worst and most dangerous sort of it. For we impose upon ourselves, which is the strongest imposition of all others; and we impose upon ourselves in that part which ought with the greatest care to be kept free from all imposition. The world is apt to cast great blame on those who have an indifferency for opinions, especially in religion. I fear this is the foundation of great error and worse consequences. To be indifferent which of two opinions is true, is the right temper of the mind that preserves it from being imposed on, and disposes it to examine with that indifferency, until it has done its best to find the truth, and this is the only direct and safe way to it. But to be indifferent whether we embrace falsehood or truth or no, is the great road to error. Those who are not indifferent which opinion is true are guilty of this; they suppose, without examining, that what they hold is true, and then think they ought to be zealous for it. Those, it is plain by their warmth and eagerness, are not indifferent for their own opinions, but methinks are very indifferent whether they be true or false, since they cannot endure to have any doubts raised or objections made against them; and it is visible they never have made any themselves, and so, never having examined them, know not nor are concerned, as they should be, to know whether they be true or false.

These are the common and most general miscarriages which I think men should avoid or rectify in a right conduct of their understandings, and should be particularly taken care of in education. The business whereof in respect of knowledge is not, as I think, to perfect a learner in all or any one of the sciences, but to give his mind that freedom, that disposition, and those habits that may enable him to attain any part of knowledge he shall apply himself to, or stand in need of, in the future course of his life.

This and this only is well principling, and not the instilling a reverence and veneration for certain dogmas under the specious title of principles, which are often so remote from that truth and evidence which belongs to principles that they ought to be rejected as false and erroneous, and is often the cause, to men so educated, when they come abroad into the world, and find they cannot maintain the principles so taken up and rested in, to cast off all principles and turn perfect skeptics, regardless of knowledge and virtue.

There are several weaknesses and defects in the understanding, either from the natural temper of the mind or ill habits taken up, which hinder it in its progress to knowledge. Of these there are as many possibly to be found, if the mind were thoroughly studied, as there are diseases of the body, each whereof clogs and disables the understanding to some degree, and therefore deserves to be looked after and cured. I shall set down some few to excite men, especially those who make knowledge their business, to look into themselves, and observe whether they do not indulge some weakness, allow some miscarriages in the management of their intellectual faculty, which is prejudicial to them in the search of truth.

§13. Particular matters of fact are the undoubted foundations on *Observation.* which our civil and natural knowledge is built; the benefit the understanding makes of them is to draw from them conclusions, which may be as standing rules of knowledge, and consequently of practice. The mind often makes not that benefit it should of the information it receives from the accounts of civil or natural historians, in being too forward or too slow in making observations on the particular facts recorded in them.

There are those who are very assiduous in reading, and yet do not much advance their knowledge by it. They are delighted with the stories that are told, and perhaps can tell them again, for they make all they read nothing but history to themselves; but not reflecting on it, not making to themselves observations from what they read, they are very little improved by all that crowd of particulars that either pass through or lodge themselves in their understandings. They dream on in a constant course of reading and cramming themselves, but, not digesting anything, it produces nothing but a heap of crudities.

If their memories retain well, one may say they have the materials of knowledge, but, like those for building, they are of no advantage, if there be no other use made of them but to let them lie heaped up together. Opposite to these there are others who lose the improvement they should make of matters of fact by a quite contrary conduct. They are apt to draw general conclusions, and raise axioms from every particular they meet with. These make as little true benefit of history as the other, nay, being of forward and active spirits, receive more harm by it; it being of worse consequence to steer one's thoughts by a wrong rule than to have none at all, error doing to busy men much more harm than ignorance to the slow and sluggish. Between these, those seem to do best who taking material and useful hints, sometimes from single matters of fact, carry them in their minds to be judged of by what they shall find in history to confirm or reverse these imperfect observations; which may be established into rules fit to be relied on, when they are justified by a sufficient and wary induction of particulars. He that makes no such reflections on what he reads, only loads his mind with a rhapsody of tales fit in winter nights for the entertainment of others; and he that will improve every matter of fact into a maxim, will abound in contrary observations, that can be of no other use but to perplex and pudder him, if he compares them, or else to misguide him, if he gives himself up to the authority of that which for its novelty, or for some other fancy, best pleases him.

*Bias.*     §14. Next to these we may place those who suffer their own natural tempers and passions they are possessed with to influence their judgments, especially of men and things that may any way relate to their present circumstances and interest. Truth is all simple, all pure, will bear no mixture of anything else with it. It is rigid and inflexible to any bye interests; and so should the understanding be, whose use and excellency lies in conforming itself to it. To think of everything just as it is in itself is the proper business of the understanding, though it be not that which men always employ it to. This all men, at first hearing, allow is the right use everyone should make of his understanding. Nobody will be at such an open defiance with common sense, as to profess that we should not endeavor to know and think of things as they are in themselves, and yet there is nothing more frequent than to do the contrary. And men are apt to excuse themselves, and think they have reason to do so, if they have but a pretense that it is for God, or a good cause, that is, in effect, for themselves, their own persuasion, or party; for to those in their turns the several sects of men, especially in matters of religion, entitle God and a good cause. But God requires not men to wrong or misuse their faculties for Him, nor to lie to others or themselves for His sake; which they purposely do, who will not suffer their understandings to have right conceptions of the things proposed to them, and designedly restrain themselves from having just thoughts of everything, as far as they are concerned to enquire. And as for a good cause, that needs not such ill helps, if it be good, truth will support it, and it has no need of fallacy or falsehood.

§15. Very much of kin to this is the hunting after arguments to make *Arguments.* good one side of a question, and wholly to neglect and refuse those which favor the other side. What is this but wilfully to misguide the understanding? And [it] is so far from giving truth its due value, that it wholly debases it. [Men] espouse opinions that best comport with their power, profit, or credit, and then seek arguments to support them. Truth, light upon this way, is of no more avail to us than error; for what is so taken up by us may be false as well as true, and he has not done his duty who has thus stumbled upon truth in his way to preferment.

There is another, but more innocent way of collecting arguments, very familiar among bookish men, which is to furnish themselves with the arguments they meet with pro and con in the questions they study. This helps them not to judge right, nor argue strongly, but only to talk copiously on either side, without being steady and settled in their own judgments: for such arguments gathered from other men's thoughts, floating only in the memory, are there ready indeed to supply copious talk with some appearance of reason, but are far from helping us to judge right. Such variety of arguments only distract the understanding that relies on them, unless it has gone farther than such a superficial way of examining; this is to quit truth for appearance, only to serve our vanity. The sure and only way to get true knowledge is to form in our minds clear settled notions of things, with names annexed to those determined ideas. These we are to consider, and with their several relations and habitudes, and not amuse[23] ourselves with floating names, and words of undetermined signification, which we can use in several senses to serve a turn. It is in the perception of the habitudes and respects our ideas have one to another that real knowledge con-

23. Beguile, or mislead.

sists; and when a man once perceives how far they agree or disagree one
with another, he will be able to judge of what other people say, and will not
need to be led by the arguments of others, which are many of them nothing
but plausible sophistry. This will teach him to state the question right, and
see whereon it turns; and thus he will stand upon his own legs, and know
by his own understanding. Whereas by collecting and learning arguments
by heart, he will be but a retainer to others; and when anyone questions the
foundations they are built upon, he will be at a nonplus, and be fain to give
up his implicit knowledge.

*Haste.*        §16. Labor for labor['s] sake is against nature. The understanding, as
well as all the other faculties, chooses always the shortest way to its end,
would presently obtain the knowledge it is about, and then set upon some
new inquiry. But this whether laziness or haste often misleads it, and
makes it content itself with improper ways of search and such as will not
serve the turn. Sometimes it rests upon testimony, when testimony of
right has nothing to do, because it is easier to believe than to be scientifi-
cally instructed. Sometimes it contents itself with one argument, and rests
satisfied with that, as [if] it were a demonstration; whereas the thing under
proof is not capable of demonstration, and therefore must be submitted to
the trial of probabilities, and all the material arguments pro and con be
examined and brought to a balance. In some cases the mind is determined
by probable topics in inquiries, where demonstration may be had. All
these, and several others, which laziness, impatience, custom, and want of
use and attention lead men into, are misapplications of the understanding
in the search of truth. In every question, the nature and manner of the
proof it is capable of should first be considered to make our inquiry such
as it should be. This would save a great deal of frequently misemployed
pains, and lead us sooner to that discovery and possession of truth we are
capable of. The multiplying variety of arguments, especially frivolous
ones, such as are all that are merely verbal, is not only lost labor, but cum-
bers the memory to no purpose, and serves only to hinder it from seizing
and holding of the truth in all those cases which are capable of demonstration. In such a way of proof the truth and certainty is seen, and the mind
fully possesses itself of it; when in the other way of assent, it only hovers
about it, is amused with uncertainties. In this superficial way, indeed, the
mind is capable of more variety of plausible talk, but is not enlarged as it
should be in its knowledge. It is to this same haste and impatience of the
mind also that a not due tracing of the arguments to their true foundation
is owing; men see a little, presume a great deal, and so jump to the conclusion. This is a short way to fancy and conceit, and (if firmly embraced) to

opinionatedness, but is certainly the farthest way about to knowledge. For he that will know must by the connection of the proofs see the truth, and the ground it stands on; and, therefore, if he has for haste skipped over what he should have examined, he must begin and go over all again, or else he will never come to knowledge.

§17. Another fault of as ill consequence as this, which proceeds also *Desultory.* from laziness with a mixture of vanity, is the skipping from one sort of knowledge to another. Some men's tempers are quickly weary of any one thing. Constancy and assiduity is what they cannot bear: the same study long continued in is as intolerable to them, as the appearing long in the same clothes or fashion is to a court lady.

§18. Others, that they may seem universally knowing, get a little *Smattering.* smattering in everything. Both these may fill their heads with superficial notions of things, but are very much out of the way of attaining truth or knowledge.

§19. I do not here speak against the taking a taste of every sort of *Universality.* knowledge; it is certainly very useful and necessary to form the mind, but then it must be done in a different way and to a different end. Not for talk and vanity to fill the head with shreds of all kinds, that he, who is possessed of such a frippery, may be able to match the discourses of all he shall meet with, as if nothing could come amiss to him, and his head was so well stored a magazine, that nothing could be proposed which he was not master of and was readily furnished to entertain anyone on. This is an excellency indeed, and a great one too, to have a real and true knowledge in all or most of the objects of contemplation. But it is what the mind of one and the same man can hardly attain unto; and the instances are so few of those who have in any measure approached towards it, that I know not whether they are to be proposed as examples in the ordinary conduct of the understanding. For a man to understand fully the business of his particular calling in the commonwealth, and of religion, which is his calling as he is a man in the world, is usually enough to take up his whole time; and there are few that inform themselves in these, which is every man's proper and peculiar business, so to the bottom as they should do. But though this be so, and there are very few men that extend their thoughts towards universal knowledge, yet I do not doubt but if the right way were taken, and the methods of enquiry were ordered as they should be, men of little business and great leisure might go a great deal farther in it than is usually done. To return to the business in hand, the end and use of a little insight in those parts of knowledge, which are not a man's proper business, is to accustom our minds to all sorts of ideas and the proper ways of examining their habitudes and relations. This gives the mind a freedom, and the exercising the understanding in the several ways of inquiry and reasoning, which the most skilful have made use of, teaches the mind sagacity and wariness, and a suppleness to apply itself more closely and dexterously to the bents and turns of the matter in all its researches. Besides, this universal taste of all the sciences, with an indifferency before the mind is possessed with any-one in particular and grown into love and admiration of what is made its darling, will prevent another evil very commonly to be observed in those who have from the beginning been seasoned only by one part of knowl-edge. Let a man be given up to the contemplation of one sort of knowledge, and that will become everything. The mind will take such a tincture from a familiarity with that object, that everything else, how remote soever, will be brought under the same view. A metaphysician will bring plowing and gardening immediately to abstract notions; the history of nature shall sig-nify nothing to him. An alchemist, on the contrary, shall reduce divinity to the maxims of his laboratory, explain morality by sal, sulphur, and mer-cury, and allegorize the Scripture itself, and the sacred mysteries thereof, into the philosopher's stone.[24] And I heard once a man, who had a more than ordinary excellency in music, seriously accommodate Moses' seven days of the first week to the notes of music, as if from thence had been taken the measure and method of the creation. It is of no small conse-quence to keep the mind from such a possession, which I think is best done by giving it a fair and equal view of the whole intellectual world, wherein it may see the order, rank, and beauty of the whole, and give a just allow-ance to the distinct provinces of the several sciences in the due order and usefulness of each of them.

If this be that which old men will not think necessary, nor be easily brought to, it is fit at least that it should be practiced in the breeding of the young. The business of education, as I have already observed, is not, as I think, to make them perfect in any one of the sciences, but so to open and dispose their minds as may best make them capable of any, when they shall apply themselves to it. If men are for a long time accustomed only to one sort or method of thoughts, their minds grow stiff in it, and do not readily turn to another. It is therefore to give them this freedom, that I think they should be made [to] look into all sorts of knowledge, and exercise their understandings in so wide a variety and stock of knowledge. But I do not

24. A stone or substance sought by alchemists, who believed that it would have the power to turn base metals into gold; by analogy, a principle or concept capable of achieving the spiritual regeneration of man.

propose it as a variety and stock of knowledge, but a variety and freedom of thinking, as an increase of the powers and activity of the mind, not as an enlargement of its possessions.

§20. This is that which I think great readers are apt to be mistaken in. *Reading.* Those who have read of everything are thought to understand everything too; but it is not always so. Reading furnishes the mind only with materials of knowledge; it is thinking makes what we read ours. We are of the ruminating kind, and it is not enough to cram ourselves with a great load of collections; unless we chew them over again, they will not give us strength and nourishment. There are indeed in some writers visible instances of deep thoughts, close and acute reasoning, and ideas well pursued. The light these would give, would be of great use, if their readers would observe and imitate them; all the rest at best are but particulars fit to be turned into knowledge, but that can be done only by our own meditation, and examining the reach, force, and coherence of what is said; and then, as far as we apprehend and see the connection of ideas, so far it is ours; without that, it is but so much loose matter floating in our brain. The memory may be stored, but the judgment is little better, and the stock of knowledge not increased, by being able to repeat what others have said or produce the arguments we have found in them. Such a knowledge as this is but knowledge by hearsay, and the ostentation of it is at best but talking by rote, and very often upon weak and wrong principles. For all that is to be found in books is not built upon true foundations, nor always rightly deduced from the principles it is pretended to be built on. Such an examination as is requisite to discover that, every reader's mind is not forward to make; especially in those who have given themselves up to a party, and only hunt for what they can scrape together that may favor and support the tenets of it. Such men wilfully exclude themselves from truth and from all true benefit to be received by reading. Others of more indifferency often want attention and industry. The mind is backward in itself to be at the pains to trace every argument to its origin, and to see upon what basis it stands, and how firmly; but yet it is this that gives so much the advantage to one man more than another in reading. The mind should, by severe rules, be tied down to this at first uneasy task; use and exercise will give it facility. So that those who are accustomed to it, readily, as it were with one cast of the eye, take a view of the argument, and presently, in most cases, see where it bottoms. Those who have got this faculty, one may say, have got the true key of books, and the clue to lead them through the mizmaze of variety of opinions and authors to truth and certainty. This young beginners should be entered in, and showed the use of, that they might profit by their reading.

Those who are strangers to it will be apt to think it too great a clog in the way of men's studies, and they will suspect they shall make but small progress, if, in the books they read, they must stand to examine and unravel every argument and follow it step by step up to its origin.

I answer, this is a good objection, and ought to weigh with those whose reading is designed for much talk and little knowledge, and I have nothing to say to it. But I am here inquiring into the conduct of the understanding in its progress towards knowledge; and to those who aim at that, I may say that he, who fair and softly goes steadily forward in a course that points right, will sooner be at his journey's end, than he that runs after everyone he meets, though he gallop all day full speed.

To which let me add, that this way of thinking on and profiting by what we read will be a clog and rub to anyone only in the beginning; when custom and exercise has made it familiar, it will be dispatched in most occasions, without resting or interruption in the course of our reading. The motions and views of a mind exercised that way are wonderfully quick; and a man, used to such sort of reflections, sees as much at one glimpse as would require a long discourse to lay before another and make out in an entire and gradual deduction. Besides, that when the first difficulties are over, the delight and sensible advantage it brings mightily encourages and enlivens the mind in reading, which without this is very improperly called study.

*Intermediate*     §21. As a help to this, I think it may be proposed that, for the saving
*Principles.*     the long progression of the thoughts to remote and first principles in every case, the mind should provide itself several stages; that is to say, intermediate principles, which it might have recourse to in the examining those positions that come in its way. These, though they are not self-evident principles, yet, if they have been made out from them by a wary and unquestionable deduction, may be depended on as certain and infallible truths, and serve as unquestionable truths to prove other points depending on them by a nearer and shorter view than remote and general maxims. These may serve as landmarks to show what lies in the direct way of truth, or is quite besides it. And thus mathematicians do, who do not in every new problem run it back to the first axioms, through all the whole train of intermediate propositions. Certain theorems, that they have settled to themselves upon sure demonstration, serve to resolve to them multitudes of propositions which depend on them, and are as firmly made out from thence, as if the mind went afresh over every link of the whole chain that ties them to first self-evident principles. Only in other sciences great care is to be taken that they establish those intermediate principles with as

much caution, exactness, and indifference, as mathematicians use in the settling any of their great theorems. When this is not done, but men take up the principles in this or that science upon credit, inclination, interest, &c. in haste, without due examination and most unquestionable proof, they lay a trap for themselves, and as much as in them lies captivate their understandings to mistake, falsehood, and error.

§22. As there is a partiality to opinions, which, as we have already   *Partiality.* observed, is apt to mislead the understanding, so there is often a partiality to studies, which is prejudicial also to knowledge and improvement. Those sciences which men are particularly versed in they are apt to value and extol, as if that part of knowledge which everyone has acquainted himself with were that alone which was worth the having, and all the rest were idle and empty amusements, comparatively of no use or importance. This is the effect of ignorance and not knowledge, the being vainly puffed up with a flatulency arising from a weak and narrow comprehension. It is not amiss that everyone should relish the science that he has made his peculiar study; a view of its beauties and a sense of its usefulness carries a man on with the more delight and warmth in the pursuit and improvement of it. But the contempt of all other knowledge, as if it were nothing in comparison of law or physic, of astronomy or chemistry, or perhaps some yet meaner part of knowledge, wherein I have got some smattering, or am somewhat advanced, is not only the mark of a vain or little mind, but does this prejudice in the conduct of the understanding, that it coops it up within narrow bounds, and hinders it from looking abroad into other provinces of the intellectual world, more beautiful possibly, and more fruitful than that which it had until then labored in; wherein it might find, besides new knowledge, ways or hints whereby it might be enabled the better to cultivate its own.

§23. There is indeed one science (as they are now distinguished) incom-   *Theology.* parably above all the rest, where it is not by corruption narrowed into a trade or faction, for mean or ill ends and secular interests; I mean theology, which, containing the knowledge of God and His creatures, our duty to Him and our fellow-creatures, and a view of our present and future state, is the comprehension of all other knowledge directed to its true end, i.e. the honor and veneration of the Creator and the happiness of mankind. This is that noble study which is every man's duty, and everyone that can be called a rational creature is capable of. The works of nature and the words of revelation display it to mankind in characters so large and visible, that those who are not quite blind may in them read and see the first principles and most necessary parts of it; and from thence, as they have time and industry, may be enabled to go on to the more abstruse parts of it, and penetrate into those infinite depths filled with the treasures of wisdom and knowledge. This is that science which would truly enlarge men's minds, were it studied, or permitted to be studied, everywhere with that freedom, love of truth and charity, which it teaches, and were not made, contrary to its nature, the occasion of strife, faction, malignity, and narrow impositions. I shall say no more here of this, but that it is undoubtedly a wrong use of my understanding to make it the rule and measure of another man's; a use which it is neither fit for nor capable of.

*Partiality.*     §24. This partiality, where it is not permitted an authority to render all other studies insignificant or contemptible, is often indulged so far as to be relied upon and made use of in other parts of knowledge, to which it does not at all belong, and wherewith it has no manner of affinity. Some men have so used their heads to mathematical figures that, giving a preference to the methods of that science, they introduce lines and diagrams into their study of divinity or politic enquiries, as if nothing could be known without them; and others, accustomed to retired speculations, run natural philosophy into metaphysical notions and the abstract generalities of logic; and how often may one meet with religion and morality treated of in the terms of the laboratory, and thought to be improved by the methods and notions of chemistry. But he that will take care of the conduct of his understanding, to direct it right to the knowledge of things, must avoid those undue mixtures, and not by a fondness for what he has found useful and necessary in one transfer it to another science, where it serves only to perplex and confound the understanding. It is a certain truth that *res nolunt male administrari*; it is no less certain, *res nolunt male intelligi.*[25] Things themselves are to be considered as they are in themselves, and then they will show us in what way they are to be understood. For to have right conceptions about them, we must bring our understandings to the inflexible natures and unalterable relations of things, and not endeavor to bring things to any preconceived notions of our own.

There is another partiality very commonly observable in men of study, no less prejudicial nor ridiculous than the former; and that is a fantastical and wild attributing all knowledge to the ancients alone, or to the moderns. This raving upon antiquity in matter of poetry, Horace has wittily described and exposed in one of his satires. The same sort of madness may be found in reference to all the other sciences. Some will not admit an

25. "Things are unwilling to be badly managed" and "things are unwilling to be badly understood."

opinion not authorized by men of old, who were then all giants in knowledge: nothing is to be put into the treasury of truth or knowledge, which has not the stamp of Greece or Rome upon it; and since their days will scarce allow that men have been able to see, think, or write. Others, with a like extravagancy, contemn all that the ancients have left us, and, being taken with the modern inventions and discoveries, lay by all that went before, as if whatever is called old must have the decay of time upon it, and truth too were liable to mould and rottenness. Men, I think, have been much the same for natural endowments in all times. Fashion, discipline, and education have put eminent differences in the ages of several countries, and made one generation much differ from another in arts and sciences: but truth is always the same; time alters it not, nor is it the better or worse for being of ancient or modern tradition. Many were eminent in former ages of the world for their discovery and delivery of it; but though the knowledge they have left us be worth our study, yet they exhausted not all its treasure; they left a great deal for the industry and sagacity of after ages, and so shall we. That was once new to them which anyone now receives with veneration for its antiquity; nor was it the worse for appearing as a novelty, and that which is now embraced for its newness will, to posterity, be old, but not thereby be less true or less genuine. There is no occasion on this account to oppose the ancients and the moderns to one another, or to be squeamish on either side. He that wisely conducts his mind in the pursuit of knowledge will gather what lights, and get what helps he can, from either of them, from whom they are best to be had, without adoring the errors or rejecting the truths which he may find mingled in them.

Another partiality may be observed, in some to vulgar, in others to heterodox tenets: some are apt to conclude that what is the common opinion cannot but be true; so many men's eyes they think cannot but see right; so many men's understandings of all sorts cannot be deceived, and therefore [they] will not venture to look beyond the received notions of the place and age, nor have so presumptuous a thought as to be wiser than their neighbors. They are content to go with the crowd, and so go easily, which they think is going right, or at least serves them as well. But however *vox populi vox Dei*[26] has prevailed as maxim, yet I do not remember wherever God

26. "The voice of the people is the voice of God." The phrase generally referred to the political will of the people. It had been used as the text of a sermon by Walter Reynolds, Archbishop of Canterbury, early in the fourteenth century, at the coronation of Edward III.

delivered his oracles by the multitude, or Nature truths by the herd. On the other side, some fly all common opinions as either false or frivolous. The title of many-headed beast is a sufficient reason to them to conclude that no truths of weight or consequence can be lodged there. Vulgar opinions are suited to vulgar capacities, and adapted to the ends of those that govern. He that will know the truth of things must leave the common and beaten track,[27] which none but weak and servile minds are satisfied to trudge along continually in. Such nice palates relish nothing but strange notions quite out of the way: whatever is commonly received has the mark of the beast on it, and they think it a lessening to them to hearken to it, or receive it; their mind runs only after paradoxes; these they seek, these they embrace, these alone they vent, and so, as they think, distinguish themselves from the vulgar. But common or uncommon are not the marks to distinguish truth or falsehood, and therefore should not be any bias to us in our enquiries. We should not judge of things by men's opinions, but of opinions by things. The multitude reason but ill, and therefore may be well suspected, and cannot be relied on, nor should be followed as a sure guide, but philosophers who have quitted the orthodoxy of the community, and the popular doctrines of their countries, have fallen into as extravagant and as absurd opinions as ever common reception countenanced. It would be madness to refuse to breathe the common air, or quench one's thirst with water, because the rabble use them to these purposes; and, if there are conveniences of life which common use reaches not, it is not reason to reject them, because they are not grown into the ordinary fashion of the country, and every villager does not know them.

Truth, whether in or out of fashion, is the measure of knowledge, and the business of the understanding; whatsoever is besides that, however authorized by consent or recommended by rarity, is nothing but ignorance, or something worse.

Another sort of partiality there is, whereby men impose upon themselves, and by it make their reading little useful to themselves; I mean the making use of the opinions of writers, and laying stress upon their authorities, wherever they find them to favor their own opinions.

There is nothing almost has done more harm to men dedicated to letters than giving the name of study to reading, and making a man of great reading to be the same with a man of great knowledge, or at least to be a title of honor. All that can be recorded in writing are only facts or reasonings. Facts are of three sorts:

27. In the original, the word here is "tract."

1. Merely of natural agents, observable in the ordinary operations of bodies one upon another, whether in the visible course of things left to themselves, or in experiments made by men applying agents and patients to one another, after a peculiar and artificial manner.

2. Of voluntary agents, more especially the actions of men in society, which makes civil and moral history.

3. Of opinions.

In these three consists, as it seems to me, that which commonly has the name of learning; to which perhaps some may add a distinct head of critical writings, which indeed at bottom is nothing but matter of fact, and resolves itself into this, that such a man, or set of men, used such a word or phrase in such a sense, i.e. that they made such sounds the marks of such ideas.

Under reasonings I comprehend all the discoveries of general truths made by human reason, whether found by intuition, demonstration, or probable deductions. And this is that which is, if not alone knowledge (because the truth or probability of particular propositions may be known too), yet is, as may be supposed, most properly the business of those who pretend to improve their understandings and make themselves knowing by reading.

Books and reading are looked upon to be the great helps of the understanding and instruments of knowledge, as it must be allowed that they are; and yet I beg leave to question whether these do not prove a hindrance to many, and keep several bookish men from attaining to solid and true knowledge. This, I think, I may be permitted to say, that there is no part wherein the understanding needs a more careful and wary conduct than in the use of books; without which they will prove rather innocent amusements than profitable employments of our time, and bring but small additions to our knowledge.

There is not seldom to be found even amongst those who aim at knowledge, who with an unwearied industry employ their whole time in books, who scarce allow themselves time to eat or sleep, but read, and read, and read on, but yet make no great advances in real knowledge, though there be no defect in their intellectual faculties, to which their little progress can be imputed. The mistake here is, that it is usually supposed that, by reading, the author's knowledge is transfused into the reader's understanding; and so it is, but not by bare reading, but by reading and understanding what he wrote. Whereby I mean, not barely comprehending what is affirmed or denied in each proposition (though that great readers do not always think themselves concerned precisely to do), but to see and follow

the train of his reasonings, observe the strength and clearness of their connection, and examine upon what they bottom. Without this, a man may
read the discourses of a very rational author, writ in a language and in
propositions that he very well understands, and yet acquire not one jot of
his knowledge; which consisting only in the perceived, certain, or probable
connection of the ideas made use of in his reasonings, the reader's knowledge is no farther increased than he perceives that, so much as he sees of
this connection, so much he knows of the truth or probability of that
author's opinions.

All that he relies on without this perception, he takes upon trust upon
the author's credit, without any knowledge of it at all. This makes me not
at all wonder to see some men so abound in citations, and build so much
upon authorities, it being the sole foundation on which they bottom most
of their own tenets; so that in effect they have but a second hand or implicit
knowledge, i.e. are in the right, if such an one from whom they borrowed
it were in the right in that opinion which they took from him, which
indeed is no knowledge at all. Writers of this or former ages may be good
witnesses of matters of fact which they deliver, which we may do well to
take upon their authority; but their credit can go no farther than this, it
cannot at all affect the truth and falsehood of opinions, which have no
other sort of trial but reason and proof, which they themselves made use
of to make themselves knowing, and so must others too that will partake in
their knowledge. Indeed it is an advantage that they have been at the pains
to find out the proofs, and lay them in that order that may show the truth
or probability of their conclusions; and for this we owe them great
acknowledgments for saving us the pains in searching out those proofs
which they have collected for us, and which possibly, after all our pains,
we might not have found, nor been able to have set them in so good a light
as that which they left them us in. Upon this account we are mightily
beholden to judicious writers of all ages for those discoveries and discourses they have left behind them for our instruction, if we know how to
make a right use of them; which is not to run them over in a hasty perusal,
and perhaps lodge their opinions or some remarkable passages in our
memories, but to enter into their reasonings, examine their proofs, and
then judge of the truth or falsehood, probability or improbability of what
they advance, not by any opinion we have entertained of the author, but by
the evidence he produces and the conviction he affords us, drawn from
things themselves. Knowing is seeing, and, if it be so, it is madness to persuade ourselves that we do so by another man's eyes, let him use ever so
many words to tell us that what he asserts is very visible. Until we our-

selves see it with our own eyes, and perceive it by our own understandings, we are as much in the dark and as void of knowledge as before, let us believe any learned author as much as we will.

Euclid[28] and Archimedes[29] are allowed to be knowing, and to have demonstrated what they say; and yet, whoever shall read over their writings without perceiving the connection of their proofs, and seeing what they show, though he may understand all their words, yet he is not the more knowing: he may believe indeed, but does not know what they say, and so is not advanced one jot in mathematical knowledge by all his reading of those approved mathematicians.

§25. The eagerness and strong bent of the mind after knowledge, if not warily regulated, is often a hindrance to it. It still presses into farther discoveries and new objects, and catches at the variety of knowledge, and therefore often stays not long enough on what is before it to look into it as it should, for haste to pursue what is yet out of sight. He that rides post through a country may be able, from the transient view, to tell how in general the parts lie, and may be able to give some loose description of here a mountain and there a plain, here a morass and there a river, woodland in one part and savannas in another. Such superficial ideas and observations as these he may collect in galloping over it. But the more useful observations of the soil, plants, animals, and inhabitants, with their several sorts and properties, must necessarily escape him; and it is seldom men ever discover the rich mines, without some digging. Nature commonly lodges her treasure and jewels in rocky ground. If the matter be knotty, and the sense lies deep, the mind must stop and buckle to it, and stick upon it with labor and thought and close contemplation, and not leave it until it has mastered the difficulty, and got possession of truth. But here care must be taken to avoid the other extreme: a man must not stick at every useless nicety, and expect mysteries of science in every trivial question or scruple that he may raise. He that will stand to pick up and examine every pebble that comes in his way is as unlikely to return enriched and loaded with jewels, as the other that travelled full speed. Truths are not the better nor the worse for their obviousness or difficulty, but their value is to be measured by their usefulness and tendency. Insignificant observations should not take up any of our minutes, and those that enlarge our view, and give light towards far-

*Haste.*

28. Euclid (ca. 300 B.C.) was a Greek geometrician and educator in Alexandria. His famous book of geometrical proofs is called the *Elements*.

29. Archimedes (ca. 287–212 B.C.) was a Greek mathematician, physicist, and inventor noted for his discovery of the principle of the lever.

ther and useful discoveries, should not be neglected, though they stop our course, and spend some of our time in a fixed attention.

There is another haste that does often and will mislead the mind, if it be left to itself and its own conduct. The understanding is naturally forward, not only to learn its knowledge by variety (which makes it skip over one to get speedily to another part of knowledge), but also eager to enlarge its views by running too fast into general observations and conclusions, without a due examination of particulars enough whereon to found those general axioms. This seems to enlarge their stock, but it is of fancies not realities; such theories built upon narrow foundations stand but weakly, and, if they fall not of themselves, are at least very hard to be supported against the assaults of opposition. And thus men, being too hasty to erect to themselves general notions and ill-grounded theories, find themselves deceived in their stock of knowledge, when they come to examine their hastily assumed maxims themselves, or to have them attacked by others. General observations drawn from particulars are the jewels of knowledge, comprehending great store in a little room; but they are therefore to be made with the greater care and caution, lest, if we take counterfeit for true, our loss and shame be the greater when our stock comes to a severe scrutiny. One or two particulars may suggest hints of enquiry, and they do well who take those hints; but if they turn them into conclusions, and make them presently general rules, they are forward indeed, but it is only to impose on themselves by propositions assumed for truths without sufficient warrant. To make such observations is, as has been already remarked, to make the head a magazine of materials which can hardly be called knowledge, or at least it is but like a collection of lumber not reduced to use or order; and he that makes everything an observation has the same useless plenty and much more falsehood mixed with it. The extremes on both sides are to be avoided, and he will be able to give the best account of his studies who keeps his understanding in the right mean between them.

*Anticipation.*   §26. Whether it be a love of that which brings the first light and information to their minds, and want of vigor and industry to enquire, or else that men content themselves with any appearance of knowledge, right or wrong, which, when they have once got, they will hold fast: this is visible, that many men give themselves up to the first anticipations of their minds, and are very tenacious of the opinions that first possess them; they are often as fond of their first conceptions as of their first born, and will by no means recede from the judgment they have once made, or any conjecture or conceit which they have once entertained. This is a fault in the conduct of the understanding, since this firmness or rather stiffness of the mind is not from an adherence to truth but a submission to prejudice. It is an unreasonable homage paid to prepossession, whereby we show a reverence not to (what we pretend to seek) truth; but what by hap-hazard we chance to light on, be it what it will. This is visibly a preposterous use of our faculties, and is a downright prostituting of the mind to resign it thus, and put it under the power of the first comer. This can never be allowed or ought to be followed as a right way to knowledge, until the understanding (whose business it is to conform itself to what it finds on the objects without) can by its own opinionatedness change that, and make the unalterable nature of things comply with its own hasty determinations, which will never be. Whatever we fancy, things keep their course; and their habitudes, correspondences, and relations keep the same to one another.

§27. Contrary to these, but by a like dangerous excess on the other *Resignation.* side, are those who always resign their judgment to the last man they heard or read. Truth never sinks into these men's minds, nor gives any tincture to them, but, chameleon-like, they take the color of what is laid before them, and as soon lose and resign it to the next that happens to come in their way. The order wherein opinions are proposed or received by us is no rule of their rectitude, nor ought to be a cause of their preference. First or last in this case is the effect of chance, and not the measure of truth or falsehood. This everyone must confess, and therefore should, in the pursuit of truth, keep his mind free from the influence of any such accidents. A man may as reasonably draw cuts for his tenets, regulate his persuasion by the cast of a die, as take it up for its novelty, or retain it because it had his first assent and he was never of another mind. Well-weighed reasons are to determine the judgment; those the mind should be always ready to hearken and submit to, and by their testimony and suffrage entertain or reject any tenet indifferently, whether it be a perfect stranger or an old acquaintance.

§28. Though the faculties of the mind are improved by exercise, yet *Practice.* they must not be put to a stress beyond their strength. *Quid valeant humeri, quid ferre recusent,*[30] must be made the measure of everyone's understanding, who has a desire not only to perform well, but to keep up the vigor of his faculties, and not to balk his understanding by what is too hard for it. The mind by being engaged in a task beyond its strength, like the body strained by lifting at a weight too heavy, has often its force broken, and thereby gets an inaptness or an aversion to any vigorous attempt ever after. A sinew cracked seldom recovers its former strength, or at least the ten-

30. "What shoulders are strong enough for, what they refuse to bear," Horace *De Arte Poetica* 39–40.

derness of the sprain remains a good while after, and the memory of it longer, and leaves a lasting caution in the man not to put the part quickly again to any robust employment. So it fares in the mind once jaded by an attempt above its power; it either is disabled for the future, or else checks at any vigorous undertaking ever after, at least is very hardly brought to exert its force again on any subject that requires thought and meditation. The understanding should be brought to the difficult and knotty parts of knowledge, that try the strength of thought and a full bent of the mind, by insensible degrees; and in such a gradual proceeding nothing is too hard for it. Nor let it be objected, that such a slow progress will never reach the extent of some sciences. It is not to be imagined how far constancy will carry a man; however, it is better walking slowly in a rugged way, than to break a leg and be a cripple. He that begins with the calf may carry the ox; but he that will at first go to take up an ox, may so disable himself, as not [to] be able to lift a calf after that. When the mind, by insensible degrees, has brought itself to attention and close thinking, it will be able to cope with difficulties, and master them without any prejudice to itself, and then it may go on roundly. Every abstruse problem, every intricate question will not baffle, discourage, or break it. But though putting the mind unprepared upon an unusual stress that may discourage or damp it for the future ought to be avoided, yet this must not run it, by an over great shyness of difficulties, into a lazy sauntering about ordinary and obvious things that demand no thought or application. This debases and enervates the understanding, makes it weak and unfit for labor. This is a sort of hovering about the surface of things, without any insight into them or penetration; and, when the mind has been once habituated to this lazy recumbency and satisfaction on the obvious surface of things, it is in danger to rest satisfied there, and go no deeper, since it cannot do it without pains and digging. He that has for some time accustomed himself to take up with what easily offers itself at first view, has reason to fear he shall never reconcile himself to the fatigue of turning and tumbling things in his mind to discover their more retired and more valuable secrets.

It is not strange that methods of learning, which scholars have been accustomed to in their beginning and entrance upon the sciences, should influence them all their lives, and be settled in their minds by an overruling reverence, especially if they be such as universal use has established. Learners must at first be believers, and, their masters' rules having been once made axioms to them, it is no wonder they should keep that dignity, and, by the authority they have once got, mislead those who think it sufficient to excuse them, if they go out of their way in a well beaten track.

§29. I have copiously enough spoken of the abuse of words in another place, and therefore shall upon this reflection, that the sciences are full of them, warn those that would conduct their understandings right, not to take any term, howsoever authorized by the language of the Schools, to stand for anything until they have an idea of it.[31] A word may be of frequent use and great credit with several authors, and be by them made use of, as if it stood for some real being; but yet if he that reads cannot frame any distinct idea of that being, it is certainly to him a mere empty sound without a meaning, and he learns no more by all that is said of it or attributed to it, than if it were affirmed only of that bare empty sound. They who would advance in knowledge, and not deceive and swell themselves with a little articulated air, should lay down this as a fundamental rule, not to take words for things, nor suppose that names in books signify real entities in nature, until they can frame clear and distinct ideas of those entities. It will not perhaps be allowed if I should set down *substantial forms* and *intentional species*,[32] as such that may justly be suspected to be of this kind of insignificant terms. But this I am sure, to one that can form no determined ideas of what they stand for, they signify nothing at all; and all that he thinks he knows about them is to him so much knowledge about nothing, and amounts at most but to a learned ignorance. It is not without all reason supposed, that there are many such empty terms to be found in some learned writers, to which they had recourse to etch out their systems where their understandings could not furnish them with conceptions from things. But yet I believe the supposing of some realities in nature, answering those and the like words, have much perplexed some, and quite misled others in the study of nature. That which in any discourse signifies, *I know not what*, should be considered *I know not when*. Where men have any conceptions, they can, if they are ever so abstruse or abstracted, explain them, and the terms they use for them. For our conceptions being nothing but ideas, which are all made up of simple ones, if they cannot give us the ideas their words stand for, it is plain they have none. To what purpose can it be to hunt after his conceptions, who has none, or none distinct? He that knew not what he himself meant by a learned term, cannot make us know anything by his use of it, let us beat our heads about it ever so long. Whether we are able to comprehend all the operations of nature and the manners of them, it matters not to enquire; but this is certain, that we can

31. See *Essay*, III x.

32. These terms were associated with established philosophical doctrines in the Schools. See note 2 above and *Essay*, III vi 10, 24.

comprehend no more of them than we can distinctly conceive; and therefore to obtrude terms where we have no distinct conceptions, as if they did
contain or rather conceal something, is but an artifice of learned vanity, to
cover a defect in a hypothesis or our understandings. Words are not made
to conceal, but to declare and show something; where they are by those,
who pretend to instruct, otherwise used, they conceal indeed something,
but that which they conceal is nothing but the ignorance, error, or sophistry of the talker, for there is, in truth, nothing else under them.

*Wandering.*  §30. That there is constant succession and flux of ideas in our minds, I
have observed in the former part of this essay, and everyone may take
notice of it in himself. This I suppose may deserve some part of our care
in the conduct of our understandings; and I think it may be of great advantage, if we can by use get that power over our minds as to be able to direct
that train of ideas, that so, since there will new ones perpetually come into
our thoughts by a constant succession, we may be able by choice so to
direct them, that none may come in view, but such as are pertinent to our
present enquiry, and in such order as may be most useful to the discovery
we are upon; or at least, if some foreign and unsought ideas will offer
themselves, that yet we might be able to reject them, and keep them from
taking off our minds from its present pursuit, and hinder them from running away with our thoughts quite from the subject in hand. This is not, I
suspect, so easy to be done as perhaps may be imagined; and yet, for all I
know, this may be, if not the chief, yet one of the great differences that
carry some men in their reasoning so far beyond others, where they seem
to be naturally of equal parts. A proper and effectual remedy for this wandering of thoughts I would be glad to find. He that shall propose such an
one would do great service to the studious and contemplative part of mankind, and perhaps help unthinking men to become thinking. I must
acknowledge that hitherto I have discovered no other way to keep our
thoughts close to their business, but the endeavoring as much as we can,
and by frequent attention and application getting the habit of attention and
application. He that will observe children, will find that, even when they
endeavor their uttermost, they cannot keep their minds from straggling.
The way to cure it, I am satisfied, is not angry chiding or beating, for that
presently fills their heads with all the ideas that fear, dread, or confusion
can offer to them. To bring back gently their wandering thoughts, by leading them into the path and going before them in the train they should pursue, without any rebuke, or so much as taking notice (where it can be
avoided) of their roving, I suppose would sooner reconcile and inure them
to attention, than all those rougher methods which more distract their

thought, and, hindering the application they would promote, introduce a contrary habit.

§31. Distinction and division are (if I mistake not the import of the *Distinctions.* words) very different things: the one being the perception of a difference that nature has placed in things; the other our making a division where there is yet none. At least, if I may be permitted to consider them in this sense, I think I may say of them, that one of them is the most necessary and conducive to true knowledge that can be, the other, when too much made use of, serves only to puzzle and confound the understanding. To observe every the least difference that is in things argues a quick and clear sight, and this keeps the understanding steady and right in its way to knowledge. But though it be useful to discern every variety [that] is to be found in nature, yet it is not convenient to consider every difference that is in things, and divide them into distinct classes under every such difference. This will run us, if followed, into particulars (for every individual has something that differences it from another), and we shall be able to establish no general truths, or else at least shall be apt to perplex the mind about them. The collection of several things into several classes gives the mind more general and larger views; but we must take care to unite them only in that and so far as they do agree, for so far they may be united under the consideration. For entity itself, that comprehends all things, as general as it is, may afford us clear and rational conceptions. If we would well weigh and keep in our minds what it is we are considering, that would best instruct us when we should or should not branch into farther distinctions, which are to be taken only from a due contemplation of things; to which there is nothing more opposite than the art of verbal distinctions, made at pleasure, in learned and arbitrarily invented terms to be applied at a venture, without comprehending or conveying any distinct notions, and so altogether fitted to artificial talk or empty noise in dispute, without any clearing of difficulties or advance in knowledge. Whatsoever subject we examine and would get knowledge in, we should, I think, make as general and as large as it will bear; nor can there be any danger of this, if the idea of it be settled and determined: for, if that be so, we shall easily distinguish it from any other idea, though comprehended under the same name. For it is to fence against the entanglements of equivocal words, and the great art of sophistry which lies in them, that distinctions have been multiplied, and their use thought so necessary. But had every distinct abstract idea a distinct known name, there would be little need of these multiplied scholastic distinctions, though there would be nevertheless as much need still of the mind's observing the differences that are in things, and discriminating them thereby one from another. It is not therefore the right way to knowledge, to hunt after, and fill the head with, abundance of artificial and scholastic distinctions, wherewith learned men's writings are often filled; and we sometimes find what they treat of so divided and subdivided, that the mind of the most attentive reader loses the sight of it, as it is more than probable the writer himself did; for in things crumbled into dust it is in vain to affect or pretend order, or expect clearness. To avoid confusion by too few or too many divisions, is a great skill in thinking as well as writing, which is but the copying our thoughts; but what are the boundaries of the mean between the two vicious excesses on both hands, I think is hard to set down in words: clear and distinct ideas is all that I yet know able to regulate it. But as to verbal distinctions received and applied to common terms, i.e. equivocal words, they are more properly, I think, the business of criticism and dictionaries than of real knowledge and philosophy, since they, for the most part, explain the meaning of words, and give us their several significations. The dexterous management of terms, and being able to *fend* and *prove*[33] with them, I know has and does pass in the world for a great part of learning; but it is learning distinct from knowledge, for knowledge consists only in perceiving the habitudes and relations of ideas one to another, which is done without words; the intervention of a sound helps nothing to it. And hence we see that there is least use of distinctions where there is most knowledge; I mean in mathematics, where men have determined ideas with known names to them; and so, there being no room for equivocations, there is no need of distinctions. In arguing, the opponent uses as comprehensive and equivocal terms as he can, to involve his adversary in the doubtfulness of his expressions: this is expected, and therefore the answerer on his side makes it his play to distinguish as much as he can, and thinks he can never do it too much; nor can he indeed in that way wherein victory may be had without truth and without knowledge. This seems to me to be the art of disputing. Use your words as captiously as you can in your arguing on one side, and apply distinctions as much as you can, on the other side, to every term, to nonplus your opponent; so that in this sort of scholarship, there being no bounds set to distinguishing, some men have thought all acuteness to have lain in it; and therefore in all they have read or thought on, their great business has been to amuse themselves with distinctions, and multiply to themselves divisions, at least more than the nature of the thing required. There seems to me, as I said, to be no other rule for this, but a due and right consideration of things as they are in

33. "Fend" and "prove" are fencing terms.

themselves. He that has settled in his mind determined ideas, with names affixed to them, will be able both to discern their differences one from another, which is really distinguishing; and, where the penury of words affords not terms answering every distinct idea, will be able to apply proper distinguishing terms to the comprehensive and equivocal names he is forced to make use of. This is all the need I know of distinguishing terms; and, in such verbal distinctions, each term of the distinction, joined to that whose signification it distinguishes, is but a new distinct name for a distinct idea. Where they are so, and men have clear and distinct conceptions that answer their verbal distinctions, they are right, and are pertinent as far as they serve to clear anything in the subject under consideration. And this is that which seems to me the proper and only measure of distinctions and divisions; which he that will conduct his understanding right must not look for in the acuteness of invention, nor the authority of writers, but will find only in the consideration of things themselves, whether they are led into it by their own meditations or the information of books.

An aptness to jumble things together, wherein can be found any likeness, is a fault in the understanding on the other side, which will not fail to mislead it, and, by thus lumping of things, hinder the mind from distinct and accurate conceptions of them.

§32. To which let me here add another near of kin to this, at least in name, and that is, letting the mind, upon the suggestion of any new notion, run immediately after similes to make it the clearer to itself; which, though it may be a good way and useful in the explaining our thoughts to others, yet it is by no means a right method to settle true notions of anything in ourselves, because similes always fail in some part, and come short of that exactness which our conceptions should have to things, if we would think aright. This indeed makes men plausible talkers; for those are always most acceptable in discourse, who have the way to let in their thoughts into other men's minds with the greatest ease and facility. Whether those thoughts are well formed and correspond with things, matters not; few men care to be instructed but at an easy rate. They who in their discourse strike the fancy, and take the hearers' conceptions along with them as fast as their words flow, are the applauded talkers, and go for the only men of clear thoughts. Nothing contributes so much to this as similes, whereby men think they themselves understand better, because they are the better understood. But it is one thing to think right, and another thing to know the right way to lay our thoughts before others with advantage and clearness, be they right or wrong. Well chosen similes, metaphors and allegories, with method and order, do this the best of anything, because, being

*Similes.*

taken from objects already known and familiar to the understanding, they are conceived as fast as spoken; and, the correspondence being concluded, the thing they are brought to explain and elucidate is thought to be understood too. Thus fancy passes for knowledge, and what is prettily said is mistaken for solid. I say not this to decry metaphor, or with design to take away that ornament of speech; my business here is not with rhetoricians and orators, but with philosophers and lovers of truth; to whom I would beg leave to give this one rule whereby to try whether, in the application of their thoughts to anything for the improvement of their knowledge, they do in truth comprehend the matter before them really such as it is in itself. The way to discover this is to observe whether, in the laying it before themselves or others, they make use only of borrowed representations and ideas foreign to the thing, which are applied to it by way of accommodation, as bearing some proportion or imagined likeness to the subject under consideration. Figured and metaphorical expressions do well to illustrate more abstruse and unfamiliar ideas which the mind is not yet thoroughly accustomed to; but then they must be made use of to illustrate ideas that we already have, not to paint to us those which we yet have not. Such borrowed and allusive ideas may follow real and solid truth, to set it off when found, but must by no means be set in its place and taken for it. If all our search has yet reached no farther than simile and metaphor, we may assure ourselves we rather fancy than know, and are not yet penetrated into the inside and reality of the thing, be it what it will, but content ourselves with what our imaginations, not things themselves, furnish us with.

*Assent.*     §33. In the whole conduct of the understanding, there is nothing of more moment than to know when, and where, and how far to give assent, and possibly there is nothing harder. It is very easily said, and nobody questions it, that giving and withholding our assent, and the degrees of it, should be regulated by the evidence which things carry with them; and yet we see men are not the better for this rule; some firmly embrace doctrines upon slight grounds, some upon no grounds, and some contrary to appearance. Some admit of certainty, and are not to be moved in what they hold: others waver in everything, and there want not those that reject all as uncertain. What then shall a novice, an enquirer, a stranger do in the case? I answer, use his eyes. There is a correspondence in things, and agreement and disagreement in ideas, discernible in very different degrees, and there are eyes in men to see them if they please, only their eyes may be dimmed or dazzled, and the discerning sight in them impaired or lost. Interest and passion dazzle, the custom of arguing on any side, even against our persuasions, dims the understanding, and makes it by degrees lose the faculty of discerning clearly between truth and falsehood, and so of adhering to the right side. It is not safe to play with error, and dress it up to ourselves or others in the shape of truth. The mind by degrees loses its natural relish of real solid truth, is reconciled insensibly to anything that can but be dressed up into any faint appearance of it; and, if the fancy be allowed the place of judgment at first in sport, it afterwards comes by use to usurp it, and what is recommended by this flatterer (that studies but to please) is received for good. There are so many ways of fallacy, such arts of giving colors, appearances, and resemblances by this court dresser, the fancy, that he who is not wary to admit nothing but truth itself, very careful not to make his mind subservient to anything else, cannot but be caught. He that has a mind to believe, has half assented already; and he that, by often arguing against his own sense, imposes falsehoods on others, is not far from believing himself. This takes away the great distance there is between truth and falsehood; it brings them almost together, and makes it no great odds, in things that approach so near, which you take; and when things are brought to that pass, passion or interest, etc. easily, and without being perceived, determine which shall be the right.

§34. I have said above that we should keep a perfect indifferency for *Indifferency.* all opinions, not wish any of them true, or try to make them appear so; but, being indifferent, receive and embrace them according as evidence, and that alone, gives the attestation of truth. They that do thus, i.e. keep their minds indifferent to opinions, to be determined only by evidence, will always find the understanding has perception enough to distinguish between evidence or no evidence, between plain and doubtful; and if they neither give nor refuse their assent but by that measure, they will be safe in the opinions they have. Which being perhaps but few, this caution will have also this good in it, that it will put them upon considering, and teach them the necessity of examining more than they do; without which the mind is but a receptacle of inconsistencies, not the storehouse of truths. They that do not keep up this indifferency in themselves for all but truth, not supposed, but evidenced in themselves, put colored spectacles before their eyes, and look on things through false glasses, and then think themselves excused in following the false appearances, which they themselves put upon them. I do not expect that by this way the assent should in everyone be proportioned to the grounds and clearness wherewith every truth is capable to be made out, or that men should be perfectly kept from error: that is more than human nature can by any means be advanced to. I aim at no such unattainable privilege. I am only speaking of what they should do who would deal fairly with their own minds, and make a right use of their faculties in the pursuit of truth; we fail them a great deal more than they fail us. It is mismanagement more than want of abilities that men have reason to complain of, and which they actually do complain of in those that differ from them. He that, by an indifferency for all but truth, suffers not his assent to go faster than his evidence, nor beyond it, will learn to examine and examine fairly instead of presuming, and nobody will be at a loss or in danger for want of embracing those truths which are necessary in his station and circumstances. In any other way but this, all the world are born to orthodoxy: they imbibe at first the allowed opinions of their country and party, and so, never questioning their truth, not one of a hundred ever examines. They are applauded for presuming they are in the right. He that considers is a foe to orthodoxy, because possibly he may deviate from some of the received doctrines there. And thus men, without any industry or acquisition of their own, inherit local truths (for it is not the same everywhere), and are inured to assent without evidence. This influences farther than is thought; for what one of a hundred of the zealous bigots in all parties ever examined the tenets he is so stiff in, or ever thought it his business or duty so to do? It is suspected of lukewarmness to suppose it necessary, and a tendency to apostasy to go about it. And if a man can bring his mind once to be positive and fierce for positions whose evidence he has never once examined, and that in matters of greatest concernment to him, what shall keep him from this short and easy way of being in the right in cases of less moment? Thus we are taught to clothe our minds as we do our bodies after the fashion in vogue, and it is accounted fantasticalness, or something worse, not to do so. This custom (which who dares oppose?) makes the short-sighted bigots, and the warier skeptics, as far as it prevails. And those that break from it are in danger of heresy; for, taking the whole world, how much of it doth truth and orthodoxy possess together? Though it is by the last alone (which has the good luck to be everywhere) that error and heresy are judged of; for argument and evidence signify nothing in the case, and excuse nowhere, but are sure to be borne down in all societies by the infallible orthodoxy of the place. Whether this be the way to truth and right assent, let the opinions, that take place and prescribe in the several habitable parts of the earth, declare. I never saw any reason yet why truth might not be trusted to its own evidence; I am sure, if that be not able to support it, there is no fence against error, and then truth and falsehood are but names that stand for the same things. Evidence therefore is that by which alone every man is (and should be) taught to regulate his assent, who is then and then only in the right way when he follows it.

Men deficient in knowledge, are usually in one of these three states: either wholly ignorant; or as doubting of some proposition they have either embraced formerly, or at present are inclined to; or, lastly, they do with assurance hold and profess, without ever having examined and been convinced by well grounded arguments.

The first of these are in the best state of the three, by having their minds yet in their perfect freedom and indifferency, the likelier to pursue truth the better, having no bias yet clapped on to mislead them.

§35. For ignorance with an indifferency for truth is nearer to it, than    *Indifferency.* opinion with ungrounded inclination, which is the great source of error; and they are more in danger to go out of the way who are marching under the conduct of a guide, that it is a hundred to one will mislead them, than he that has not yet taken a step and is likelier to be prevailed on to enquire after the right way. The last of the three sorts are in the worst condition of all; for if a man can be persuaded and fully assured of anything for a truth, without having examined, what is there that he may not embrace for truth? And if he has given himself up to believe a lie, what means is there left to recover one who can be assured without examining? To the other two this I crave leave to say, that as he that is ignorant is in the best state of the two, so he should pursue truth in a method suitable to that state, i.e. by enquiring directly into the nature of the thing itself, without minding the opinions of others, or troubling himself with their questions or disputes about it, but to see what he himself can, sincerely searching after truth, find out. He that proceeds upon other principles in his enquiry into any sciences, though he be resolved to examine them and judge of them freely, does yet at least put himself on that side, and post himself in a party which he will not quit until he be beaten out; by which the mind is insensibly engaged to make what defence it can, and so is unawares biased. I do not say but a man should embrace some opinion when he has examined, else he examines to no purpose; but the surest and safest way is to have no opinion at all until he has examined, and that without any the least regard to the opinions or systems of other men about it. For example, were it my business to understand physic, would not the safer and readier way be to consult nature herself, and inform myself in the history of diseases and their cures, than espousing the principles of the dogmatists, methodists, or chemists, engage in all the disputes concerning either of those systems, and suppose it true, until I have tried what they can say to beat me out of it. Or, supposing that Hippocrates, or any other book, infallibly contains the whole art of physic, would not the direct way be to study, read and consider that book, weigh and compare the parts of it to find the truth, rather than espouse the doctrines of any party, who, though they acknowledge his authority, have already interpreted and wiredrawn all his text to their own sense; the tincture whereof when I have imbibed, I am more in danger to misunderstand his true meaning, than if I had come to him with a mind unprepossessed by doctors and commentators of my sect, whose reasonings, interpretation, and language, which I have been used to, will of course make all chime that way, and make another and perhaps the genuine meaning of the author seem harsh, strained,[34] and uncouth to me. For words, having naturally none of their own, carry that signification to the hearer that he is used to put upon them, whatever be the sense of him that uses them. This, I think, is visibly so; and if it be, he that begins to have any doubt of any of his tenets, which he received without examination, ought, as much as he can, to put himself wholly into this state of ignorance in reference to that question, and throwing wholly by all his former notions, and the opinions of others, examine, with a perfect indifferency, the question in its source, without any inclination to either side, or any regard to his or others' unexamined opinions. This I own is no easy thing to do, but I am not enquiring the easy way to opinion, but the right way to truth; which they must follow who will deal fairly with their own understandings and their own souls.

*Question.*    §36. The indifferency that I here propose will also enable them to state the question right, which they are in doubt about, without which they can never come to a fair and clear decision of it.

*Perseverance.*    §37. Another fruit from this indifferency and the considering things in themselves, abstract from our own opinions and other men's notions and discourses on them, will be that each man will pursue his thoughts in that method which will be most agreeable to the nature of the thing and to his apprehension of what it suggests to him; in which he ought to proceed with regularity and constancy, until he come to a well-grounded resolution wherein he may acquiesce. If it be objected that this will require every man to be a scholar, and quit all his other business, and betake himself wholly to study; I answer, I propose no more to anyone than he has time for. Some men's state and condition requires no great extent of knowledge; the necessary provision for life swallows the greatest part of their time. But one man's want of leisure is no excuse for the oscitancy and ignorance of those who have time to spare; and everyone has enough to get as much knowledge as is required and expected of him, and he that does not that is in love with ignorance, and is accountable for it.

34. The editors have replaced the original "stained" with "strained."

§38. The variety of distempers in men's minds is as great as of those   *Presumption.*
in their bodies; some are epidemic, few escape them, and everyone too, if
he would look into himself, would find some defect of his particular
genius. There is scarce anyone without some idiosyncrasy that he suffers
by. This man presumes upon his parts, that they will not fail him at time
of need, and so thinks it superfluous labor to make any provision beforehand. His understanding is to him like Fortunatus's purse,[35] which is
always to furnish him without ever putting anything into it beforehand;
and so he sits still satisfied, without endeavoring to store his understanding with knowledge. It is the spontaneous product of the country, and
what need of labor in tillage? Such men may spread their native riches
before the ignorant; but they were best not come to stress and trial with the
skilful. We are born ignorant of everything. The superficies of things that
surround them make impressions on the negligent, but nobody penetrates
into the inside without labor, attention, and industry. Stones and timber
grow of themselves, but yet there is no uniform pile with symmetry and
convenience to lodge in without toil and pains. God has made the intellectual world harmonious and beautiful without us; but it will never come
into our heads all at once; we must bring it home piecemeal, and there set
it up by our own industry, or else we shall have nothing but darkness and
a chaos within, whatever order and light there be in things without us.

§39. On the other side, there are others that depress their own minds,   *Despondency.*
despond at the first difficulty, and conclude that the getting an insight in
any of the sciences or making any progress in knowledge farther than
serves their ordinary business, is above their capacities. These sit still,
because they think they have not legs to go; as the others I last mentioned
do, because they think they have wings to fly, and can soar on high when
they please. To these latter one may for answer apply the proverb, *Use legs
and have legs.* Nobody knows what strength of parts he has until he has
tried them. And of the understanding one may most truly say, that its force
is greater generally than it thinks, until it is put to it. *Viresque acquirit
eundo.*[36]

And therefore the proper remedy here is but to set the mind to work,
and apply the thoughts vigorously to the business; for it holds in the strug-
gles of the mind, as in those of war, *dum putant se vincere, vicere;*[37] a per-

---

35. Fortunatus was a character in a popular legend who received from the god-
dess of Fortune a purse which could never be emptied.

36. "It acquires force as it goes," Virgil, *Aeneid* IV 175.

37. "While reckoning themselves conquered, they conquered," Livy II 64.

suasion that we shall overcome any difficulties that we meet with in the sciences seldom fails to carry us through them. Nobody knows the strength of his mind and the force of steady and regular application, until he has tried. This is certain, he that sets out upon weak legs will not only go farther, but grow stronger too than one who, with a vigorous constitution and firm limbs, only sits still.

Something of kin to this men may observe in themselves, when the mind frights itself (as it often does) with anything reflected on in gross, and transiently viewed confusedly and at a distance. Things, thus offered to the mind, carry the show of nothing but difficulty in them, and are thought to be wrapped up in impenetrable obscurity. But the truth is, these are nothing but specters that the understanding raises to itself to flatter its own laziness. It sees nothing distinctly in things remote and in a huddle, and therefore concludes too faintly that there is nothing more clear to be discovered in them. It is but to approach nearer, and that mist of our own raising that enveloped them will remove; and those that in that mist appeared hideous giants, not to be grappled with, will be found to be of the ordinary and natural size and shape. Things that in a remote and confused view seem very obscure, must be approached by gentle and regular steps; and what is most visible, easy, and obvious in them first considered. Reduce them into their distinct parts; and then, in their due order, bring all that should be known concerning everyone of those parts into plain and simple questions; and then what was thought obscure, perplexed, and too hard for our weak parts, will lay itself open to the understanding in a fair view, and let the mind into that which before it was awed with and kept at a distance from, as wholly mysterious. I appeal to my reader's experience, whether this has never happened to him, especially when, busy on one thing, he has occasionally reflected on another. I ask him, whether he has never thus been scared with a sudden opinion of mighty difficulties, which yet have vanished, when he has seriously and methodically applied himself to the consideration of this seeming terrible subject; and there has been no other matter of astonishment left, but that he amused himself with so discouraging a prospect of his own raising about a matter which, in the handling, was found to have nothing in it more strange nor intricate than several other things which he had long since and with ease mastered? This experience should teach us how to deal with such bugbears another time, which should rather serve to excite our vigor than enervate our industry. The surest way for a learner, in this as in all other cases, is not to advance by jumps and large strides; let that which he sets himself to learn next be indeed the next, i.e. as nearly conjoined with what he knows already as is possible; let it be distinct but not remote from it: let it be new and what he did not know before, that the understanding may advance; but let it be as little at once as may be, that its advances may be clear and sure. All the ground that it gets this way it will hold. This distinct gradual growth in knowledge is firm and sure, it carries its own light with it in every step of its progression in an easy and orderly train, than which there is nothing of more use to the understanding. And though this perhaps may seem a very slow and lingering way to knowledge, yet I dare confidently affirm that whoever will try it in himself, or anyone he will teach, shall find the advances greater in this method than they would, in the same space of time, have been in any other he could have taken. The greatest part of true knowledge lies in a distinct perception of things in themselves distinct. And some men give more clear light and knowledge by the bare distinct stating of a question, than others by talking of it in gross whole hours together. In this, they who so state a question do no more but separate and disentangle the parts of it one from another, and lay them, when so disentangled, in their due order. This often, without any more ado, resolves the doubt, and shows the mind where the truth lies. The agreement or disagreement of the ideas in question, when they are once separated and distinctly considered, is, in many cases, presently perceived, and thereby clear and lasting knowledge gained; whereas things in gross taken up together, and so lying together in confusion, can produce in the mind but a confused, which in effect is no knowledge, or at least, when it comes to be examined and made use of, will prove little better than none. I therefore take the liberty to repeat here again what I have said elsewhere, that, in learning anything, as little should be proposed to the mind at once as is possible; and, that being understood and fully mastered, to proceed to the next adjoining part yet unknown, simple, unperplexed proposition belonging to the matter in hand, and tending to the clearing what is principally designed.

§40. Analogy is of great use to the mind in many cases, especially in natural philosophy, and that part of it chiefly which consists in happy and successful experiments. But here we must take care that we keep ourselves within that wherein the analogy consists. For example, the acid oil of vitriol is found to be good in such a case, therefore the spirit of nitre or vinegar may be used in the like case. If the good effect of it be owing wholly to the acidity of it, the trial may be justified; but if there be something else besides the acidity in the oil of vitriol, which produces the good we desire in the case, we mistake that for analogy, which is not, and suffer our under-

*Analogy.*

standing to be misguided by a wrong supposition of analogy where there is none.

*Association.*    §41. Though I have, in the second book of my *Essay Concerning Human Understanding*, treated of the association of ideas;[38] yet having done it there historically, as giving a view of the understanding in this as well as its several other ways of operating, rather than designing there to enquire into the remedies [that] ought to be applied to it: it will, under this latter consideration, afford other matter of thought to those who have a mind to instruct themselves thoroughly in the right way of conducting their understandings; and that the rather, because this, if I mistake not, is as frequent a cause of mistake and error in us as perhaps anything else that can be named, and is a disease of the mind as hard to be cured as any; it being a very hard thing to convince anyone that things are not so, and naturally so, as they constantly appear to him.

By this one easy and unheeded miscarriage of the understanding, sandy and loose foundations become infallible principles, and will not suffer themselves to be touched or questioned: such unnatural connections become by custom as natural to the mind, as sun and light. Fire and warmth go together, and so seem to carry with them as natural an evidence as self-evident truths themselves. And where then shall one with hopes of success begin the cure? Many men firmly embrace falsehood for truth; not only because they never thought otherwise, but also because, thus blinded as they have been from the beginning, they never could think otherwise; at least without a vigor of mind able to contest the empire of habit, and look into its own principles, a freedom which few men have the notion of in themselves, and fewer are allowed the practice of by others; it being the great art and business of the teachers and guides in most sects, to suppress, as much as they can, this fundamental duty which every man owes himself, and [which] is the first steady step towards right and truth in the whole train of his actions and opinions. This would give one reason to suspect that such teachers are conscious to themselves of the falsehood or weakness of the tenets they profess, since they will not suffer the grounds whereon they are built to be examined; whereas those who seek truth only, and desire to own and propagate nothing else, freely expose their principles to the test, are pleased to have them examined, give men leave to reject them if they can, and, if there be anything weak and unsound in them, are willing to have it detected, that they themselves, as well as others, may not lay any stress upon any received proposition beyond what the evidence of its truth will warrant and allow.

38. See *Essay*, II xxxiii.

There is, I know, a great fault among all sorts of people of principling their children and scholars; which at last, when looked into, amounts to no more but making them imbibe their teachers' notions and tenets by an implicit faith, and firmly to adhere to them whether true or false. What colors may be given to this, or of what use it may be when practiced upon the vulgar, destined to labor and given up to the service of their bellies, I will not here enquire. But as to the ingenuous part of mankind, whose condition allows them leisure, and letters, and enquiry after truth, I can see no other right way of principling them, but to take heed, as much as may be, that, in their tender years, ideas that have no natural cohesion come not to be united in their heads, and that this rule be often inculcated to them to be their guide in the whole course of their lives and studies, viz. that they never suffer any ideas to be joined in their understandings in any other or stronger combination than what their own nature and correspondence give them; and that they often examine those that they find linked together in their minds, whether this association of ideas be from the visible agreement that is in the ideas themselves, or from the habitual and prevailing custom of the mind joining them thus together in thinking.

This is for caution against this evil, before it be thoroughly riveted by custom in the understanding; but he that would cure it, when habit has established it, must nicely observe the very quick and almost imperceptible motions of the mind in its habitual actions. What I have said in another place about the change of the ideas of sense into those of judgment may be proof of this. Let anyone not skilled in painting be told when he sees bottles and tobacco pipes, and other things so painted, as they are in some places shown, that he does not see protuberances, and you will not convince him but by the touch: he will not believe that, by an instantaneous legerdemain of his own thoughts, one idea is substituted for the other. How frequent instances may one meet with of this in the arguings of the learned, who not seldom, in two ideas that they have been accustomed to join in their minds, substitute one for the other; and, I am apt to think, often without perceiving it themselves. This, whilst they are under the deceit of it, makes them incapable of conviction, and they applaud themselves as zealous champions for truth, when indeed they are contending for error. And the confusion of two different ideas, which a customary connection of them in their minds has made to them almost one, fills their heads with false views, and their reasonings with false consequences.

§42. Right understanding consists in the discovery and adherence to *Fallacies.* truth, and that in the perception of the visible or probable agreement or disagreement of ideas, as they are affirmed and denied one of another.

From whence it is evident that the right use and conduct of the understanding, whose business is purely truth and nothing else, is that the mind
should be kept in a perfect indifferency, not inclining to either side, any
farther than evidence settles it by knowledge, or the overbalance of probability gives it the turn of assent and belief; but yet it is very hard to meet
with any discourse, wherein one may not perceive the author not only
maintain (for that is reasonable and fit) but inclined and biased to one side
of the question, with marks of a desire that that should be true. If it be
asked me, how authors who have such a bias and lean to it may be discovered, I answer, by observing how, in their writings or arguings, they are
often led by their inclinations to change the ideas of the question, either by
changing the terms, or by adding and joining others to them, whereby the
ideas under consideration are so varied as to be more serviceable to their
purpose, and to be thereby brought to an easier and nearer agreement or
more visible and remoter disagreement one with another. This is plain and
direct sophistry; but I am far from thinking that, wherever it is found, it is
made use of with design to deceive and mislead the readers. It is visible
that men's prejudices and inclinations by this way impose often upon
themselves; and their affections for truth, under their prepossession in
favor of one side, is the very thing that leads them from it. Inclination suggests and slides into their discourse favorable terms, which introduce
favorable ideas, until at last, by this means, that is concluded clear and evident, thus dressed up, which taken in its native state, by making use of
none but the precise determined ideas, would find no admittance at all.
The putting these glosses on what they affirm, these, as they are thought,
handsome, easy, and graceful explications of what they are discoursing on,
is so much the character of what is called and esteemed writing well, that
it is very hard to think that authors will ever be persuaded to leave what
serves so well to propagate their opinions and procure themselves credit in
the world, for a more jejune and dry way of writing, by keeping to the same
terms precisely annexed to the same ideas, a sour and blunt stiffness tolerable in mathematicians only, who force their way and make truth prevail
by irresistible demonstration.

But yet if authors cannot be prevailed with to quit the looser, though
more insinuating, ways of writing, if they will not think fit to keep close to
truth and instruction by unvaried terms and plain unsophisticated arguments, yet it concerns readers not to be imposed on by fallacies and the
prevailing ways of insinuation. To do this, the surest and most effectual
remedy is to fix in the mind the clear and distinct ideas of the question
stripped of words; and so likewise, in the train of argumentation, to take

up the author's ideas, neglecting his words, observing how they connect or separate those in the question. He that does this will be able to cast off all that is superfluous; he will see what is pertinent, what coherent, what is direct to, what slides by the question. This will readily show him all the foreign ideas in the discourse, and where they were brought in; and though they perhaps dazzled the writer, yet he will perceive that they give no light nor strength to his reasonings.

This, though it be the shortest and easiest way of reading books with profit, and keeping one's self from being misled by great names or plausible discourses, yet, it being hard and tedious to those who have not accustomed themselves to it, it is not to be expected that everyone (amongst those few who really pursue truth) should this way guard his understanding from being imposed on by the wilful or, at least, undesigned sophistry, which creeps into most of the books of argument. They that write against their conviction, or that next to them are resolved to maintain the tenets of a party they are engaged in, cannot be supposed to reject any arms that may help to defend their cause, and therefore such should be read with the greatest caution. And they who write for opinions they are sincerely persuaded of, and believe to be true, think they may so far allow themselves to indulge their laudable affection to truth, as to permit their esteem of it to give it the best colors, and set it off with the best expressions and dress they can, thereby to gain it the easiest entrance into the minds of their readers and fix it deepest there.

One of those being the state of mind we may justly suppose most writers to be in, it is fit their readers, who apply to them for instruction, should not lay by that caution which becomes a sincere pursuit of truth and should make them always watchful against whatever might conceal or misrepresent it. If they have not the skill of representing to themselves the author's sense by pure ideas separated from sounds, and thereby divested of the false lights and deceitful ornaments of speech, this yet they should do, they should keep the precise question steadily in their minds, carry it along with them through the whole discourse, and suffer not the least alteration in the terms, either by addition, subtraction, or substituting any other. This everyone can do who has a mind to it: and he that has not a mind to it, it is plain makes his understanding only the warehouse of other men's lumber; I mean, false and unconcluding reasonings, rather than a repository of truth for his own use, which will prove substantial and stand him in stead when he has occasion for it. And whether such an one deals fairly by his own mind, and conducts his own understanding right, I leave to his own understanding to judge.

*Fundamental*        §43. The mind of man being very narrow, and so slow in making
*Verities.*       acquaintance with things and taking in new truths that no one man is capable, in a much longer life than ours, to know all truths; it becomes our prudence, in our search after knowledge, to employ our thoughts about
fundamental and material questions, carefully avoiding those that are trifling, and not suffering ourselves to be diverted from our main even purpose by those that are merely incidental. How much of many young men's
time is thrown away in purely logical enquiries, I need not mention. This
is no better than if a man, who was to be a painter, should spend all his time
in examining the threads of the several cloths he is to paint upon, and
counting the hairs of each pencil and brush he intends to use in the laying
on of his colors. Nay, it is much worse than for a young painter to spend
his apprenticeship in such useless niceties; for he, at the end of all his pains
to no purpose, finds that it is not painting, nor any help to it, and so is really
to no purpose. Whereas men designed for scholars have often their heads
so filled and warmed with disputes on logical questions, that they take
those airy useless notions for real and substantial knowledge, and think
their understandings so well furnished with science that they need not look
any farther into the nature of things, or descend to the mechanical drudgery of experiment and inquiry. This is so obvious a mismanagement of the
understanding, and that in the professed way to knowledge, that it could
not be passed by; to which might be joined abundance of questions, and the
way of handling of them in the Schools. What faults in particular of this
kind every man is, or may be guilty of, would be infinite to enumerate; it
suffices to have shown that superficial and slight discoveries and observations that contain nothing of moment in themselves, nor serve as clues to
lead us into farther knowledge, should be lightly passed by, and never
thought worth our searching after. There are fundamental truths that lie at
the bottom, the basis upon which a great many others rest, and in which
they have their consistency. These are teeming truths, rich in store, with
which they furnish the mind, and, like the lights of heaven, are not only
beautiful and entertaining in themselves, but give light and evidence to
other things that without them could not be seen or known. Such is that
admirable discovery of Mr. Newton,[39] that all bodies gravitate to one
another, which may be counted as the basis of natural philosophy; which
of what use it is to the understanding of the great frame of our solar system,
he has to the astonishment of the learned world shown, and how much far-

39. Sir Isaac Newton (1642–1727), author of *Principia*, became a personal friend
of Locke's.

ther it would guide us in other things, if rightly pursued, is not yet known. Our Savior's great rule, that *we should love our neighbor as ourselves,* is such a fundamental truth for the regulating human society, that I think by that alone one might without difficulty determine all the cases and doubts in social morality. These, and such as these, are the truths we should endeavor to find out and store our minds with. Which leads me to another thing in the conduct of the understanding that is no less necessary, viz.

§44. To accustom ourselves in any question proposed to examine and *Bottoming.* find out upon what it bottoms. Most of the difficulties that come in our way, when well considered and traced, lead us to some proposition which, known to be true, clears the doubt, and gives an easy solution of the question, whilst topical and superficial arguments, of which there is store to be found on both sides, filling the head with variety of thoughts and the mouth with copious discourse, serve only to amuse the understanding, and entertain company, without coming to the bottom of the question, the only place of rest and stability for an inquisitive mind whose tendency is only to truth and knowledge.

For example, if it be demanded, whether the Grand Seignior[40] can lawfully take what he will from any of his people, this question cannot be resolved without coming to a certainty, whether all men are naturally equal; for upon that it turns, and that truth, well settled in the understanding and carried in the mind through the various debates concerning the various rights of men in society, will go a great way in putting an end to them and showing on which side the truth is.

§45. There is scarce anything more for the improvement of knowl- *Transferring* edge, for the ease of life, and the dispatch of business, than for a man to *of Thoughts.* be able to dispose of his own thoughts; and there is scarce anything harder in the whole conduct of the understanding, than to get a full mastery over it. The mind, in a waking man, has always some object that it applies itself to; which, when we are lazy or unconcerned, we can easily change, and at pleasure transfer our thoughts to another, and from thence to a third, which has no relation to either of the former. Hence men forwardly conclude, and frequently say, nothing is so free as thought, and it were well it were so; but the contrary will be found true in several instances; and there are many cases wherein there is nothing more restive and ungovernable than our thoughts: they will not be directed what objects to pursue, nor be

40. The ruler of the Turkish empire. Locke refers to the Grand Seignior as an example of an illegitimate ruler wielding absolute power. See, for example, *Second Treatise,* par. 91.

taken off from those they have once fixed on, but run away with a man in pursuit of those ideas they have in view, let him do what he can.

I will not here mention again what I have above taken notice of, how hard it is to get the mind, narrowed by a custom of thirty or forty years standing to a scanty collection of obvious and common ideas, to enlarge itself to a more copious stock, and grow into an acquaintance with those that would afford more abundant matter of useful contemplation; it is not of this I am here speaking. The inconvenience I would here represent and find a remedy for, is the difficulty there is sometimes to transfer our minds from one subject to another, in cases where the ideas are equally familiar to us.

Matters that are recommended to our thoughts by any of our passions take possession of our minds with a kind of authority, and will not be kept out or dislodged, but, as if the passion that rules were, for the time, the sheriff of the place, and came with all the posse, the understanding is seized and taken with the object it introduces, as if it had a legal right to be alone considered there. There is scarce anybody, I think, of so calm a temper who has not sometime found this tyranny on his understanding, and suffered under the inconvenience of it. Who is there almost whose mind, at some time or other, love or anger, fear or grief, has not so fastened to some clog, that it could not turn itself to any other object? I call it a clog, for it hangs upon the mind so as to hinder its vigor and activity in the pursuit of other contemplations, and advances itself little or not [at] all in the knowledge of the thing which it so closely hugs and constantly pores on. Men thus possessed are sometimes as if they were so in the worst sense, and lay under the power of an enchantment. They see not what passes before their eyes; hear not the audible discourse of the company; and when by any strong application to them they are roused a little, they are like men brought to themselves from some remote region; whereas in truth they come no farther than their secret cabinet within, where they have been wholly taken up with the puppet, which is for that time appointed for their entertainment. The shame that such dumps cause to well-bred people, when it carries them away from the company, where they should bear a part in the conversation, is a sufficient argument that it is a fault in the conduct of our understanding, not to have that power over it as to make use of it to those purposes and on those occasions wherein we have need of its assistance. The mind should be always free and ready to turn itself to the variety of objects that occur, and allow them as much consideration as shall for that time be thought fit. To be engrossed so by one object, as not to be prevailed on to leave it for another that we judge fitter for our contemplation, is to make it of no use to us. Did this state of mind remain always so, everyone would, without scruple, give it the name of perfect madness; and while it does last, at whatever intervals it returns, such a rotation of thoughts about the same object no more carries us forwards towards the attainment of knowledge, than getting upon a mill-horse while he jogs on in his circular track would carry a man a journey.

I grant something must be allowed to legitimate passions and to natural inclinations. Every man, besides occasional affections, has beloved studies, and those the mind will more closely stick to; but yet it is best that it should be always at liberty, and under the free disposal of the man, to act how and upon what he directs. This we should endeavor to obtain, unless we would be content with such a flaw in our understandings, that sometimes we should be as it were without it; for it is very little better than so in cases where we cannot make use of it to those purposes we would and which stand in present need of it.

But before fit remedies can be thought on for this disease, we must know the several causes of it, and thereby regulate the cure, if we will hope to labor with success.

One we have already instanced in, whereof all men that reflect have so general a knowledge, and so often an experience in themselves, that nobody doubts of it. A prevailing passion so pins down our thoughts to the object and concern of it, that a man passionately in love cannot bring himself to think of his ordinary affairs, or a kind mother, drooping under the loss of a child, is not able to bear a part as she was wont in the discourse of the company or conversation of her friends.

But though passion be the most obvious and general, yet it is not the only cause that binds up the understanding, and confines it for the time to one object from which it will not be taken off.

Besides this, we may often find that the understanding, when it has a while employed itself upon a subject which either chance, or some slight accident, offered to it without the interest or recommendation of any passion, works itself into a warmth, and by degrees gets into a career, wherein, like a bowl down a hill, it increases its motion by going, and will not be stopped or diverted, though, when the heat is over, it sees all this earnest application was about a trifle not worth a thought, and all the pains employed about it lost labor.

There is a third sort, if I mistake not, yet lower than this; it is a sort of childishness, if I may so say, of the understanding, wherein, during the fit, it plays with and dandles some insignificant puppet to no end, nor with any design at all, and yet cannot easily be got off from it. Thus some trivial sentence, or a scrap of poetry, will sometimes get into men's heads, and make such a chiming there, that there is no stilling of it; no peace to be obtained, nor attention to anything else, but this impertinent guest will take up the mind and possess the thoughts in spite of all endeavors to get rid of it. Whether everyone has experimented in themselves this troublesome intrusion of some striking ideas which thus importune the understanding, and hinder it from being better employed, I know not. But persons of very good parts, and those more than one, I have heard speak and complain of it themselves. The reason I have to make this doubt is from what I have known in a case something of kin to this, though much odder, and that is of a sort of visions that some people have lying quiet but perfectly awake in the dark, or with their eyes shut. It is a great variety of faces, most commonly very odd ones, that appear to them in a train one after another; so that having had just the sight of one, it immediately passes away to give place to another that the same instant succeeds and has as quick an exit as its leader, and so they march on in a constant succession; nor can anyone of them by any endeavor be stopped or retained beyond the instant of its appearance, but is thrust out by its follower, which will have its turn. Concerning this fantastical phenomenon I have talked with several people, whereof some have been perfectly acquainted with it, and others have been so wholly strangers to it, that they could hardly be brought to conceive or believe it. I knew a lady of excellent parts, who had got past thirty without having ever had the least notice of any such thing; she was so great a stranger to it that, when she heard me and another talking of it, [she] could scarce forbear thinking we bantered her; but sometime after, drinking a large dose of dilute tea (as she was ordered by a physician) going to bed, she told us at next meeting, that she had now experimented what our discourse had much ado to persuade her of. She had seen a great variety of faces in a long train, succeeding one another, as we had described; they were all strangers and intruders, such as she had no acquaintance with before, nor sought after then, and as they came of themselves they went too; none of them stayed a moment, nor could be detained by all the endeavors she could use, but went on in their solemn procession, just appeared and then vanished. This odd phenomenon seems to have a mechanical cause, and to depend upon the matter and motion of the blood or animal spirits.

When the fancy is bound by passion, I know no way to set the mind free and at liberty to prosecute what thoughts the man would make choice of, but to allay the present passion, or counterbalance it with another, which is an art to be got by study and acquaintance with the passions.

Those who find themselves apt to be carried away with the spontaneous current of their own thoughts, not excited by any passion or interest, must be very wary and careful in all the instances of it to stop it, and never humor their minds in being thus triflingly busy. Men know the value of their corporal liberty, and therefore suffer not willingly fetters and chains to be put upon them. To have the mind captivated is, for the time, certainly the greater evil of the two, and deserves our utmost care and endeavors to preserve the freedom of our better part. And in this case our pains will not be lost; striving and struggling will prevail, if we constantly, in all such occasions, make use of it. We must never indulge these trivial attentions of thought; as soon as we find the mind makes itself a business of nothing, we should immediately disturb and check it, introduce new and more serious considerations, and not leave until we have beaten it off from the pursuit it was upon. This, at first, if we have let the contrary practice grow to a habit, will perhaps be difficult; but constant endeavors will by degrees prevail, and at last make it easy. And when a man is pretty well advanced, and can command his mind off at pleasure from incidental and undesigned pursuits, it may not be amiss for him to go on farther, and make attempts upon meditations of greater moment, that at the last he may have a full power over his own mind, and be so fully master of his own thoughts, as to be able to transfer them from one subject to another with the same ease that he can lay by anything he has in his hand and take something else that he has a mind to in the room of it. This liberty of mind is of great use both in business and study, and he that has got it will have no small advantage of ease and despatch in all that is the chosen and useful employment of his understanding.

The third and last way which I mentioned the mind to be sometimes taken up with, I mean the chiming of some particular words or sentence in the memory, and, as it were, making a noise in the head, and the like, seldom happens but when the mind is lazy or very loosely and negligently employed. It were better indeed be without such impertinent and useless repetitions; any obvious idea, when it is roving causelessly at a venture, being of more use and apter to suggest something worth consideration, than the insignificant buzz of purely empty sounds. But since the rousing of the mind, and setting the understanding on work with some degrees of vigor, does for the most part presently set it free from these idle companions; it may not be amiss, whenever we find ourselves troubled with them, to make use of so profitable a remedy that is always at hand.